# DOWN DEEP
# IN MY SOUL

# DOWN DEEP
# IN MY SOUL

## An African American Catholic Theology of Preaching

Maurice J. Nutt, CSsR

ORBIS BOOKS

Maryknoll, New York 10545

ORBIS BOOKS
Maryknoll, New York 10545

Fathers and Brothers
MARYKNOLL™

Founded in 1970, Orbis Books endeavors to publish works that enlighten the mind, nourish the spirit, and challenge the conscience. The publishing arm of the Maryknoll Fathers and Brothers, Orbis seeks to explore the global dimensions of the Christian faith and mission, to invite dialogue with diverse cultures and religious traditions, and to serve the cause of reconciliation and peace. The books published reflect the views of their authors and do not represent the official position of the Maryknoll Society. To learn more about Maryknoll and Orbis Books, please visit our website at www.orbisbooks.com

### Library of Congress Cataloging-in-Publication Data

Names: Nutt, Maurice J., author.
Title: Down deep in my soul : an African American Catholic theology of preaching / Maurice J. Nutt.
Description: Maryknoll, NY : Orbis Books, [2022] | Includes bibliographical references and index. | Summary: "A comprehensive treatment of preaching in the Black Catholic tradition"—Provided by publisher.
Identifiers: LCCN 2022015606 (print) | LCCN 2022015607 (ebook) | ISBN 9781626984943 (trade paperback) | ISBN 9781608339563 (epub)
Subjects: LCSH: Catholic preaching. | African American preaching.
Classification: LCC BX1795.P72 N88 2022 (print) | LCC BX1795.P72 (ebook) | DDC 251.0089/96073—dc23/eng/20220506
LC record available at https://lccn.loc.gov/2022015606
LC ebook record available at https://lccn.loc.gov/2022015607

*To the predominantly Black Catholic faith communities
where I served as pastor:*

*St. Alphonsus Liguori "Rock" Catholic Church
in St. Louis, Missouri (1993–2002)*

*and*

*Holy Names of Jesus and Mary Catholic Church
in Memphis, Tennessee
(2005–2011)*

*Your faith, faithfulness, and love of God's word nurtured, formed,
encouraged, challenged, and prepared me for my preaching ministry.
You made me the preacher I am today. May you continue
to celebrate the Good News and remain word-bearers
and word-sharers to all whom you encounter.*

*To my fellow Redemptorist missionaries throughout the world:
As devoted sons of St. Alphonsus Liguori may we remain
ever devoted to witnessing to the Redeemer by preaching
Good News to the poor and most abandoned. May we remain
on fire in our mission to preaching explicitly to and being in
solidarity with the poor by advocating for their fundamental rights
to justice and liberation in our wounded world.*

*Faith comes from what is heard, and what is heard comes by the preaching of Christ.*

—Romans 10:17


*Christ's message must truly penetrate and possess the preacher, not just intellectually but in his entire being. The Holy Spirit, who inspired the word, today, just as at the beginning of the Church, acts in every evangelizer who allows himself to be possessed and led by him. The Holy Spirit places on his lips the words which he could not find by himself.*

—Pope Francis
*Evangelii Gaudium* (The Joy of the Gospel)


*By a lived witness of uncommon faithfulness, Black Catholics have much to offer the millions of European American Catholics in the United States and beyond who are determined to keep the faith but also committed to change the church. Indeed, Black Catholics have kept the faith, and in doing so they have changed the church. They have done this by being Black Catholics: by prayer and sacrifice, discipline and fasting; by healing and creating in their own circumstances, by making and wading in rivers of music; by striving for excellence in all that they do for the greater honor and glory of God; by teaching and sharing the strengths and weaknesses, lessons and achievements of nearly 450 years of uncommon faithfulness.*

—M. Shawn Copeland, PhD
*Uncommon Faithfulness: The Black Catholic Experience*

*There's beauty in my brokenness*
*I've got true love instead of pain*
*There's freedom though you've captured me*
*I've got joy instead of mourning*
*You give me joy*
*Down deep in my soul*
*Down deep in my soul*
*Down deep in my soul.*

—VaShawn Mitchell
From the Gospel song *Joy*

# Contents

# Acknowledgments

The wisdom, research, instruction, pastoral application, stories, truth-telling, and challenges in this book are the culmination of many years of listening, learning, living, observing, being, and becoming all that I inherited from my ancestors and all that was instilled in me by the Black Catholic community.

*Down Deep in My Soul* emanated from my being named a Delaplane Preaching Scholar by Aquinas Institute of Theology through a grant from the Lilly Foundation to produce literature that strengthened Christian preaching. The lexicon of Christian preaching literature was bereft of a monograph on the Black preaching style from a Roman Catholic perspective. I am most appreciative to the Delaplane Preaching Scholars' writing cohort, particularly to Dr. Deborah L. Wilhelm, Rev. Dr. Kay L. Northcutt, Rev. Dr. Vince Pastro, and Rev. Dr. Gregory Heille, O.P.—thank you for your constructive suggestions and belief in the necessity of this book. I owe a debt of gratitude to Dr. Diana L. Hayes, not only for her blessing me by writing the foreword to this book but for her influence and intellectual prowess in African American Catholic theology and spirituality. I am extremely indebted to Robert Ellsberg, publisher of Orbis Books, for reading my manuscript and immediately catching the vision and import of this book. Robert presided over the creation of this book with percipient expertise, encouragement, and benevolence. I humbly stand in the wake of great preachers, Protestant and Catholic, women and men, living and those gone to Glory, too numerous to name, who have inspired me by their practice and scholarly pursuits of preaching.

To my beloved family and cherished friends who love, support, encourage, and pray for me through the joys and challenges of life: Cordell Nutt, Michael and Princilla Nutt, Eunice Jett-Day, Andrea Franklin Davis, Dr. Brenda L. Walker and Andre Walker, Adrian D. Hall, my nephews, nieces, and myriad of cousins, Verona A. Bowers, Harry and Karen Johnson, Michael P. McMillan, Lynn Woolfolk, Dr. Randy Glean, Michael Jones and Kathy Conley Jones, Rev. Renee Fenner, Rev. Darryl F. James, Rev. Dr. Bryan Massingale, Rev. Manuel Williams, CR, Jesse Cox, Rev. Dr.

Joseph A. Brown, SJ, Rev. Paul Whittington, OP, Rev. Tom Jackson, OP, Rev. Jeffrey Ott, OP, Veronica Downs-Dorsey, Ralph McCloud, Carolyn D. Thomas, Kristine Stremel, Dr. Norman C. Francis, Dr. Loren J. Blanchard, Dr. Pamela Franco, Learnard Dickerson, Dr. Ansel Augustine, Monsignor Wallace Harris, Carla A. Harris, Victor Franklin, Ron and Beverly Riddick, Samantha Dulaney, Rev. Dr. Ronald Bobo, Rev. Dr. Louis Forsythe, Rev. Dr. Anthony Witherspoon, Beatriz Ramoutarsingh, Dr. Reginald K. Ellis, McKinley Martin, Edward Howard, Dr. Brian L. Turner, Dr. Marcus S. Cox, Dr. Karla Scott, Paul and Shirley Foster, Richard and Larissa Banks, Sheila Banks, Michael and Gail Holmes, Ron and Dana Redwing, Helene LaBerta, Bonita Cornute, Geri Mitchell, Robin Boyce, Sr. Sylvia Thibodeaux, SSF, Sr. Monica Ellerbush, RSM, Sr. Jane Briseno, RSM, Dr. Donald Nichols, Phillandas Thompson, Perri and Stephanie Johnson, Kathy McGinnis, Dr. Ernest L. Gibson, III, Will Jemison, Jesse Vincent Johnson, Dr. Rochelle Catus, Sharon Hawthrone, Dr. Robert and Marie Scott, Luis Dogue, Reggie and Beth Moore, Drs. John and Carmel Wright, Dr. Christi Griffin, Dr. Ken McKay, Gloria Taylor, Deacon Dunn and Magnolia Cumby, Deacon Larry and Loretta Chatmon, Deacon Allen and Edith Stevens, Deacon Lawrence and Erica Houston.

To my Redemptorist confreres, especially my classmates, and the Black Redemptorist Caucus, your unwavering fraternal support and friendship has nurtured, sustained, and helped me to persevere in my vocation. To my fraternity brothers, the distinguished gentlemen of Alpha Phi Alpha Fraternity, Inc., for your insistence that our members be scholars and thought leaders always advocating for the advancement of African American communities. To Joseph Cardinal Tobin, CSsR, Wilton Cardinal Gregory, Bishop J. Terry Steib, SVD, Bishop Joseph Perry, and Bishop Fernand J. Cheri, OFM, thank you for your episcopal leadership and personal guidance and support—I am forever grateful.

To the faculty, staff, students, and alumni of the Institute for Black Catholic Studies, the members of the Black Catholic Theological Symposium, the National Black Catholic Clergy Caucus, the National Black Sisters Conference, the National Association of Black Catholic Deacons, and the National Black Catholic Seminarians Association, and the Knights and Ladies of Peter Claver—remain steadfast to your faithful witness and ever committed to your work for justice in the church and society.

I give honor to the cloud of witnesses who constantly watch over me: Haller and Beatrice Nutt, Haller Edward Nutt, Edward and Hattie Duvall, Oliver Calvin and Inez Nutt, Oliver and Louise Nutt, Maurice and Elizabeth Duvall, Fred and Mary Jett, Edward and Ellen Duvall, Marshall and Eva Duvall, Lawrence Duvall, Bill and Roberta Franklin, Michael A. Davis, Rev. Ronald B. Packnett, Rev. Joseph T. Campbell, CSsR, Rev. Robert L. Wirth, CSsR, Rev. Tony Judge, CSsR, Brother Duane A. Brown, OP, Archbishop James P. Lyke, OFM, Bishop Joseph A. Francis, SVD, Brother Martin de Porres Smith, CSsR, Rev. Carlyle Blake, CSsR, Rev. Jacky Merilan, CSsR, Deacon Kevin Bellot, CSsR, Sister Antona Ebo, FSM, Rev. Tony Clark, SVD, Rev. Chester Smith, SVD, Rev. George Clements, Rev. James E. Goode, OFM, Dr. Kirk P. Gaddy, Leon Henderson, Louis Evans, James and Ollie Johnson, John and Ann Holmes, Vashti Ransom, Willie Tyler, Julia Jones, Ruth Jones, Lucille Grimes, Oscar and Dorothy Bennett, Stephen LaBerta, Willie D. Cunningham, and finally my spiritual mother and mentor, Servant of God Sister Thea Bowman, FSPA—may you all rest on in peace and power.

# Foreword

In the last fifty or so years, we have had the benefit of research and books done by new scholars, persons of color, whose readings and interpretations of doctrine and tradition as well as history have made us rethink much of what we know today. One of the most important insights has been in liturgy, which is being reinterpreted to include the history, traditions, stories, songs, and so on, of persons of color, especially African Americans. This is Dr. Maurice J. Nutt's contribution in this deeply researched and highly educational work on Black preaching, a topic on which little has been written and of which there is much for us to learn. As he notes: "For effective evangelization to occur in African American Catholic parishes, aspects and techniques of the Black preaching style must be utilized by those called upon to preach." And this is true regardless of the race or ethnicity of the preacher. So, what is this unique style of preaching known as Black preaching? In the next 200-plus pages, Nutt clearly and carefully lays out what he is talking about.

Preaching is at the very heart of worship in Christianity, whether Protestant or Catholic. It takes many forms, but all preachers attempt to help those in the pews understand the Word of God. Some do so with theological treatises that may or may not reach the hearts and minds of their followers while others let loose all the bells and whistles in order to attract and keep their attention. Historically, when people speak of Black preaching, they are speaking of those preachers who are a part of the historically Black Church, the Protestant churches. But there are other preachers who have been recovering their voices and proclaiming the Gospel in ways that may surprise but that also enlighten and invigorate their listeners. These are Black Catholic preachers, male and female, ordained and lay, who have heard the voice of God speak to them and are now attempting to share that Word with all around them.

Preaching is an important aspect of worship, especially for persons of African descent. As Father Nutt reveals in this work, it is a means of sharing the Good News of Jesus Christ with his followers. Like their Protestant brothers and sisters, Black Catholic preachers seek to enlighten the hearts and minds of their parishioners with the treasures that unfold from scripture. It is a way of helping them to make it in the days and weeks ahead as they deal with the obstacles and pleasures of today's material world.

In this wonderful and challenging book, Fr. Maurice J. Nutt provides what has been long overdue: an incisive, clear, and vibrant discussion of Black preaching in the Roman Catholic Church. For some this book will be an eye-opener. They knew Blacks were in the Catholic Church but never paid much attention to their preaching styles or the style of worship in which Black preachers found themselves. Many assumed they preached similarly to white and other Catholic preachers. In some ways, they were correct, but this has to change, Dr. Nutt argues.

What does it mean to be a Black preacher in the Roman Catholic Church today? For many, it simply means reading the daily readings from the lectionary and then attempting to clarify their meaning, usually in less than fifteen or so minutes! This is not satisfactory and does not, claims Nutt, respond to the needs, voiced and unvoiced, of Black Catholics who hunger for the word of God spoken clearly, fervently, and with honesty. He calls on those who are ordained, whether Black or of other ethnicities, to learn how to preach in what he calls the Black style of preaching, a style that responds to the needs of persons of African descent but also of others looking for a more fervent, colorful, rich vocalization of God's word.

At the opening of his text, Fr. Nutt shares the words of Scripture (Paul), Pope Francis, theologian M. Shawn Copeland, and gospel singer VaShawn Mitchell to reveal the depth, richness, and variety of preaching as it should be, He quotes Paul: "Faith comes from what is heard, and what is heard comes by the preaching of Jesus" (Romans 10:17). He cites Pope Francis: "Christ's message must truly penetrate and possess the preacher, not just intellectually but in his entire being." Copeland connects the gifts of Black folk to the richness of their lives, as revealed in an "uncommon faithfulness" that seeks to change the church into one that truly lives out its catholicity (universality).

The book has seven chapters plus an introduction and conclusion. In the introduction, we read of the passionate preaching of two quite different men, Pope Francis, the Vicar of Christ, and Barack Obama, the former President of the United States. Yet both have sought to heal a nation and a world with their words of hope and faith. Fr. Nutt is attempting to bring their words to life in the Church for Black and, if possible, all Catholics. He notes: "This is a book about race, religion, rhetoric, and ritual," but it is also "a book authenticating, validating, and encouraging the use of the Black preaching style" in Catholic parishes. He speaks of the importance of evangelism as well as the challenges facing those trying to bring life back into deteriorating, small, and underfunded inner-city parishes. Most of the church's money now flows to the suburbs, yet there are thousands of faithful still active and engaged and seeking a word of hope in the cities. They should not be ignored.

This book is a massive undertaking. To my knowledge, it is the first in-depth effort to present a theology of Black preaching from a Roman Catholic perspective. Beginning with its roots in Africa and reviewing all that has happened to the present day, this text provides insight on the development and growth of Black preaching. It is long overdue and makes a wonderful contribution to the growing numbers of books finally being written from the perspective of Black Catholics, long present but also long unheard from and almost voiceless in the church. This is a clarion call to Catholics, regardless of their ethnicity, that Black Catholics are a critical part of the Roman Catholic Church and have much to offer it. It is also a proclamation to Black Protestants that there is a richness in the voices of Black Catholics from which they too can learn.

Diana L. Hayes, JD, PhD, STD
Emerita Professor
Georgetown University

# Introduction

During the past decade (2010–2019) of the twenty-first century many throughout the world experienced a rare phenomenon of having two world leaders capture, captivate, and most importantly keep our attention not only through their inspiring humanitarian deeds but also by their sincere and riveting rhetoric—their words. The persuasive eloquence of both the former United States president (2009–2016), Barack Obama, and the leader of the Roman Catholic Church (2013–), Pope Francis. President Obama and Pope Francis both possess the ability to engage their listeners in a familiar way without being ostentatious given their position and authority. Their words, whether in an address, oration, disquisition, or homily, are seamlessly intelligent, relevant, clear, and compassionate. By and large people want to listen to these two contrasting figures, men varying in age, ethnicity, religion, and profession not only because of *what* they say but *how* they say it. Both politician and pontiff are passionate about their beliefs and convictions, and it is apparent in their rhetoric. I believe their speaking and preaching styles (although not ordained, Barack Obama has a preaching style) are honed by their cultural identities. The spirited rhetoric of Latin Americans and African Americans, persuasively evoking passion, emotion, and certitude, are evidenced by both of these prominent leaders.

Although there are undeniable differences and challenges between American laws, political positions, and Roman Catholic teachings, without compromising their personal and institutional values they respected each other and coalesced around their commonalities. This was never more in evidence than when Pope Francis made a papal visit to the United States and was invited by Mr. and Mrs. Obama to visit the White House on September 23, 2015. As a way of welcome President Obama spoke first, and after his initial customary pleasantries, he took on the semblance and rhetoric of a preacher. He didn't have a scriptural text but with rhythmic diction, moving cadence, and reverberating repetition of the phrase, "you remind us," President Obama in part shared these sentiments regarding Pope Francis's papacy:

You remind us that the Lord's most powerful message is mercy. That means welcoming the stranger with empathy and a truly open heart—from the refugee who flees war-torn lands, to the immigrant who leaves home in search of a better life. It means showing compassion and love for the marginalized and the outcast, those who have suffered, and those who seek redemption.[1]

Having just promulgated his encyclical, *Laudato Si'*, Pope Francis spoke next, offering a salient admonition about caring for the environment by caring for our common home. He said:

Such change demands on our part a serious and responsible recognition not only of the kind of world we may be leaving to our children, but also to the millions of people living under a system which has overlooked them. Our common home has been part of this group of the excluded which cries out to heaven and which today powerfully strikes our homes, our cities and our societies. To use a telling phrase of the Reverend Martin Luther King, we can say that we have defaulted on a promissory note and now is the time to honor it.[2]

Knowing to whom he was addressing his comments, this first pope from Latin America was saying to the first African American president that we share common ground with our concern for marginalized and excluded people because we have worked with and ministered to them in our respective countries. Pope Francis contextualized this global environmental crisis for the American people by invoking the name and words of Dr. King, an American champion for the oppressed and downtrodden.

Many who were present on the White House's South Lawn that day commented that they felt like they were at a church service rather than a meeting of two world leaders. How could you not feel that way when immediately after Pope Francis finished his remarks / "sermon" a robe-clad African American gospel choir rose from their seats and with full voice sang a "sermonic song" typical of a Black church service. They sang the stirring song "Total Praise" by composer Richard Smallwood. However, the choir was not from a Protestant church. No, they were a gospel choir from St. Augustine Catholic Church, the "mother church" of African American Catholics in Washington, DC. This Black Catholic

---

[1]President Barack Obama's Remarks: https://obamawhitehouse.archives.gov/the-press-office/2015/09/23/remarks-president-obama-and-his-holiness-pope-francis-arrival-ceremony.
[2]Ibid., Pope Francis's Remarks.

gospel choir delighted both pope and president as they rejoiced together in praise to God at the conclusion of the song. In an unassuming meeting beginning a papal visit to the United States, something happened on the White House's South Lawn that both secular and Catholic news commentators and political pundits apparently missed—the occurrence was manifested in both symbol and substance—that race, religion, rhetoric, and ritual all matter.

This is a book about race, religion, rhetoric, and ritual. The racial group considered consists of African Americans who are members of the Roman Catholic Church who generally appreciate sound theological, biblically grounded, and culturally astute rhetoric known as the Black preaching style utilized during their time of worship at eucharistic liturgies and prayer services. More succinctly, this is a book authenticating, validating, and encouraging the use of the Black preaching style by those who are blessed to preach in African American Catholic settings as well as other cultural settings.

## Preaching and Evangelism

When the Black[3] preacher is moving the hearts and souls of his or her Black congregation through his or her powerful teaching, a loud shout of "tell the story, preacher" may be heard from some satisfied soul sitting in the pew. One of the most interesting and faith-filled stories within the Catholic Church in America is that told by African American Catholics. It is a story that tells of a people who were both faith-filled and faithful to a God who never fails. It is a story of persistence and perseverance under discouraging circumstances. It is a story fraught with racial hatred and racial injustice, opposition and oppression, and blatant disregard and disrespect. And yet it is also a story of a people who held tight to God's unchanging hands when the dark clouds of racism clouded their way. With great self-determination and steadfast activism, African Americans carved a place for themselves within the Roman Catholic Church in America. Once known as a mission church and a mission people, the African American Catholics of today are a people committed to the work of spreading the good news of the Gospel among themselves and

---

[3]Although it is most common to use the term "African American" in referring to the children of the African Diaspora, for the purpose of this work "Black" and "African American" will be used interchangeably. Note also the term "Negro" will be used in citing references prior to the Civil Rights Movement of the 1960s.

others—while acknowledging that this is no easy task as membership at Black Catholic parishes continues to decline.

African American Catholics experience a double invisibility. In the Black world, they are marginalized because of their religious identity as Catholics; in the Catholic world, they are marginalized because of their racial and cultural identity. Yet African American Catholics have not allowed their perceived double invisibility to deter their mission of evangelization.

In their pastoral letter *What We Have Seen and Heard*, addressed to the Catholics of the United States, ten African American bishops made the bold statement that African American Catholics have "come of age." African American Catholics had matured to adulthood and were no longer the helpless missionary children of the predominantly white Catholic Church of America. Although the tone of the pastoral letter was respectful and appreciative of the many gifts that had been shared with African American Catholics, the African American Catholic bishops nonetheless affirmed that they, too, as African Americans, had gifts to share with the universal Catholic Church. The African American Catholic bishops wrote: "Evangelization means not only preaching but witnessing; not only conversion but renewal; not only community but the building up of the community; not only hearing the Word but sharing it."[4]

There remains today a great vitality among African American Catholics to spread the Word of God among themselves and others. African Americans are a biblical people. The Word of God has been a tremendous source of support and consolation through the anguish and afflictions that they have had to endure. Many times, it has been "a word from the Lord" that has sustained them throughout their struggle with the evils of racism. However, in most cases the Word of God is not effectively preached to many African American Catholics. Every Sunday, many African American Catholics endure homilies that are not Holy Spirit filled, not relevant to their situations or life circumstances. The homilies are not based on the scripture readings and do not inspire the people to be a witness to the goodness of Jesus. It is truly a mystery how African American Catholics continue to return to the liturgies that give them neither life nor the hope of eternal life. Some African Americans contend that Mass has always been fairly boring. Others maintain that their love for the Eucharist calls them back to the Catholic Church every Sunday. Some also acknowledge that their faith is so strong that even if the priest or deacon doesn't have the Word, the Word of God is still deep within them.

---

[4] *What We Have Seen and Heard: A Pastoral Letter on Evangelization from the Black Bishops of the United States* (Cincinnati: St. Anthony Messenger Press, 1984), 2.

For the most part, preaching in our Catholic churches is notoriously uninspired. African Americans throughout this country almost unanimously will attest to this fact. Those who feel called to minister to African American congregations must see it as their duty to develop the art of effective, spirit-filled preaching. Black preaching is a Black folk art, but this does not mean that preachers from other ethnicities cannot be trained in certain techniques of this Black liturgical art. Some white pastors have acquired the ability to preach in the Black genre without doing a disservice to the integrity of their white identities. Conversely, many preachers who are not African American use their cultural identity as an unacceptable excuse for mediocrity. Preaching in the Black genre implies preaching with an eloquence that exegetes both the scriptural text and the congregation. The "Good News" must be addressed to this particular people, and the hermeneutical application of it must be made to their own situation.

## Challenges

The Catholic Church in urban neighborhoods throughout the United States is faced with a serious challenge. Many urban neighborhoods are plagued by deterioration and decay. Where once stood thriving communities with stable neighborhood residences, corner grocery stores, and other economic endeavors, now remain abandoned buildings, vacant lots, and the ruins of former successful businesses. In some neighborhoods the large beautiful Catholic church buildings remain, signs of a once-flourishing immigrant Catholic community. The once strong immigrant neighborhoods (German, Irish, Polish, and Italian) are now inhabited, in many cases, by a struggling and depressed African American community. In some instances, the ornate edifices dedicated to God and once populated by the Roman Catholic faithful have been sold to growing Protestant and non-denominational congregations in desperate need of extra space. Familiar Catholic names, such as "St. Mark's," "Most Holy Name of Jesus," and "St. Ann Shrine," have been replaced by new names reflective of new congregations, names such as "Emmaus Way Missionary Baptist Church," "New Jerusalem Cathedral Church of God in Christ," and "Transformation Christian Church." These once densely populated former Roman Catholic churches are now standing-room-only-churches. The Word of God is powerfully preached, the music ministry moves the congregation to make a joyful noise unto the Lord, the doors of the church are opened, and a call to discipleship is extended; the congregants have the Good News about Jesus Christ to take with them to share all week long, and the Word of God leads them to service within and outside their church.

In most cases the Catholic churches in African American neighborhoods throughout this nation have remained. However, there are significantly fewer parishioners. Dioceses and archdioceses have closed or merged many of their parishes in urban communities. Lack of parishioners and lack of funds have topped the list of reasons for the increased mergers. Pastors have somberly noted that all of the Catholics have moved to the suburbs. Yet there remains in our urban communities a vast number of African Americans who are unchurched or lapsed Catholics or inactive baptized believers. For too long there has been the perception that any semblance of Blackness must be left on the front steps of Catholic churches and that admittance means assimilating to the dominant Eurocentric expressions of Roman Catholic liturgy and worship. There have been few methods and/or models of inculturated evangelization of African Americans to the Catholic Church. In short, there is a great harvest of souls among African Americans for which the Catholic Church *must* find ways of effectively evangelizing.

According to the late Glenn Jeanmarie, preaching plays an important role in the evangelization of African Americans:

> We Blacks are people of the Word. We are by culture, by history, preaching orientated. We come from a preaching tradition. Preaching sustained and nurtured us during the days of slavery. Preaching gave us hope "in days when hope unborn had died." Preaching enables us to keep on keeping on. Preaching enables us to be truly opened to receive Eucharist, the bread of life. So, one of the greatest gifts, we, as Black people, can give to the Church today is preaching. For in authentic Black preaching the spirit is renewed.[5]

The Holy Spirit calls us all to the work of evangelization. It is important that those who have received the Gospel of Jesus Christ spread the Good News. Like Paul, Christians must be compelled to confess, "Preaching the gospel is not the subject of a boast; I am under compulsion and have no choice. I am ruined if I do not preach it!" (1 Cor. 9:16).

Evangelization is both a call and a response. It is the call of Jesus reverberating down the centuries: "Go into the whole world and proclaim the good news to all creation" (Mark 16:15). The response is, "Conduct

---

[5]Glenn Jeanmarie, "Black Catholic Worship: Celebrating Roots and Wings," in *Portrait in Black: Black Catholic Theological Symposium*, ed. Thaddeus J. Posey (Washington, DC: National Black Catholic Clergy Caucus, 1978), 85.

yourselves, then, in a way worthy of the gospel of Christ" (Phil. 1:27). Evangelization means not only preaching but witnessing, not only conversion but renewal, not only entry into the community but the building up of the community, not only hearing the Word but sharing it.

The Good News of the gospel not only transforms those who hear it, but it must also transform those who preach it. "The person who has been evangelized," Pope Paul VI wrote, "goes on to evangelize others."[6] However, evangelization is not done in a vacuum; it is performed within a particular context. Pope Paul VI in writing on the subject of evangelization in the modern world states:

> The obvious importance of the content of evangelization must not overshadow the importance of the ways and means. This question of "how to evangelize" is permanently relevant, because the methods of evangelizing vary according to the different circumstances of time, place and culture, and because they thereby present a certain challenge to our capacity for discovery and adaptation. On us particularly, the pastors of the Church, rests the responsibility for reshaping with boldness and wisdom, but in complete fidelity to the content of evangelization, the means that are most suitable and effective for communicating the Gospel message to the men and women of our times.[7]

The *National Black Catholic Pastoral Plan* promulgated by the National Black Catholic Congress in 1987, while stating that its primary purpose was to discuss issues relating to the evangelization of African Americans on the local level (within dioceses and parishes), never adequately addressed the need of a model of inculturated evangelization of African Americans to Catholicism. The National Black Catholic Pastoral Plan merely encourages the development of evangelization programs that are rooted in the Black spiritual experience. I submit that the preaching of the Word of God in a style that speaks to the heart and soul of the African American community is vital and must precede any programs of evangelization. In the great commission, Jesus did not instruct us to "go ye therefore" and set up programs, policies, and procedures. He instructed us to go preach!

---

[6]Pope Paul VI, *Evangelii Nuntiandi* [*On Evangelization in the Modern World*], apostolic exhortation (December 8, 1975), no. 24.

[7]*Evangelii Nuntiandi*, no. 40.

## Outline of *Down Deep in My Soul*

In this book I maintain that for effective evangelization to occur in African American Catholic parishes, aspects and techniques of the Black preaching style must be utilized by those called upon to preach. When Catholic preachers, African American, and non–African American, preach the Word of God in a manner that speaks to both the heart and the experience of the African American community, then there will be fewer empty pews in African American Catholic parishes. My fundamental goal in writing this book is to prepare *all* preachers—African Americans and those of other cultures called to preach in African American Catholic parishes—and thus enable a growth of African Americans embracing the Catholic faith. However, this stated endeavor presupposes both a willingness of the preacher to minister to African Americans and an openness to immerse himself or herself into the African American culture.

*Down Deep in My Soul* consists of seven chapters that offer a deeper understanding of the African American culture and preaching style. Chapter 1, titled "The Uniqueness of African American Culture, Spirituality, and Religious Experience," is an exposé of the uniqueness of African American culture and the richness of African American spirituality. I also give an extensive review of slavery and the slave religion. One cannot speak of Black preaching apart from Black spirituality. I demonstrate that spirituality is one's attempt to encounter God or the Divine Other. From a Christian perspective, when we speak of spirituality, we acknowledge a way of personally encountering or experiencing God in our lives. Spirituality is "faith lived." This means simply that as Christians we strive to live out that which we believe. In this first chapter the specific characteristics of Black spirituality are named. Black spirituality is characterized and explained as contemplative, holistic, biblical, joyful, and communal. Finally, I illustrate how each characteristic of Black spirituality relates to Black preaching.

Chapter 2 examines the very origins of Black preaching. The chapter is titled "The Black Preaching Style: Its Origins, Language, Method, and Techniques." The origins of the Black preaching style are discussed, with an analysis of the African oral tradition, the effects of slavery on the modes of communications among enslaved Africans, and the creation of the Black English dialect. The purpose of this chapter is to present a brief historic overview of the origins of the Black preaching style, an operative definition of Black preaching, and an observation of the literary and artistic forms of the Black preaching style. A methodology for Black preaching is offered, including an expansive description of the various techniques of the Black preaching style (e.g., call and response, rhythm, alliteration, repetition, and musicality).

The third chapter raises the question and is aptly titled "Will It Preach?" This chapter considers the purpose of the homily in Catholic worship. Essential to the foundation of preaching is to examine the stages of homily preparation, homily development, and delivering the homily. I offer four objectives of homily preparation germane to an African American Catholic liturgical context. These rudiments of homily preparation are information, inspiration, motivation, and celebration. The structure and movements of a homily are addressed as they pertain to homily development. I highlight the value of lectionary preaching in Catholic worship and the advantage of having several biblical texts to consider. Although there are various homiletical methods that are useful, I delve into the expository and narrative preaching methods that are commonly used in the Black preaching tradition. It is vital to gain the skills necessary to effectively deliver a homily. I review the significance of finding and owning one's voice as well as one's preaching presence.

Evangelization is the focus of Chapter 4. This chapter, titled "The Black Preaching Style as an Effective Means of Inculturated Evangelization," defines evangelization and its meaning and impact on the Roman Catholic Church and the African American community. Since the advent of his papacy, Pope Francis has emphasized the importance of preaching in the ministry of the Catholic Church. I assess the writings of Pope Francis on preaching by briefly considering his two apostolic encyclicals that uplift preaching as paramount to the work of evangelization, *The Joy of the Gospel* and *Rejoice and Be Glad*. I also appraise the import of "Word of God Sunday" promulgated by Pope Francis. The concept of "inculturated evangelization" is explored in depth. In what follows, I elucidate the importance of the role and image portrayed by the Catholic Church within the African American community. The image of the Catholic Church and its impact on any local community often reflect the dedication of the persons representing the Catholic Church who minister in that community. For the most part, people do not relate to abstract institutions. Rather, they identify with ministers working among them on matters important to them and their families. The same could be said for the place and purpose of preaching. African Americans generally seek a preached Word that will have a significant impact and relevance in their lives. They look to hear a powerfully preached message that leads them to the Lord and assists them in their daily Christian journey. If this is not accomplished in the context of worship, they leave the worship service feeling unfed and frustrated. I put forth practical suggestions for effective inculturated evangelization in African American Catholic parishes, demonstrating proven ways in which the Black preaching style can lead to amazing growth in African American Catholic parishes. Conversely, I conclude this chapter without negating what not only hinders evangelization but has attempted and at times succeeded in destroying the faith of African American Catholics, namely racism, indifference, and injustice within the Church.

Chapter 5 queries a probing and provocative question, "Whom Shall I Send?" This chapter strives to achieve clarity regarding who can and who should preach. Although the Church is clear canonically that ordained male presbyters and deacons are the persons who are granted faculties to preach at Eucharistic liturgies by the local Ordinary, I briefly examine other occasions that the non-ordained are permitted to "break open the Word." This chapter also explores the many and varied contributions that women offer as gift to the Church specifically in the African American Catholic community. This chapter culminates by highlighting lay preaching as an intrinsic value and an indubitable necessity within the African American Catholic community.

The sixth chapter addresses the transformative power of words and how they successfully effect societal change. The agency of the Black prophetic tradition is commonly embodied in preached sermons, pronouncements, declarations, and resolutions. The prophetic practices and actions of Black people seeking justice derive from the Black prophetic tradition. This study of rhetorical agency in the Black prophetic tradition, while not ground-breaking, is one that has not been considered by the Roman Catholic rhetorical or religious tradition. On several occasions, Pope Francis has acknowledged the transformative rhetoric of Martin Luther King Jr. I hope that this exposition of the Black prophetic tradition will cause it to be valued and utilized more widely within mainstream Catholicism.

*Down Deep in My Soul*, draws to a close with Chapter 7, "Toward an African American Catholic Theology of Preaching." It establishes the common ground between a developing Catholic theology of preaching and the tenets of the Black preaching style. The essential tenets of the Black preaching style are complementary to the principles of effective Catholic preaching promoted by the United States Catholic Bishops. Topics addressed in this formulation of an African American Catholic theology of preaching include: The Holy Spirit and Preaching, Preaching and

Ecumenism, Preaching as Celebration, and Preaching for Liberation. An appropriate understanding regarding *true* liberation for African Americans cannot remain abstract or nebulous; no, it demands praxis. A familiar adage of Black folks is the admonition "to practice what you preach." This is precisely what is expected in any tenable African American theology of preaching: preaching must make liberation and justice real for all God's children. From the pulpits of African American Catholic parishes, issues of social injustice must be preached; avoidance or disregard of topics pertaining to the social maladies plaguing the African American community is antithetical to the Gospel. This chapter serves not only as a concise personal operative theology of preaching but is intended also to facilitate further discussion between Catholic theology and Black theology as they relate to preaching.

The aims of *Down Deep in My Soul: An African American Catholic Theology of Preaching* are met only when preachers ministering in African American Catholic settings effectively understand that they must preach in a way that is relevant and brings their listeners to a greater commitment to following Jesus and witnessing to others about it. Then, and only then, will the resounding cry come from some satisfied soul sitting in a pew, "You've told the story, preacher; you've told the story!"

1

# The Uniqueness
# of African American Culture,
# Spirituality, and Religious Experience

## PART I: FROM AFRICAN TRADITIONAL RELIGION
## TO BLACK CHRISTIANITY

The enslavement of an estimated twelve million Africans over a period of almost four centuries in the Atlantic slave trade was a tragedy of such scope that it is difficult to imagine, much less comprehend.[1] When these Africans were brought to slavery in the mines, plantations, and households of the New World, they were torn away from the political, social, and cultural systems that had ordered their lives. Tribal and linguistic groups were broken up, either on the coasts of Africa or in the slave pens across the Atlantic. Most brutal of all, the dehumanizing system of slavery did not allow the preservation of family or kinship ties.

In the New World, slave control was based on the eradication of all forms of African culture because of their power to unify the slaves and thus enable them to resist or rebel. Nevertheless, African beliefs and customs persisted and were transmitted by slaves to their descendants. Shaped and modified by a new environment, elements of African folklore, music, language, and religion were transplanted in the New World by the African Diaspora. Influenced by colonial European and Indigenous Native American cultures, aspects of the African heritage have contributed, in greater or lesser degree, to the formation of various African American cultures in the New World. One of the most durable and adaptable elements of the slave culture, linking African past with American present, was

---

[1]For estimates of the volume of the slave trade, see Philip D. Curtin, *The Atlantic Slave Trade: A Census* (Madison: University of Wisconsin Press, 1969). Curtin's figures have been challenged as excessively low by J. E. Inikori, "Measuring the Atlantic Slave Trade," *Journal of African History*,17, no. 2 (1976): 197–223.

African religion. It is important to realize, however, that in the Americas the religions of Africa have not been merely preserved as static "African-isms" or as archaic "retentions." African styles of worship, forms of ritual, systems of belief, and fundamental perspectives have remained vital on this side of the Atlantic not because they were preserved in a pure ortho-doxy but because they were transformed. Adaptability, based on respect for spiritual power wherever it originated, accounted for the ability of African religions to resonate with other religious traditions and for the continuity of a distinctively African religious consciousness.

## Traditional African Religion

In the traditional religion of West Africa, the perceived power of the gods and spirits was effectively present in the lives of the people on every level—environmental, individual, social, national, and cosmic. The gods and people related to one another through the mediation of sacrifice, through the mechanism of divination, and through the phenomenon of spirit possession. Widely shared by diverse West African societies were several fundamental beliefs concerning the relationship of the divine and human: belief in a transcendent, benevolent God, creator and ultimate source of providence; belief in a number of immanent gods, to whom people must sacrifice in order to make life propitious; belief in the power of spirits to affect the welfare of people; belief in priests and others who were expert in practical knowledge of the gods and spirits; belief in spirit possession, in which gods, through their devotees, spoke to individuals as well as to the community. Again, it must be understood that not every West African society shared all these beliefs. Nonetheless, this is an ac-curate description of the theological perspectives of a wide range of West African peoples.

In addition to the gods, the ancestors are a powerful class of spirits in the world of traditional West African religions.[2] Throughout West Africa, the ancestors, both those who died long ago and those of recent memory, are revered as founders of villages and kinship groups. These esteemed ancestors play a prominent role in human agency. Diana L. Hayes states in her book *Forged in the Fiery Furnace: African American Spirituality*, "The ancestors are integral to the African cosmology because they serve as the connection between the living and the dead in the cycle of life,

---

[2]Benjamin Ray, *African Religions* (Englewood Cliffs, NJ: Prentice-Hall, 1976), 17–26.

death, and rebirth. They serve as intermediaries for their living relatives, as guides and often as goads to living a good life."[3] It is believed that, as custodians of custom and law, the ancestors have the power to intervene in present affairs and, moreover, to grant fertility and health to their descendants, for whom they mediate with the gods. Among the Mende, for example, "The mediator role of the ancestors is assumed to be possible because they are spirit and therefore already have access to God who is also spirit."[4] Indeed, some gods are said to be the divinized ancestors of living members of the tribe.

In his book *Theology Brewed in an African Pot*, Agbonkhianmeghe E. Orobator delineates the five essential traits of African ancestorship:

- An ancestor maintains some binding blood ties with the living members of his or her family, clan, or community.
- The experience of death offers the ancestor a privileged place of closeness to God.
- He or she is able to mediate or intercede on behalf of the living family or clan members.
- He or she [as a mediator] is entitled to mandatory and regular communication and consultation (invocation, libation, ritual offerings, sacrifices, etc.) with the living.
- To become an ancestor [the living dead], a person must have distinguished himself or herself in service and led an exemplary life in community.[5]

Albert J. Raboteau in his landmark book, *Slave Religion,* quotes M. J. Field in reference to the beliefs of the Africans of the Ga or Gan tribe from the southeast coast of Ghana: "Most people are, in practice, more afraid of offending these [dead forefathers and foremothers] than of offending the gods, though in theory . . . they give the higher place to the gods."[6] It was clear to the Ga people that in order to avoid harm, sickness, and perhaps even death, they were expected to offer homage and veneration to their ancestors. They believed that if they dishonored the ancestors in any way, especially by not offering veneration, the ancestors would visit them

---

[3]Diana L. Hayes, *Forged in the Fiery Furnace* (Maryknoll, NY: Orbis Books, 2012), 25.

[4]W. T. Hanis and Henry Sawyer, *The Springs of the Mende Belief and Conduct* (Freetown: Sierra Leone University Press, 1968), 15.

[5]Agbonkhianmeghe E. Orobator, *Theology Brewed in an African Pot* (Maryknoll, NY: Orbis Books, 2008), 141.

[6]Albert J. Raboteau, *Slave Religion* (Oxford: Oxford University Press, 1978), citing M.J. Field, *Religion and Medicine of the Ga* (Oxford: Oxford University Press, 1961, 197), 12.

in their dreams and express their displeasure and disapproval of them.[7]

Raboteau is emphatic that the ancestors carefully attend to the observance of African ritualistic traditions. If there was any digression from what was normative, the perpetrator was possibly penalized.[8] Once again, he cites M. J. Field's work, *Religion and Medicine from the Ga*:

> The living never forget that they are the trustees of the dead. The continuity of customs must be faithfully preserved. A custom, rite, or ceremony is a link with the dead who instituted it quite as much as it is the right of the god who received it. The dead are always watching to see that the living preserve what their forefathers established. And since the dead have power to bestow either blessing or adversity . . . the welfare of the living is felt to be bound up with the faithful performance of ancient customs.[9]

Thus, we have witnessed in brief that the religious background and briefs of the enslaved West Africans[10] were considered complicated and intricate. Within the African community's daily life there was an undeniable connection between the natural and the supernatural, the sacred and the profane.[11] According to Pierre Verger, there was no apparent distance between the heavenly world and the earthly world.[12] Verger states, "African traditional religion enables Africans to speak directly with their gods and benefit from their benevolence."[13] African traditional religions adhered to the understanding that they must without exception commune with the ones whom they considered the "divine," including the ancestors. To further explain this understanding, J. F. Ajayi notes in his book *Christian Missions in Nigeria, 1841–1891*, that the sacredness of meticulously following the custom of maintaining an abiding generational relationship with the divine and ancestors are "expressed in laws and customs hallowed by time and myth."[14]

Plantation life in the New World was where the enslaved Africans' sense

---

[7] Ibid.

[8] Ibid.

[9] Raboteau, 13, citing M. J. Field, *Religion and Medicine of the Ga*, 197.

[10] It has long been debated that the use of the term "slaves" is neither culturally nor politically correct. Thus, as much as possible I will use the term "enslaved Africans" to denote the undisputed fact that slaves were not brought to the New World from Africa, but rather free Africans were forcibly transplanted from the continent of Africa.

[11] Raboteau, 32.

[12] Pierre Verger, *Dieux d'Afrique* (Paris: Paul Hartmann, 1954), 9.

[13] Ibid.

[14] J. F. Ajayi, *Christian Missions in Nigeria, 1841–1891* (Evanston, IL: Northwestern University Press, 1965), 4–5.

of humanity was systematically expunged and obliterated. Strict apartheid practices were observed on large Southern plantations, generally disallowing personal contact except on rare occasions. Consequently, it was virtually impossible for the Africans to communicate without the presence of a white overseer or the master of the plantation himself. Slavery in the United States consisted of not only the chains of physical bondage but also the psychological chains of mental bondage.[15]

Slave owners, primarily through their overseers, made sure that newly purchased Africans entering plantation life were indoctrinated into the quotidian customs and rules of the plantation. They were mentored or advised by older, well-assimilated enslaved persons on the plantations. This formation process was inclusive of work, personal hygiene, behavior within the slave quarters, adherence to expressed rules and regulations, and times of recreation.[16]

E. Franklin Frazier posits in *The Negro Church in America* that it was necessary to acquire some knowledge of the language of whites for communication.[17] Any attempt on the part of the slaves to preserve or use their native language was discouraged or prohibited. They were set to tasks in order to acquire the necessary skills for the production of cotton or sugarcane. On the small farms very often the slaves worked in the fields with their white owners. On the larger plantations they were under the strict discipline of the overseers who not only supervised their work but also maintained a strict surveillance over all their activities in the interest of security. It was a general rule that there could be no assembly of five or more slaves without the presence of a white man.[18] This applied especially to their gathering for religious purposes. All of this tended to bring about as completely as possible a loss of the enslaved Africans' cultural and religious heritage.

## The Loss of Social Cohesion

It is evident, then, that the manner in which Africans were captured, enslaved, and inducted into the plantation system loosened all social bonds among them and destroyed the traditional basis of social cohesion. In addition, the organization of labor and the system of social control and discipline on the plantation also hindered the development of social

---

[15] E. Franklin Frazier, *The Negro Church in America* (New York: Schocken Books, 1974), 10.
[16] Ibid., 10–11.
[17] Frazier, 11.
[18] Ibid.

cohesion either on the basis of whatever remnants of African culture might have survived or on the basis of the Africans' role in the plantation economy. Although the enslaved Africans were organized in work gangs, labor lost its traditional African meaning as a cooperative undertaking with communal significance. In fact, there was hardly a community among the slaves despite the fact that on the larger plantations there were slave quarters. In reality, these living arrangements were designed to accommodate heavy surveillance by the overseer or master.

The possibility of establishing some basis for social cohesion was further reduced because of the difficulty of communication among the slaves. If by chance slaves who spoke the same African language were thrown together, it was the policy on the part of the masters to separate them. In any case, it was necessary for the operation of the plantation that the slaves should learn the language of their masters, and communication among slaves themselves was generally carried on in English.

Africans are a communal people. Even in the midst of a brutal enslavement, Africans found ways to communicate with one another. The use of gestures, body language, words, or phrases had common meaning, as well as songs, music, and drum playing. Their indomitable spirit refused to allow physical separation to keep them from finding alternative ways of communicating. The recognition of taking on the oppressor's language as their own language was a way of restoring a customary intimacy among the enslaved Africans. Possessing a shared language, enslaved Africans could find again a way to make community and a means to create the political solidarity necessary to resist their oppression, as well as their oppressors.

The enslavement of the Africans not only destroyed the traditional African system of kinship and other forms of organized social life, but it also made insecure and precarious the most elementary form of social life which tended to sprout anew on American soil, the family. There was no legal marriage, and the relation of the husband and father to his wife and children was a temporary relationship, subject to the will of the white masters and the pressing needs of the plantation regime. Although it was necessary to show some regard for the biological tie between slave mother and her children, even this relationship was not always respected by the masters. Nevertheless, under the most favorable conditions of slavery as, for example, among the privileged skilled artisans and the favored house servants, some stability in family relations and a feeling of solidarity among the members of the slave households did develop. This represented the maximum social cohesion that was permitted to exist among the transplanted Africans.[19]

---

[19]Ibid., 13.

There has been some debate over this issue of the loss of social cohesion among the Africans brought to these shores. Some scholars have argued that social cohesion among the enslaved Africans was not destroyed completely. W. E. B. Du Bois believed that social cohesion among the enslaved Africans was totally destroyed. Du Bois, the first African American graduate of Harvard University, asserts, "The Black church was the only social institution among the Negroes which started in the African forest and survived slavery." He also noted that "under the leadership of the priest and medicine man," the church preserved the remnants of African tribal life. However, B. Franklin Frazier, refuting this position, states, "From the available evidence, including what we know of the manner in which slaves were Christianized and the character of their churches, it is impossible to establish any continuity between African religious practices and the Black church in the United States."[20] It is Frazier's belief that with the breaking up or destruction of the clan and kinship organization, the religious myths and cults lost their significance. He contends that in America the destruction of the clan and kinship organization was devastating, and the Africans were plunged into an alien civilization in which whatever remained of their religious myths and cults had no meaning whatever.

In my opinion, there is a middle ground in this debate of how much was lost in the religious expressions of the enslaved Africans. We cannot say that all of the primitive cultural and religious traditions were maintained throughout the period of slavery. In many ways the elders were prohibited from passing on the devotions and worship patterns from their beloved homeland. However, to say that everything of the African traditional religious belief system was totally lost is also untrue. I contend that many contemporary religious expressions such as singing, shouting, witnessing, "calling on the ancestors," and "telling the story" have all been retained from a rich African past. Though not purely African, the prayers and devotion of those of the African Diaspora are expressed with African hearts and an African sacred memory.

## Christian Religion as a New Basis of Social Cohesion

E. Franklin Frazier suggests that it was not what remained of African culture or African religious experience but the Christian religion that provided the new basis of social cohesion. It follows, then, that in order to understand the religion of the enslaved Africans, one must study the

---

[20]Ibid.

influence of Christianity on creating solidarity among a people who lacked social cohesion and a structured social life.

From the earliest days of their importation to the colonies, Africans received Christian baptism. The initial opposition to the baptism of Africans gradually disappeared when laws made it clear that they did not become free through the acceptance of the Christian faith and baptism.[21] Although the enslaved Africans were regularly baptized and taken into the Anglican Church during the seventeenth century, it was not until the beginning of the eighteenth century that a systematic attempt was made on the part of the Church of England to Christianize the Africans in America. This missionary effort was carried out by the Society for the Propagation of the Gospel in Foreign Parts, which was chartered in England in 1701.[22] Unfortunately, there are not very detailed or accurate accounts of the early Christian evangelization efforts toward the African people. So it is difficult to assess the extent to which the converted Africans resumed their practice of the traditional African religions. It may even be plausible that they combined their acceptance of Christianity with their former ways of prayer and worship. In this connection it should be noted that the missionaries recognized the difficulty of converting adult Africans and concentrated their efforts on the children. The African children were much more inclined to learn and accept Christianity.[23]

Theologian Diana L. Hayes submits that there was a stark distinction between the ways Catholics and Protestants introduced Christianity to the enslaved Africans:

> Those Africans who found themselves on Catholic plantations, especially in the Caribbean and South America, were introduced to Christianity from the very beginning of their enslavement. Finding much in Catholicism to suit them, they, in most instances, simply layered the Christian faith onto already existing beliefs, seeing no conflict in doing so. At the same time many African Catholics, especially in the Carolinas and Louisiana, came to the American colonies/states with prior knowledge of and experience of Catholicism, especially those from Kongo (today's Angola), the first West African nation voluntarily to convert to Roman Catholicism (1491) and to establish independent relations with the Vatican State.

---

[21]Ibid., 14.

[22]C. F. Pascoe, *Two Hundred Years of the Society for the Propagation of the Gospel: An Historical Account of the Society for the Propagation of the Gospel in Foreign Parts*, vol. 1 (Oxford: Oxford University Press, 1901), 1–7.

[23]Ibid.

On Protestant plantations, however, conversion to Christianity was not initially welcomed or encouraged due to the owners' fears that the newly baptized slaves would have to be freed. . . .The delay, however, allowed slaves to retain and pass on African understandings and habits, often for generations.[24]

However, by the eve of the Civil War, Christianity had pervaded the enslaved African community.[25] The vast majority of Africans were American-born, and the cultural and linguistic barriers that impeded the evangelization of earlier generations of African-born slaves were generally not a problem. The widespread opposition of the planters to the catechizing of slaves had been largely dissipated due to the efforts of the churches and missionaries of the South. Not all enslaved Africans were Christian, nor were all those who accepted Christianity members of a church. Still, doctrines, symbols, and the vision of life preached by Christianity were familiar to most.[26] Albert J. Raboteau asserts that during the end of the antebellum era the so-called invisible institution of slave religion or slave Christianity came to maturity. This assertion is well documented by sources from the enslaved Africans themselves.[27]

## Slave Religion

At first glance it seems strange to refer to the religion of the enslaved Africans as an invisible institution, since independent Black churches with slave members did not exist in the South before emancipation. In racially mixed churches, it was not uncommon for the Africans to outnumber masters in attendance at Sunday services. But the religious experience of the Africans was by no means fully contained in the visible structures of the institutional church. From the abundant testimony of fugitive and freed Africans it is clear that the enslaved African community had an extensive religious life of its own that was hidden from the eyes of the master. In the secrecy of the quarters or the brush arbors or "hush harbors" the enslaved Africans made Christianity truly their own.

Albert J. Raboteau, professor emeritus of religion at Princeton University, concisely describes the unique nature and function of the slave

---

[24]Hayes, *Forged in the Fiery Furnace*, 27.
[25]Raboteau, 212.
[26]Ibid.
[27]Ibid., 213.

religion as a religion that was in many ways indefinable so as to protect the Africans from being caught by their master. Raboteau states:

> The religion of the slaves was both institutional and noninstitutional, visible and invisible, formally organized and spontaneously adapted. Regular Sunday worship in the local church was paralleled by illicit, or at least informal, prayer meetings on weeknights in the slave cabins. Preachers licensed by the church and hired by the master were supplemented by slave preachers licensed only by the spirit.
>
> Texts from the Bible which most slaves could not read were explicated by verses from the spirituals. Slaves forbidden by masters to attend church or, in some cases, even to pray risked floggings to attend secret gatherings to worship God.[28]

Wash Wilson, a former slave, recalls his own experience of the "invisible institution":

> When de [negroes] go round singin' "Steal Away to Jesus," dat mean dere gwine be a 'ligious meeting: dat night. De masters . . . didn't like dem 'ligious meetin's, so us natcherly slips off at night, down in de bottoms or somewhere. Sometimes us sing and pray all night.[29]

Into that all-night singing and praying the slaves poured the sufferings and needs of their days. Like "Steal Away" and the rest of the spirituals, Christianity was fitted by the enslaved African community to its own particular experience. At the same time the symbols, myths, and values of the Judeo-Christian tradition helped form the slave community's image of itself.

The enslaved Africans frequently were moved to hold their own religious meetings out of disgust for the pseudo-gospel preached by their masters' preachers. Sermons urging them to be obedient and docile to their masters were repeated *ad nauseam*. The type of sermon to which he and the others enslaved were constantly subjected was paraphrased by former slave Frank Roberson in John B. Cade's account, "Out of the Mouths of Ex-Slaves":

---

[28]Raboteau, 212–13.
[29]Dorothy Scarborough, *On the Trail of Negro Folk-Songs* (Cambridge, MA: Harvard University Press, 1925), 22–23.

You slaves will go to heaven if you are good, but don't ever think you will be close to your mistress and master. No! No! There will be a wall between; but there will be holes in it that will permit you to look out and see your mistress when she passes by. If you want to sit behind this wall, you must do the language of the text, "Obey your masters."[30]

Often the enslaved Africans would complain (among themselves) about the content of the sermons that the white preachers preached. It seemed that "going to church" only meant going to hear the preacher talk about slaves obeying their masters and avoiding lying and stealing. There was nothing said about Jesus, and the overseer stood there to see that the preacher preached what was expected of him. Thus, the need arose for an "invisible church" so that the real Word could be preached, and a relevant message could be heard.

Looking back at these secret and risky religious gatherings, an ex-slave declared, "Meetings back there meant more than they do now. Then everybody's heart was in tune, and when they called on God they made Heaven ring. It was more than just Sunday meeting and then no godliness for a week. They would steal off to the fields and in the thickets and there . . . they called on God out of heavy hearts."[31] Truly these meetings needed no preacher, because "everyone was so anxious to have a word to say that a preacher did not have a chance. All of them would sing and pray."[32]

Raboteau offers a keen insight into the spirituality and religious practice of the enslaved African community with a compelling description of the secret prayer meeting recorded by Peter Randolph, a slave in Prince George County, Virginia, until he was freed in 1847. It is interesting to note and compare many of the similarities found in the slave religion and what evolved into the contemporary African American praise and worship. From all observations the slave religion was an inviting and inclusive style of worship. It seemed as if everyone was encouraged and even expected to participate by offering a song, a prayer, a witness, or a testimony. This was indeed the time, in the stillness and secrecy of the dark night, to speak and express the need for God's deliverance from the pain and brutality of slavery. Randolph observed:

---

[30]John B. Cade, "Out of the Mouths of Ex-Slaves," *Journal of Negro History* 20 (July 1935): 329. Another common notion preached was that slaves would occupy the "kitchen" of heaven and would continue there to serve their white masters as on earth.

[31]George P. Rawick, *God Struck Me Dead* (Philadelphia: Pilgrim Press, 1969), 134–135.

[32]Ibid.

Not being allowed to hold meetings on the plantation, the slaves assembled in the swamp, out of reach of the patrols. They have an understanding among themselves as to the time and place of getting together. This is often done by the first one arriving breaking boughs from the trees and bending them in the direction of the selected spot. Arrangements are then made for conducting the exercises. They first ask each other how they feel, the state of their minds, etc. The male members then select a certain space, in separate groups, for the division of the meeting. Preaching . . . by the brethren, then praying and singing all around, until they generally feel quite happy. The speaker usually commences by calling himself unworthy, and talks very slowly, until feeling the spirit, he grows excited, and in a short time, there fall to the ground twenty or thirty men and women under its influence.[33]

Randolph went on to make clear the importance of these gatherings for the life of the slave community:

The slave forgets all his sufferings, except to remind others of the trials during the past week, exclaiming: "Thank God, I shall not live here always!" Then they pass from one to another, shaking hands, and bidding each other farewell. . . . As they separate, they sing a parting hymn of praise.[34]

It is well documented that prayer, preaching, song, communal support, and especially "feeling the spirit" refreshed the slaves and consoled them in their times of distress. By imagining their lives in the context of a different future they gained hope in the present.

Annual revival meetings were social occasions for Blacks, as well as whites. Masters were known to enjoy the singing and praying and preaching of the slaves. Nevertheless, the cabin room, the overturned pot, the prayin' ground, and the "hush harbor" were the safe places where the children of Africa found a resting place where they could be one with God and God could be one with them. These safe places were the indisputable sacred spaces that witnessed the birth of Black spirituality. This sacred place, this holy ground, the captives from Africa kept to themselves. No matter how religious the master might be, the slaves knew that the master's religion did not include prayers for their freedom in this world.

---

[33]Peter Randolph, *Sketches of Slave Life or, Illustrations of the Peculiar Institution* (Boston, 1855), 30–31.
[34]Ibid.

## PART II: CHARACTERISTICS OF BLACK SPIRITUALITY

Spirituality is faith lived. As such, it encompasses the totality of personal and collective responses to religious belief, including relationships, morality, worship, and daily living. As Christians we strive to understand and to act in a way that makes us part of the reality that is the will and purpose of God. Thus, Black spirituality is "pervaded with the African American experience and awareness."[35] It is at once a response to and a reflection of African American life and culture. It is rooted in African heritage and religious traditions, with its ways of perceiving and valuing reality, its style of expression, and its modes of prayer and of contemplating the divine. It is colored by the experiences of the Middle Passage, slavery, the Caribbean and Latin experience, segregation, integration, and African Americans' ongoing struggle for justice and liberation. It is expressed in every geographic locale, whether urban or rural, Southern, Northern, Eastern, or Western. It is present in every socioeconomic level—rich, middle-class, and poor. Black spirituality is influenced by present experiences and that of African American forebears in Pentecostal, Baptist, Adventist, Episcopal, Methodist, Catholic, and other churches. Black spirituality contains elements from high churches to Spirit-filled, hand-clapping, foot stomping storefront churches. Regardless of the circumstance, wherever African Americans have sought to find meaning, purpose, identity, community, worth, and God together, Black spirituality has grown and flourished.

The late Benedictine African American Catholic historian, Father Cyprian Davis, maintained that Black spirituality is characterized by

> a contemplative approach to prayer; a sense of God's power and presence everywhere, a high value placed on emotional responses; a fundamental rejection of any "body is evil" spirituality; a sense that joy is the important spiritual good; an awareness of social justice dimensions of religion; and finally, a sense that Blacks are as a people a spiritual people [with] a heritage to pass on.[36]

Black spirituality is also characterized by a number of specific emphases and attitudes, none of which is exclusive, but which, taken together, combine to produce a unique vision and practice of the spiritual life.

---

[35]Cyprian Davis, OSB, "The Black Contributions to a North American Spirituality," *New Catholic World* 225 (July–August 1982): 184.

[36]Ibid.

Drawing from Cyprian Davis's explanation of Black spirituality, we now explore Black spirituality as contemplative, holistic, biblical, joyful, and communal.

## Black Spirituality Is Contemplative

Inherent in the contemplative dimension of Black spirituality is the sense that prayer is spontaneous and pervasive. Any place is a place for prayer because God's presence is felt in every place. Some cultures deem certain places as exclusively the place where the divine dwells. For example, churches and well-known religious sites such as Lourdes in France and Fatima in Portugal are viewed as sacred places where faith and spirituality abound. However, it is the African American religious concept that God and or the divine is not relegated merely to a certain shrine or building. God is everywhere. Therefore, drawing from the "invisible churches" of their horrific past, African Americans feel enabled and called to prayer just where they are. It could be on a city bus, while cooking dinner, or at work in a noisy factory. Black spirituality senses the awe of God's transcendence and the vital intimacy of God's closeness. The sense of God's omnipresence and power taught the African American ancestors that no one can run or hide from God.

Jamie T. Phelps, OP, African American Catholic theologian, argues that there is a uniquely African concept of the pervasive nature of God, one that is intimate and personal:

> Most Africans and members of the African Diaspora have an experience of God that is both transcendent and immanent. God is the One who is beyond us but dwells within us. Black believers know experientially ("deep down in my soul") that the Spirit of God dwells within their inner selves, directing their memory, imagination, intellect, feelings, and body. Any person born into the religious tradition of African or African Diaspora cultures is nurtured from birth into a style of life that witnesses to the belief that God is manifest everywhere and in every person, thing or event. This attitude corresponds to the traditional religions of Dahomey, in which God meets the human being at every point of life; but the involvement of God in human life by way of "the gods" has been replaced, in the Black church, by the concept of God being present by means of the Spirit sent by Jesus after his ascension. Thus, a person steeped in the Black spiritual tradition is trained, so to speak, in a particular kind

of mystical tradition. One sees God's hand in every human encounter and event in life and is conditioned by environmental nurturing to abandon oneself, in obedience to God's will, to the movements of the Holy Spirit.[37]

It is not unusual for a Black child reared in a religious home to hear family members, especially the mother, talking to Jesus as they mull over family concerns. Nor is it unusual to hear in family and community conversations testimony that a person had been led by God to use his or her talents in a specific way, even when the individual involved was initially resistant to such a course of action. The impulse in Black spirituality to abandon oneself to the divine will and the indwelling Spirit lends itself to a particularly intimate experience of God.

The nature and being of God in Black spirituality are best understood when one pictures God as the Almighty One who is all powerful, who rules the universe, and who controls all people. Almost always the traditional Black prayer opens with a line addressed specifically to "Almighty God." God is often pictured as the One who "sits high and looks low" and knows every thought and action of humanity. God is also seen in Black prayers as being "too high to get over, too low to get under, too wide to get around, so that one comes to God through the door." Over and over again, God is seen in this prayer tradition as being able to "open doors no one can close, and close doors that no one can open." The Almighty can "build up where no one can tear down and can tear down where no one can build up." All of these prayer lines are deeply rooted in the language of traditional Black prayers and may be heard repeatedly.

Benjamin E. Mays summarizes the idea of God in Black prayer as follows:

> God is in heaven. He is all powerful, the source of all things even to allowing us to go to bed and rise in the morning. In allowing us to do this, He displays mercy. God is a rock in a weary land and a shelter in a mighty storm. All that happens is God's will. God is a partial God who is to be feared and appeased. He does things arbitrarily, apparently for no other reason than the fact that He is all powerful and can do what He pleases.[38]

---

[37]Jamie T. Phelps, OP, "Black Spirituality," in *Taking Down Our Harps*, ed. Cyprian Davis, OSB, and Diana Hayes (Maryknoll, NY: Orbis Books, 1998), 191.
[38]Benjamin E. Mays, *The Negro's God* (New York: Russell & Russell, 1968), 83.

African Americans believe that a personal relationship with God is absolutely necessary. God has to be known at this level, so that the supportive sense of God's presence can provide a lift for life's burdens and unpleasant encounters. Therefore, African Americans view God as an ever-present help. While God may be referred to in prayer as being almighty, in reality God is very close and personal. Knowing God and doing God's will also provide a sense of security against the many known and unknown cruelties of life. This feeling was expressed in the following prayer lines:

> Oh, Father, you are a good God, because some are lying on their beds of affliction, some are behind bars, some are in the hospital, and some are sleeping in their graves; yet, we have been wonderfully blessed with health.[39]

In these prayers are firm beliefs that health, life, and security from disease come from God. God can extend life and health to whom God wills. There is a sense within the African American community that those who are fortunate to receive God's blessings are obligated to praise and thank God for what they have received.

African Americans' sense of God is essentially gained through experience. God is not the God of speculation. God is the One who acts in life. Within the contemplative dimension of Black spirituality God teaches, guides, protects, and remains faithful even when humanity is not faithful. Therefore, the preacher in an African American setting must use language, stories, and expressions that speak of a personal God. For example, the preacher may say in a call and response fashion, "God is good!" The Black congregation almost on cue knows to respond, "All the time!" The preacher understanding the nature of God for the African American can speak of God as the One who "walks with me, and talks with me, and tells me I am His own." In the Black preaching style and in the tenets of Black spirituality, God is seen as the One who protects and defends in time of need and thus the preacher can say of God: "He can make a way out of no way!"

## Black Spirituality Is Holistic

Black spirituality, in contrast with much of Western tradition, is holistic. This holistic characteristic of Black spirituality simply means that there

---

[39]Ibid., 84.

is no dualism. Divisions between intellect and emotion, spirit and body, action and contemplation, individual and community, sacred and secular are foreign to Africans and those of the African Diaspora.[40] In keeping with their African heritage, African Americans are not ashamed of expressing their emotions.[41] Likewise, their religious experience is an experience of the whole human being. Encounters with the divine encompass the total person including feelings and the intellect, the heart as well as the head. There is also no notion that the body is evil as is in Western culture. Therefore, when Black people pray and worship, there is a sense of the whole coming together. Feelings and emotions are commingled with cognitive reasoning. For instance, a common religious phrase in the African American religious experience used both in sermon and song is: "When I think [cognitive] of the goodness of Jesus and all He's done for me [the blessing], my soul cries out, 'Hallelujah' [the emotional response], I thank God for saving me!" Note in this simple religious expression the holistic nature of Black spirituality. In this one simple phrase there is thought and the reception of a blessing, which in turn call forth an emotional response.

Black preaching is an exercise in holistic Black spirituality. Within the context of a sermon the preacher identifies the concern, issue, or problem (the preacher sets up a thought process, or perhaps a moment of doubt or bewilderment), and then the preacher seeks a solution to the problem (usually an act of God, a healing, a miracle, deliverance, a rescue, or Jesus, himself, is the answer) which results in an emotional response (Praise the Lord; Thank you, Jesus) from both the recipient of the blessing and the congregation hearing the sermon.

The lack of distinction between the sacred and the secular is often demonstrated in the Black preaching style. It is common to hear a preacher using the Black preaching style make references to secular situations and circumstances in connection with the Word of God. For example, preaching on the scripture in which Jesus says, "It is easier for a camel to fit through the eye of a needle than it is for a rich man to enter the kingdom," the preacher may appropriately title the sermon or homily, "Sashay if you may, but you won't get in that way!" This secular phrase captures both the essence of that particular biblical passage and the attention of the congregation. The preacher, again using the dynamics of a holistic spirituality, may further illustrate his or her sermon or homily title by using his or her body to literally sashay in the pulpit. There is no

---

[40]James P. Lyke, *What We Have Seen and Heard* (Cincinnati: St. Anthony Messenger Press, 1984), 8.
[41]Ibid.

doubt that the congregation will remember this homily because it touched their mind as well as their emotions.

Once again we see that in African American culture the emotional is not the opposite of the spiritual, nor is there any separation between the emotional and the intellectual. Both the mind and the heart are needed to grasp the truth. If the preacher does not preach the truth, it will not be long before the congregation calls him or her to task.

## Black Spirituality Is Biblical

Another fundamental element of Black spirituality is its strong biblical character. In the dark days of slavery reading was forbidden, but for African Americans, the Bible was never a closed book. The stories were told and retold in sermons, spirituals, and shouts. Proverbs and turns of phrase were borrowed freely from the Bible. The Bible, to those African Americans, was not a mere record of the wonderful works of God in a bygone age, but rather a present record of what was soon to come. God will lead the Hebrew children from the bondage of Egypt. God will preserve his children in the midst of the fiery furnace. God's power will make dry bones scattered on the plain snap together, and God will breathe life into them. Above all, the birth and death, the suffering and the sorrow, the burial and the resurrection of Jesus tell how the story will end for all who are faithful despite the present tragedy.

The African American bishops eloquently expound on the significance of the sacred scriptures in the spiritual life of African Americans in their pastoral letter *What We Have Seen and Heard*:

> For Black people the story is our story; the Bible promise is our hope. Thus, when the Word of Scripture is proclaimed in the Black community, it is not a new message but a new challenge. Scripture is part of our roots; the Bible has sunk deep into our tradition; and the Good News of the Gospel has been enmeshed in our past of oppression and pain. Still the message was heard, and we learned to celebrate in the midst of sorrow, to hope in the depths of despair and to fight for freedom in the face of all obstacles. The time has now come to take this precious heritage and to go and "tell it on the mountain."[42]

---

[42]Ibid., 5.

The worship services of the traditional Black church are dominated by the dynamic and evocative preaching of the minister, and the starting point of the sermon is always the Word of God. The preacher begins by retelling an entire biblical story or dramatically announcing a few lines from a text taken from the Old or New Testament. After this vivid proclamation of the scripture, the preacher brings the biblical text to life by indicating how the story has meaning in the lives of the congregation. Often the preaching is a dialogical experience, with the congregation affirming the preacher's truth-telling by nods of the head, applause, amens, and similar responses. When the Spirit of Truth envelops the assembly, some of the worshipers respond in a manner similar to their African ancestors who experienced spirit possession. The preaching and singing are necessarily emotional, because the worshipers have been touched at the core of their being, moved by the presence of the Spirit deep in their soul.

The point of the Black church's Bible-centered worship is to hear God's word from the past as it is evidenced in the present. This interpretive principle or hermeneutic is a reflection of the African concept of time in which past and present are one and continuous. Thus, Black spirituality always situates itself firmly in the present, in the midst of the concrete daily experience. In the same way, the biblical characters are not simply heroes and heroines of long ago; they have joined the ranks of the ancestors, and their lives, like those of the biological ancestors of African Americans, influence the lives of the living community.

Further justification and validation of a Black biblical hermeneutic is given by the late African American theologian James Hal Cone, who is generally regarded as the "father of Black theology."

The hermeneutical principle for an exegesis of the Scriptures is the revelation of God in Christ as the Liberator of the oppressed from social oppression and to political struggle, wherein the poor recognize that their fight against poverty and injustice is not only consistent with the gospel but is the gospel of Jesus Christ. Any starting point that ignores God in Christ as the Liberator of the oppressed or that makes salvation as liberation secondary is *ipso facto* invalid and thus heretical. The test of the validity of this starting point, although dialectically related to Black cultural experience, is not found in the One who freely granted us freedom when we were doomed to slavery. In God's revelation in Scripture, we come to the recognition that the divine liberation of the oppressed is not determined by our perceptions but by the God of the Exodus, the prophets, and Jesus Christ who calls the oppressed into a liberated existence. Divine revelation *alone* is the test of the validity of this starting point.[43]

Observing Cone's thoughts on a Black biblical hermeneutic, one could argue that a biblical emphasis on the social and political character of God's revelation in history for the weak and the helpless has important implications not only for the spiritual life of the Christian but for the work of theology as well. Therefore, Black spirituality is biblical in that it is a retelling of what God has done in the past, is doing in the present, and has promised for the future. Finally, Black spirituality is biblical because it risks being prophetic by doing theology from the perspective of those who are helpless and voiceless in this society.

## Black Spirituality Is Joyful

A popular gospel song boldly proclaims: "This joy that I have the world didn't give it me. The world didn't give it, and the world can't take it away!" Joy is a hallmark of Black spirituality. Joy is first of all celebration. The African American Bishops assert, "Celebration is movement and song, rhythm and feeling, color and sensation, exultation and thanksgiving."[44] We celebrate the presence and the proclamation of the Word.

This joy is a sign of the faith of African Americans and especially their hope. The characteristic of joy is real. It is not a superficial emotion, nor is it an escape from reality, however harsh it may be. Indeed, this joy is often present even in the midst of deep anguish and bitter tears.

> You will weep and mourn
> while the world rejoices;
> you will grieve for a time,
> but your grief will be turned into joy.
> —John 16:20

According to Phelps, "The mystical union to which Black spirituality predisposes one is the source of an emotional, energetic, and joyful approach to life and worship. The life experiences of African Americans

---

[43]James H. Cone, *God of the Oppressed*, rev. ed. (Maryknoll, NY: Orbis Books, 1997), 74–75.
[44]Lyke, *What We Have Seen and Heard*, 9.

attest that God is reliable and benevolent, involved in the daily life of individuals and the community."[45] African Americans in touch with their spiritual traditions are confident about their ultimate well-being, because our God is a loving God, who, in the last analysis, can be trusted to give joy, power, and liberation from the debilitating oppressions of sin, racism, or any form of evil. The Black preaching style conveys this deep sense of joy that finds expression in a correspondingly deep and pervasive sense of peace, even in the midst of great adversity or trial. It is the same deep joy that overflows in quiet tears, loud shouts, exuberant or emotional songs, dancing, and clapping by choir and congregation gathered in worship.

Joy is not merely an emotional endeavor. Nor is it simply someone who "gets happy" under the influence of the Spirit. Phelps maintains that one who is possessed by the Spirit should evidence a truly sanctified life.

> While the joy of the Spirit's presence manifests itself in vivid and diverse ways in the worshiping community, such expression alone does not authenticate Black spirituality. The absolute criterion of authentic Black spirituality is its impact on the quality of the believer's life. It assumes that the true nature of our faith is reflected in the way in which we relate to other human beings and the created order, and that our concern for others will naturally generate witness and actions directed toward the realization of freedom for all human beings to live a liberated and joyful life, energized by the power of the Spirit. For example, does the person possessed by the Spirit of God treat family, neighbor, friends, and enemies with a sense of respect for the presence of God within each and every person? Does this person struggle to establish right relationships with others, regardless of race, gender, or creed? Does this person act right and call others to be right? Does this person struggle for the liberation of oppressed persons, races, nations?[46]

Accordingly, Black spirituality is a joyful spirituality that empowers humankind to love and not hate. Thus, a joyful person seeks to reconcile and will not cause division. A joyful person is troubled by the sight of another's sadness. A joyful person seeks to console, strives to encourage, and brings to all true peace.

---

[45]Phelps, 191–92.
[46]Ibid., 192.

## Black Spirituality Is Communal

The communal aspect of Black spirituality may well be the most recognized of all the characteristics. Why? Anyone with any idea whatsoever of African American culture and spirituality can readily identify its communal nature. Blacks, by and large, are a social and family-oriented people. This may seem unusual, given their history of separation, segregation, rejection, and abuse even to this very day. However, since the center and organizing principle of all African religion is the preservation and strengthening of the life-force or power of the community, in Black spirituality, too, the central focus is the preservation and strengthening of the life-force or power that dwells within each individual and in the community. This life-force is the Spirit of God.

The communal dimension of Black spirituality permeates our experience of liturgy and worship. Worship is always a celebration of community. No one stands in prayer alone. In communal worship the assembly gathers up the experiences of its individual members and transforms them into the experience and concerns of the entire community. The suffering caused by unemployment, poverty, hunger, homelessness, rejection, and racism is all brought to church to be transformed. All of it is indeed transformed by offering the entire community to God for healing, relief, and strengthening.

The role of the preacher in African American congregations is vital. It is the preacher's responsibility to build a communal spirit among the members of the church. As shepherd of the flock, his or her words must be compassionate. He or she is called to unify his or her congregation as Christ did in addressing his Father in prayer, "And I have given them the glory you gave to me, so that they may be one, as we are one" (John 17:22).

In African culture the "I" takes its meaning in the "we." In other words, individual identity is to be found within the context of the community. This communal concept is embodied in the African proverb: "I am because we are, and we are because I am." There is a great sense among African Americans that we cannot survive if we stand alone. We have to stand together against the injustices that hinder prosperity and progress.

Authentic Black spirituality leads to prophetic action. One who is genuinely interested in the advancement of the oppressed is one who will take prophetic action and struggle for the liberation of those who are victimized by the evils of society. By its very communal nature, Black spirituality demands that if a person in the community has gained some portion of success or freedom, he or she is obligated to assist any brother or sister within the community who is in need.

Unfortunately, not all Black Christians embrace the universal and community-centered understanding of Black spirituality or the teachings of Jesus Christ. They, like some other Christians, believe that the life and death of Christ have nothing at all to do with the ecclesial and social structures of human society, even when these structures oppress the spirit of love, truth, and liberation given to each person and to the community for building up and preparing for God's kingdom.

Yes, it is unfortunate that some Black Christians who feel that they have "made it" forget their past and their ancestral sacrifices. It was illiterate Black people who marched and were beaten in the streets so that all African Americans could have an opportunity to receive a quality education. It was Black mothers who sacrificed having new dresses so that their children would have new church clothes. It was Black fathers who worked two or more jobs so that each night food would be on the table and a decent home would be maintained for his family. The challenge to the African American race is the realization that freedom is not free. A price has been paid and yet there is still a balance due. Black people do not have the luxury to believe that they have finally "made it." Sacrifices have been made, and many more need to be made until all God's children are free.

At the conclusion of this chapter, it is clear what is required. There must be a faithful remembrance of the past and an undying commitment to the future. Likewise, there must be a remembrance of a communal Black spirituality that enabled African American ancestors to *hold on just a little while longer* and a common Black spirituality that will empower their descendants to overcome some day. Hope and perseverance are what make African American culture and spirituality truly unique.

## 2

# The Black Preaching Style:
# Its Origins, Language, Method,
# and Techniques

## PART I: THE ORIGINS AND LANGUAGE
## OF THE BLACK PREACHING STYLE

One of the oldest and most familiar exercises in which we regularly
engage on Sunday mornings is the attentive, patient, serious, and reverent
listening to sermons or homilies—those ten-, twenty-, or over forty-minute
presentations of religious ideas and stimulants of moral and spiritual
sentiments. From the lofty pulpits of elegant Gothic sanctuaries to the
homemade lecterns in pulsating, tinted-window storefronts on cluttered
ghetto avenues, preaching happens.

Whether the sermon or homily is offered in a modern suburban church
to six-figure-income parishioners or in a clapboard rural chapel to simple
country folk, these exercises have common elements. Often a sermon is a
simple celebration, not new or startling, but a recitation of faithful sayings that send joy and spiritual satisfaction rippling through the pews.
Sometimes, a sermon is purely to affirm and to edify. It is a call to renewed
commitment to the faith. At other times it may be to prophesy and to
challenge. At these times preaching is a prodding to action, an effort to
break inertia, confront apathy, or rally to a just cause. Often the sermon
is somber and soothing, a balm in Gilead, a solace for troubled times, an
assurance of the mystical presence of God. Much of it is simply instructional, an exegetical homily on a Bible verse or a dramatic retelling of the
story of creation, of Samson, Ruth, Jonah, Job, the crucifixion of Jesus, or
the conversion of Saul of Tarsus to the apostle Paul. No matter the place,
time, situation, or circumstances, on Sunday morning preaching happens.

This chapter explores the origins of the Black preaching style through a
brief analysis of the African oral tradition and the effects of slavery on the

modes of Black communication, especially in regard to the slave preacher. I also will offer an operative definition of Black preaching and demonstrate the relationship between the Black English language and Black preaching. The ultimate intent of this chapter is to provide a methodology for sermon (homily) preparation in the Black preaching style within the context of the Roman Catholic liturgy. In providing this Black homiletic, it is vital to illustrate the various techniques of the Black preaching style (e.g., call and response, rhythm, alliteration, repetition, and musicality). This chapter establishes a foundation to support my thesis that it is not only possible but imperative to prepare non–African Americans to preach in African American Catholic settings.

### The African Oral Tradition and the Effects of Slavery on Modes of Communication

Africans are a communal people. Even in the midst of brutal enslavement, Africans found ways to communicate with one another. The use of gestures, body language, words or phrases had common meaning, as well as songs, music, and drum playing. The indomitable spirit of the people refused to allow physical as well as tribal separation to keep them from discovering alternative ways of communicating. And yet the enslaved Africans had to learn the oppressors' language because they needed it to speak to them. In her book *Teaching to Transgress: Education as the Practice of Freedom*, bell hooks[1] posits:

> The very sound of English had to terrify. I think of Black people meeting one another in the space away from the diverse cultures and languages that distinguished them from one another, compelled by circumstances to find ways to speak with one another in a new world where Blackness or the darkness of one's skin and not language would become space of bonding.[2]

I contend that it was not the English language that hurt the enslaved Africans but rather what the oppressors did with it, how they shaped it to become a territory that limits and defines, how they made it a weapon

---

[1] Note here that the author, bell hooks, uniquely spells her name in lowercase letters. This is her pen name. She assumed her grandmother's name because she was a strong defiant Black woman.

[2] bell hooks, *Teaching to Transgress: Education as the Practice of Freedom* (London: Routledge, 1994), 169.

that can shame, humiliate, and colonize. It was most important that Africans found value in learning English as a way of sharing a common bond. It was a language that allowed the various African tribes to communicate. The recognition of taking on the oppressors' language as their own language was a way of restoring a customary intimacy among the enslaved Africans. The author, bell hooks, states,

> A culture of resistance could be formed that would make recovery from the trauma of enslavement possible. Learning English, learning to speak the alien tongue, was one-way enslaved Africans began to reclaim their personal power within a context of domination. Possessing a shared language, Black folks could find again a way to make community and a means to create the political solidarity necessary to resist.[3]

While they learned English, they also transformed it, made it different, and made it serve their purpose. This was the beginning of Black English or what is today known as "Ebonics." It was not so much that Africans never learned standard English correctly, nor were they unable to learn to speak "proper" English. It was, in fact, that enslaved Africans were so ingenious that they developed their own way of speaking English so that they could understand one another while the oppressor could not comprehend what was being communicated. Once again they not only used verbal communication but gestures, eye contact, body language, and songs (spirituals) to convey messages to one another. Although English was meant to serve the purpose of hindering the slaves from revolt or rebellion, it ironically enabled them to gain freedom by simply adapting their oppressors' language.

To fully understand the significance of the relationship between Black preaching and Black language, one must understand the importance of culture. The operative definition of culture for the purposes of this work is that culture is the accumulation over time of all the wisdom and methods of a given cultural group for the objective of ensuring survival. Each group has a menu of acceptable foods, a collection of proper hairstyles and attire, a way to greet people, ways to sing music and tell stories, and ways to build homes and rear children. In addition to language, and included in the language, is a way to view the world—a belief system. It is fascinating that in African languages there are no gender-specific pronouns. In the African worldview, a person is a person, regardless of gender. African

---

[3]Ibid., 170.

slaves were thought of as ignorant when they used the same pronouns for everybody, but now we know they had a sophistication that esteemed the concept of inclusiveness.

The real message of this cultural consideration, then, is not the promotion of a particular culture, but the insistence that the preacher affirms and works within the culture of the congregation. Whatever the culture may be, it is utterly fruitless to try to communicate effectively outside of it. The preacher is challenged to preach in a manner that speaks to the heart and soul of the culture of the congregation.

While there are many other cultural influences that contribute to and even enhance Black sermons, the most effective cultural expression is the "mother tongue," the language and idiom of Black people. Cultural considerations in Black preaching are vital. Henry H. Mitchell, noted African American expert in homiletics, asserts, "No amount of concern for educational levels or correctness of belief should be allowed to lure the preacher into frontal engagement with the fundamental wisdom of the communal life of a group or race."[4]

In summary, the preaching tradition of the Black ancestors did not spring into existence suddenly. It developed during a long and often quite disconnected series of contacts between the Christian gospel, variously interpreted, and African men and women caught up in the Black experience of slavery and oppression. To this experience and this gospel, they brought their own culture and folkways. In a manner more unusual and powerful than they or we dreamed, until recent decades, they devised a Black preaching tradition. This preaching tradition consisted of the ways Blacks delivered and responded to sermons. In essence this is the birth of what is known as the "Black oral tradition." Culturally, so much of the rich African American tradition is preserved not in written form but in oral form. Black preaching by and large is an excellent example of the Black oral tradition, of how the story of a people was told and retold from one generation to the next.

Preaching and worship are indeed the soul of the Black Church. However, preaching *is* the center of Black folk religion. While music is critical to the overall worship structure, it does not overshadow the place and purpose of the preached Word. Neither does prayer, Holy Communion, nor any other ritual. Black folk get excited about good preaching, and the Black preacher is often a master at telling the biblical story in such a way that the church understands, appreciates, and responds.

---

[4]Henry H. Mitchell, *Black Preaching: The Recovery of a Powerful Art* (Nashville: Abingdon Press, 1990), 15.

## Licensed by the Spirit: Slave Preaching

Recapturing the spirit of slave religion and developing what Molefi Kete Asante calls an "Afrocentric Idea" will give us the foundation for an authentic African American homiletic.[5] With no thoughts of the romantic, I suggest that African Americans need to recapture the quest for freedom and liberation that preoccupied our slave foreparents.

The words to the following slave song expressed the heartfelt disdain that both preacher and layperson felt about the institution of slavery. Every time the preacher preached there was an expectation that he would offer a message of hope in the midst of their subhuman slave status. In addition, the desire to be free and the spirit of defying the status quo are equally evident in these words of liberation chanted so often among Black Christians.

> Oh Freedom! Oh, Freedom!
> Oh, Freedom over me!
> And before I'll be a slave,
> I'll be buried in my grave,
> And go home to my Lord and be free.

Religion was the nucleus of slave culture, and at the center of religion was the slave preacher and his message of freedom, often subtle and indirect, but always expressing a yearning to be free. Lewis V. Baldwin, echoing the sentiment of W. E. B. Du Bois, says that the single most important figure in the Black Christian experience was the Black preacher.[6] Many scholars have suggested that the African American preacher was sometimes radical and revolutionary as evidenced by the most well known insurrection in America's history, led by the Reverend Nat Turner in 1831 in South Hampton County, Virginia. However, more often than not the preacher was politically conservative because of the bondage of slavery. Nevertheless, freedom was a basic desire expressed or unexpressed. The preacher's message was like a two-edged sword because sin and oppression, along with evil and injustice, were the objects of his homiletic. Like the prophets of the Old Testament, the slave preacher instinctively knew that God and his African ancestors were friends of freedom. The preacher,

---

[5]See Molefi Kete Asante, *The Afrocentric Idea* (Philadelphia: Temple University Press, 1987).

[6]Lewis V. Baldwin, "Black Christianity in the South in the Nineteenth Century: Its Development and Character," in *Religion in the South Conference Papers* (Mobile: Alabama Humanities Foundation, 1986), 19.

often referred to as the "medicine man," was the one person who could exhort, comfort, and tell the old, old story.

This natural, God-given talent enabled the preacher to voice the woes and sorrows of the other slaves. He spoke directly to their quest for liberation and freedom. They could "connect" to his words. His telepathic way of describing how they felt was grounded in mutual suffering and pain and bound by the heavy chains and shackles of being perceived and treated as less than human. "Whatever the content of the sermons, the slaves preferred a Black preacher."[7] They could trust the preacher and relate to the language and symbols of freedom that he espoused. Although the preacher had to be careful not to anger the slave master, preaching enabled him to paint a vivid picture of heaven and hell and the prevailing oppressive social structure with a few simple strokes of the imagination. The slave listeners could read between the lines and understand that there was something liberating about the message and the messenger. The fact that this man or woman[8] in chains, this chattel, bound by law and custom, could venture to speak in the Lord's name, "thus says the Lord," was reason enough to hope and believe in the power of God.

As one ponders the rapid growth of the early Black church and the other evidences of the effective leadership of the early Black preacher, two significant questions arise: What was their preaching like? And where did they get their preaching style or tradition?

## The Style and Content of Early Black Preaching

Given the fact that there is little written documentation of early African American history, it is no easy task to understand the nature of Black preaching. However, Mitchell notes:

The word often used by whites to describe Black preaching was *sonorous* or *tonal*. There is good reason to believe that African culture influenced all Black preachers in their use of a tonally pleasing voice, with or without intentional moaning or chanting. This aspect is taken for granted by Blacks, but many whites report being impressed by the pleasing speaking tones of Black preachers.[9]

---

[7] John W. Blasingame, *The Slave Community* (New York: Oxford University Press, 1972), 13.

[8] From all observations it seems that the slave preachers were predominantly male. However, there were a few known and many unknown women who preached during slavery, the most notable being Sojourner Truth.

[9] Mitchell, *Black Preaching: The Recovery of a Powerful Art*, 27–28.

Early Black preachers' use of standard English must have been a combination of native skill and exposure to "standard" speech and literature. Schools open to Blacks were most unusual, even in the North. And most churches were unable to pay for a Black preacher's food, much less training. Mitchell tells the story of how Bishop Richard Allen, founder of the African Methodist Episcopal Church, was quite typical in that he had progressed to the ownership of a shoe business so that he could be independently secure. In his fifteen years as a bishop he received only eighty dollars for all of his services.[10] "In other words, early Black preachers had to make it without formal schooling or support for their ministries and with little time for study. Black preachers acquired the skillful use of English in spite of being denied education and not having time to attend school even if there had been a school open to them."[11]

To garner some idea of what early Black preaching was like and to appreciate its content, it is helpful to note an experience of Sir Charles Lyell, a British geologist, who reported on a visit to the First African Baptist Church in Savannah, Georgia, during the pastorate of the famed Black preacher Andrew Marshall. Lyell reports:

> The singing was followed by prayers, not read, but delivered without notes by a Negro of pure African blood, a gray-headed venerable-looking man, with a fine sonorous voice, named Marshall. He concluded by addressing to them a sermon, also without notes, in good style, and for the most part in good English; so much so, as to make me doubt whether a few ungrammatical phrases in the Negro idiom might not have been purposely introduced for the sake of bringing the subject home to their family thoughts. . . . He compared it to an eagle teaching her newly fledged offspring to fly, by carrying it up high into the air, then dropping it, and, if she sees it falling to earth, darting with the speed of lightning to save it before it reaches the ground. Described in animated and picturesque language, yet by no means inflated, the imagery was well calculated to keep the attention of his hearers awake. He also inculcated some good practical maxims of morality. . . . Nothing in my whole travels gave a higher idea of the capabilities of Negroes than the actual progress which they have made, even in part of a slave state . . . than this Baptist meeting . . . they were listening to a good sermon, scarcely, if at all, below the average standard of the compositions of white ministers.[12]

---

[10]Ibid., 29.
[11]Ibid.
[12]Leslie H. Fishel Jr. and Benjamin Quarles, *The Negro American: A Documentary History*

Although Lyell's statement might sound paternalistic and even racist, nonetheless it illustrates the power, passion, and eloquence of the early Black preaching style. It also demonstrates the sound scriptural basis and firm theological underpinnings of the Black preaching style. Many whites knew that the phenomenon of the Black preaching style far surpassed their own in both content as well as character. Black preaching also reveals its ability to bring souls to Jesus Christ regardless of race or ethnicity.

My consideration of Black preaching must examine its African origins. Africans speak in languages that are tonal. Many early Black preachers preached with sonority. According to Mitchell, "African rhetorical style is always very dignified as well as sophisticated. Sonority is not a sign of primitivity, as is so often assumed even today."[13]

Call and response is unquestionably the hallmark of the Black preaching style. This homiletic technique calls forth a verbal response from the congregation, as does African music and oral communication. Black preaching engages the assembly by using words that paint vivid pictures of the biblical stories and images. Mitchell maintains, "Even today, congregations of the Black masses feel cheated if no place for their response is provided."[14] For the African American community, oratory is a response-inducing event. The Word proclaimed, announcement made, or, most importantly, the sermon preached must be concrete and relevant so that the community may respond. Mitchell contends, "At no point did the African rhetorical tradition permit emphasis on abstractness."[15] The same could be said regarding Black preaching.

Participant proclamation does more than describe what is actually occurring in churches where the congregation responds orally to the preacher. It strengthens and manifests one of the central principles of the African American religious heritage: the priesthood of all believers. The dynamics of the preaching event include dialogic interaction with the congregation. The congregation's responses and participation in shaping the act of proclamation make it clear the preacher does not hold a monopoly on the Word of God. The Word is shared by the entire group.

It is significant that the literature on preaching in recent years emphasizes the congregation's investment in the sermon. My operative definition of preaching maintains that once the Word has been proclaimed (scattered like seed on good ground) it is the duty and obligation of the preacher in his or her preaching to call forth the Word dwelling in the hearts and

---

(Glenview, IL: Scott, Foresman, 1967), 135–36.

[13]Mitchell, *Black Preaching: The Recovery of a Powerful Art*, 31.

[14]Ibid.

[15]Ibid.

minds of the faithful. I believe that there is a sermon in every hearer of the Word waiting to be preached. From this unquestionably Christian yet Afrocentric stance, the preacher empowers the faithful—the priesthood of all believers—to proclaim boldly the inspired Word of God within them. In essence preaching is ushering hearers into the presence of God and sending them forth to proclaim what they have seen and heard.

## The Uniqueness of Black Preaching

*"There is in my heart, as it were, a burning fire shut up in my bones, and I am weary with holding it in, and I cannot"* (Jeremiah 20:9). Jeremiah often struggled with God about his sense of vocation. When Jeremiah saw God's overpowering majesty, Jeremiah was convinced that he should preach the word of God. Many of his contemporaries mocked him for preaching God's word, and he had to quickly decide whether he should or should not go on preaching.

In one instance he is full of the Lord's fury. He does not accept the mystery of how God can work through him as a preacher. Jeremiah lacks patience. On this occasion, Jeremiah is filled with the wrath of God. He is tired of holding his thoughts in. He wants to speak what he really feels about the power of God. The Black preacher, too, has held in much of his or her concerns. The real truth is that the Black preacher is a unique preacher.

## The Uniqueness of the Black Preacher

Black preaching is best understood within the context of the Black church and the Black family. They are interrelated in fundamental and historical ways. William Augustus Jones Jr. of Brooklyn, New York, stated in *Outstanding Black Sermons* that Black preaching is the peak place in worship for African Americans. "It is the 'Mount Zion' to which the pilgrims ascend and from whence they descend. Black preaching is a happening or an event!"[16] Thus Black preaching is the Black minister's offering in worship of a Bible-centered living drama whereby participation comes from the congregation who act as the supporting cast. Jones best defines Black preaching as "a dialogue and a response rather than a monologue without a response, and the call to have the experience is orchestral."[17]

---

[16]William A. Jones Jr., in *Outstanding Black Sermons*, vol. 1, ed. J. Alfred Smith, Walter B. Hoard, and Milton E. Owens (Valley Forge, PA: Judson Press, 1978), 27.

[17]Ibid.

To comprehend the distinctiveness of Black preaching, one must understand preaching in general. The Black preacher has a unique experience within the tradition of Christian preachers in America because he or she has unique cultural and spiritual characteristics. The Black preacher must address the vast problems that beset the Black community informing listeners that God is able to care for problems that beset the Black community. God may transform people when people believe that God is a transformer. When one is transformed, one has spiritual power to deal with crisis. According to Gene B. Bartlett, preaching goes beyond proclaiming the kerygma, those mighty events of God in the life of Jesus Christ. "It is an urgent word, vagueness corrected, and also a proclamation of the present. It is not only what God in Christ has done, but what He is doing, for the Event goes on."[18]

Preaching is a high calling in society. Most people respect preachers who sincerely preach the Gospel of Jesus Christ. Preachers proclaim the Word of God. The congregation is awaiting the Word. That Word has to do with God and one's relationship to the world. It is an event that can bring about a change in lives. Good preachers preach to set a healthy tone for community life. They aid people where they are and try to prevent or deal with crises, translating the gospel into the daily lives of the congregation.

I contend that not just Black preachers, but *all preachers* need to offer what Christian souls need most: what the Bible teaches, God's saving acts, an encounter with Christ, and to teach those who desire learning. Ministers or those who would preach must offer a gospel that sustains people week by week, day by day, to provide enough inspiration for a person until the next Sunday. Harris maintains, "The preaching should exhort the will, kindle emotions, and make one feel more deeply that God is love. This will make one feel deeply the wrongness of sin."[19] The preacher must remember that he or she is the one who is commissioned to preach, called to represent the Body of Christ, with an ability to interpret the Bible and speak with the authority of the church.

## What Is Black Preaching?

Today the modern Black preacher retains vestiges of the past. It is a past that is deeply rooted in the hearts and minds of those who dare to declare in the Lord's name, "Thus says the Lord." The veteran Black preacher

---

[18]Gene B. Bartlett, *The Audacity of Preaching* (New York: Harper and Row, 1961), 27.

[19]James Henry Harris, "Preaching Liberation: The Afro-American Sermon and the Quest for Social Change," *Journal of Religious Thought* 46 (Winter–Spring, 1995): 76.

is still an orator whose voice thunders like the roar of a mighty wind, one who naturally meshes style and content in a way that continues to touch the heartstrings of Black congregations and other races alike. When somebody says "amen," shouts, claps the hands, or stomps the feet with rhythmic cadence and perfect timing, he or she is responding to the power of the Holy Spirit and the power of the voice of God. Unquestionably, it is a voice heard through the Black preacher.

The ability to excite the emotions with the eloquence of the spoken word remains a characteristic of the preacher who ministers to the masses of Black people. Black people want to "feel something" when the preacher preaches. They want to feel joy and sorrow, guilt and acceptance. They want to feel that God hears their cries, and despite their sins, they are accepted; despite the gloom and doom of oppressive life situations, they want to be assured that "there is a bright side somewhere." They want the preacher's message to touch them, to help them understand, and to fight against poverty, oppression, racism, sexism, and all forms of hatred and injustice. Not only that, they want the preacher to speak to their individual needs, troubles, desires, and frailties. According to James H. Harris:

> Most African Americans today, like the slaves of the antebellum South, want the preacher to make connections between personal, that is, individual salvation, and communal redemption and freedom. And, after the cogitating and reflecting on the correlation between what Tillich called "scripture-situation," they want to "celebrate" in the language of Henry Mitchell.[20]

## The Evolution of Black Preaching

### Kenyatta R. Gilbert's Trivocal Preaching

In recent years there has been an abundance of Black Christian preaching literature published. Black Protestant experts in homiletics have deconstructed Black preaching in order to excavate or to dig deeper into the purpose, understanding, motivation, interpretation, structure, language, and imagination of this Black folk art. These monographs have furthered not only the understanding and appreciation of Black preaching but have made significant contributions to the evolution and

---

[20]Ibid., 75–76.

lexicon of Black preaching. Noteworthy among these recent contributions is a masterly homiletical theorem by Kenyatta R. Gilbert, professor of homiletics at Howard University School of Divinity in Washington, DC. Gilbert hails from a lineage of inspiring Baptist preachers and is certainly an impressive, anointed preacher and scholar himself. He has provided a fresh approach to Black preaching. In his book *The Journey and Promise of African American Preaching* he offers a broad historical overview of the development of Black preaching, and he challenges ways in which some preachers' proclamations have become stagnant and in some cases reduced to entertainment. He also rightfully critiques Black congregations that want to be simply entertained rather than motivated to be dedicated disciples of Jesus Christ. Inspired by his preacher-father, who viewed preaching as a sacred assignment and agency for the spiritual and social liberation of God's people, Gilbert proposes a three-dimensional preaching life or preaching in three voices. Motivated by his sacred memory of his father's preaching responsibility, he notes that as a preacher his father authentically, in his own voice, assumed three preaching personas—prophet, priest, and sage. Recalling his father's preaching, he notes that "at times the voice of prophet raged in him; other times, in spite of his afflictions, the priestly voice of compassion emerged; and still at other moments, the voice of a sage spoke wisdom to those ministers who shadowed him."[21] Gilbert's trivocal proposal understands that the substance of the gospel is conveyed by the preacher through these three distinct voices. Gilbert meticulously unpacks his homiletical approach by first offering his operative definition of African American preaching, or what he calls trivocal preaching:

African American preaching is a ministry of Christian proclamation— a theo-rhetorical discourse about God's good will toward community with regard to divine intentionality, communal care, and the active practice of hope—that finds resources internal to Black life in the North American context.[22]

Keep in mind the words *divine intentionality, communal care*, and *the active practice of hope* as prophetic Black preaching, priestly Black preaching, and sagely (wisdom) Black preaching are examined. Gilbert's

---

[21]Kenyatta R. Gilbert, *The Journey and Promise of African American Preaching* (Minneapolis: Fortress Press, 2011), 2.

[22]Ibid., 11.

argument is simple: through this trifold perspective the preacher finds his or her voice that speaks a message of "justice, recovery, and hope, telling again the church about its present situation and where it must now go."[23]

## Prophetic Black Preaching

A prophet is one who speaks on behalf of God, especially when God seeks transformation in the church and or society for the cause of justice. The prophet makes God's divine intentionality known by revealing God's demands and expectations for humanity both in the present and future. The prophetic word is directed to the people, powers, and oppressive structures that hinder justice. Prophetic Black preaching offers Black congregations the assurance that God is active in their situations in light of God's justice and what God intends. In our pluralistic, fragmented, and polarized American society it is incumbent upon the Black preacher to preach against injustices as God's prophet. God's divine intentionality has been a characteristic of prophetic Black preaching since slavery, and yet it appears that words of prophecy are often abrogated or excluded from the sermons of modern-day Black preachers. Why? I believe that while prophetic Black preaching demands oppressive people, policies, and systems to transform and justice to prevail, it also demands that the preacher speak the uncomfortable message as God intends—a prospect that not all preachers willingly accept.

Within the African American context, it might seem obvious when and where God intentionally demands justice, but sadly very few Catholic priests readily avail themselves to preach a prophetic word to their Black congregations—and Black parishioners many times simply suffer in silence. Therefore, I will illustrate a few opportunities when priests ministering in Black Catholic communities should assume their prophetic voices and preach what God intends amid unabating racism, discrimination, poverty, police brutality, unfair housing and employment practices, lack of affordable health care insurance, needed asylum for refugees and protection of undocumented immigrants, public school disparities, Catholic church and school closures in poor Black communities, the proliferation of drugs and guns within the Black community, food deserts, and ecological pollution in Black communities, Black gang violence, and the list could go on. Do we want to be a prophetic church? Divine intentionality demands that we be.

---

[23]Ibid.

## Priestly Black Preaching

According to Gilbert, the priestly voice in Black preaching "is a sacramental meditating voice of Christian spiritual formation that encourages listeners to enhance themselves morally and ethically by integrating elements of personal piety, that is, keeping devotional practices like daily prayer and Bible study, and striving after holiness through abstention from cardinal sins."[24] This priestly voice of the preacher emphasizes the obligation to promote the congregation as a worshiping community. Likewise, the preacher is the one who not only gathers the people for worship but offers intercessory prayer for the parishioners and community at large. The function of preaching as priest and offering spiritual care underscore that there is no substitution for the ministry of presence. The priestly voice is one who knows, cares, and demonstrates compassion for the congregation. This priestly compassion is also demonstrated in the attentive care given by the preacher to church administration and stewardship. The priestly Black preaching voice, like the prophetic voice, reminds the congregation of their covenantal relationship with and obligation to God, as well as understanding God's faithfulness. Gilbert sees priestly Black preaching as guiding individuals to a deeper encounter with God. The communal care is illustrated through the Black priestly preaching voice whenever the community experiences any oppressive life situation or natural disaster.

For the most part, I find that within the Black Catholic community the priest-preacher assumes this preaching function well. Generally, the Catholic priest understands his responsibility to preach about and to offer communal care through intercessory prayer, devotion, worship, church administration, and the ministry of presence, especially during times of hardship. The challenge of priestly Black preaching is not to limit communal care solely to individuals but also to those beyond the church walls. As a pastor, I was often convicted not to be so consumed with my congregation that I missed those whom Jesus called "the least of these." Priestly Black preaching in my estimation has a further obligation to lead a congregation to care for the wider society, especially the poor, the marginalized, the imprisoned, and the forgotten.

When I served as pastor in an impoverished Memphis neighborhood, our small parish reached out to care for the needs of the community through a soup kitchen, a food pantry, and a clothing closet. However, I was personally affected and found my priestly Black preaching voice

---

[24]Ibid., 13.

when I received word of a home invasion of an elderly lady and long-time parishioner, who happened to be the only remaining white parishioner living in our neighborhood. We affectionately called her "Mother Evelyn White." The vandals not only broke into her home, but brutally beat and robbed her. In my Sunday homily I told the congregation that we have to take a stand against the violence plaguing our neighborhood and we need to let our neighbors know that Mother White belonged to us. Since Mother White was afraid to leave her home to come to church, at the end of Mass our entire congregation, all fifty members led by our gospel choir singing processed down the street three blocks to her home. When Mother White came out on her porch and saw her entire church congregation in her front yard she was amazed. We prayed with her, shared God's word, gave her holy communion, and blessed her. In that instance Black priestly preaching led our congregation to take the church to the streets.

### Sagely Black Preaching

The sagely Black preaching voice is unequivocally a voice of seasoned wisdom coming from a preacher who has prayed and encountered God in prayer, who has experienced and travailed over Black pain and suffering, and yet knows that pain and suffering endure. Indeed, the sagely preacher is one who knows the communal story because he or she has received the story, lives the story, and passes the story on for generations to come. Gilbert understands sagely Black preaching as a "wisdom-focused, dialectical, communal voice of both the preacher and the hearer. Sages interpret the common life of a particular community of worshipers. The sagely voice carries an endearing function; it strongly corresponds with the voice and activity of the African *jaili*."[25] The *jaili* in West African culture is the keeper of the village's communal story—the communal wisdom handed down through the African oral tradition and relayed to the community through storytelling and song. Unfortunately, of the three preaching voices, the sagely voice is often overlooked and deemed insignificant and unrelated to contemporary circumstances. Many contemporary preachers ascribe more value to present and future preaching interests. Both Gilbert and I strongly agree that because the sagely voice is ignored by younger Black preachers in the postmodern era that the sacred historical and cultural legacy is slowly fading away.[26]

At the crux of sagely preaching is the cherished historical, cultural, and

---

[25]Ibid., 14.
[26]Ibid., 15.

religious legacy of the African American community. As one who serves as the repository of the communal story, the Black sagely preaching voice is the one who safeguards the history, traditions, archival materials, rituals, stories, songs, symbols, and prayers of the community. The one called to lead and preach to a Black congregation is tacitly assumed to know and has the ability to tell the story.

My first pastorate was of a historic Catholic parish in St. Louis; it was also my home parish where I was reared. I was assigned to lead and preach to this congregation at the age of thirty. And while I knew and loved the people, I was also cognizant of so much that I didn't know. After much prayer and discernment, I intentionally sought wise counsel from my elder priest associates as well as from the elders of the community. Realizing that wisdom didn't come from osmosis, I formed a "Council of Elders" whose purpose was to be "seats of wisdom" not only to the pastor, but to the pastoral staff and council, and to have an intimate connection with the youth and young adults. While I initially prayerfully chose the first twelve elders, six women and six men biblically representing the twelve tribes of Israel of the Hebrew scriptures and twelve apostles of the Christian scriptures, in the future they would prayerfully come together in prayer to discern any vacancies among them. It was my hope that the elders could serve lifetime appointments; however, old age and physical ailments prevented this and some elders would resign when unable to fulfill their duties. The Council of Elders was installed and affirmed by the community at Mass, emphasizing their position and esteem among us. Besides having regularly scheduled meetings with the staff, pastoral council, and the youth and young adults to offer their observations, affirmations, or concerns, the elders were often called upon to offer prayers and blessings to the community. Drawing from the African tradition of respect and honor for the elders, at meetings with the Council of Elders individuals would ask for their permission to speak before addressing them. From these dialogues with the elders not only I but the greater community benefited from their wisdom, knowledge, and spirituality.

It was also vital to appoint a church archivist to collect and preserve important documents, newspaper articles, parish event materials, pictures, and weekly church bulletins. These endeavors serve to ensure that the preacher and community cherishes its historical legacy, knows its history, and can tell the story. It is also important for a community to celebrate its cultural, historical, and spiritual legacy. I was aware that a former pastor who is credited for integrating our once racially segregated parish in 1947 against the castigations of his religious confreres and parishioners was growing old and feeble. This courageous priest was notably shy and extremely humble. He rarely spoke of that time of integration of the parish because of the pain and trauma he personally suffered—even to the point of resigning his pastorate before the end of his term. Because I was told the story of our at times tumultuous and racially divisive history, one year on the occasion of our parish patronal feast day, under the guise of having him simply join us for the liturgy, I summoned the Black sagely preaching voice during my homily to tell the congregation of this priest's actions to obtain justice and equality for Black people at the risk of his own peril. Preaching in the sagely voice also enabled me to warn the now predominantly Black congregation not to repeat the mistakes of the past, that though our Catholic worship experience is unapologetically African American, our church must always be a place of welcome and inclusivity.

The Black preaching style can be most advantageous as our nation becomes increasingly segmented and segregated, polarized and paralyzed by racism and bigotry. The Black preaching style can be an expression of God's good and perfect will for the healing and wellness of African American communities. Kenyatta Gilbert offers us a homiletical way forward through his trivocal preaching schema accentuating the Black prophetic, priestly, and sagely preaching voices that corroborate divine intentionality, communal care, and the active practice of hope.

### Non–African Americans' Commitment to Preach to the African American Community

Black preaching, when effectively done, exhilarates and fulfills the preacher as it satisfies the congregation. The preacher delivering the Word must declare that it is God who sends the preacher. While this is certainly true, Mervyn Warren, author of the landmark book on the Black preaching style, *Black Preaching: Truth and Soul,* argues that there are distinctive dimensions to Black preaching. Warren states, "The genetic dimension of Black preaching builds its house on the similar rock of race, claiming a communicative event peculiar only to the American Negro, by virtue of his indigenous cultural background and inherent humanity. Hereby, the function as conceived, limits itself to a special race or cultural group at a particular point in history. The byword here is race."[27] Warren goes on to elaborate on the genetic experience of the Black preacher: "The nuances of styles and delivery may be indigenous to the Black pulpit, but accord-

---

[27]Mervyn Warren, *Black Preaching: Truth and Soul* (Washington, DC: University Press of America, 1977), 4–5.

ing to genetics, a *person not of the Black race could possess this charisma* but without commitment to Black liberation" (emphasis mine).[28] Thus, we move to the purpose of this book, non–African Americans preaching in specifically African American Catholic settings. Warren maintains that a person who is not African American can be trained to preach in the Black preaching style but cannot have a true commitment to the cause of justice for Black people. My conviction is that it is precisely this real dedication and commitment to genuine ministry among African Americans that persuades non–African Americans to learn to preach in the Black preaching style. They realize that their preaching would be in vain without a sincere desire to immerse themselves in the lives of the sons and daughters of the African diaspora. By and large those who commit their lives to the service of the gospel and to the African American community are also committed to the African American struggle and cause for justice and racial equality.

This chapter has explored the origins and language of the Black preaching style. The Black preaching style has strong roots in the African oral tradition. This oral tradition of Black preachers has survived slavery and remains a hallmark of contemporary Black preaching. In fact, African Americans have always found alternative ways to communicate in the midst of their oppression. Liberation was the theme and objective of the slave preacher's preaching. The messages always expressed a yearning to be free.

I have acknowledged that call and response is central to the uniqueness of Black preaching. To truly understand and thus appreciate the Black preaching style, one must comprehend that call and response, or congregational participation, calls God's people to claim the Word for themselves and to share the Word with others. It is evident that the preacher does not have full ownership of the Word of God—it belongs to the entire faith community. The role of call and response in Black preaching is always spontaneous. Spontaneity in Black preaching is the ability to respond to the movement of the Spirit among preacher and congregation and to express deep feeling without shame.

Since there is no "official" definition of Black preaching that can be simply stated, one can only speak in terms of the characteristics of Black preaching. From its evolution from the oral tradition of Africa to its effects on slave religion, to the prophetic role it has played in the quest for equal power and civil rights of African Americans in this country, Black preaching has sought to heal, empower, and encourage African Americans and all others who appreciate its style.

---

[28]Ibid.

Finally, the next part of this chapter examines the method and techniques of the Black preaching style. Specifically, I explore the Black preaching style within the context of African American Roman Catholic Liturgy.

## PART II: THE METHOD AND TECHNIQUES OF THE BLACK PREACHING STYLE

Today in many African American Catholic worshiping communities we have the warmth, the openness, and the African and African American cultural symbols and artifacts (colorful vestments for the presider and ministers and crimson red or kente cloth robes for the gospel choirs), and yet the preaching remains in desperate need of transformation. Dull, lifeless preaching needs to become powerful proclamation, not only in Black Catholic churches but throughout the entire Catholic Church. Fortunately, the hunger and need for powerful preaching have come to the attention of Catholic Church officials who have encouraged and urged preachers in the Church to truly invest in the preaching ministry and to spiritually feed the hungry faithful.

In 1982, the National Conference of Catholic Bishops through its Committee on Priestly Life and Ministry published a document on the role of preaching in the Catholic Church titled *Fulfilled in Your Hearing*. This document set forth the doctrine, theology, theory, and, most important, the practical pastoral applications that would wholeheartedly promote powerful proclamation from the pulpits of our Catholic Churches. While *Fulfilled in Your Hearing* can undoubtedly be celebrated as good news for the Catholic Church, for African Americans rooted in the powerful oral tradition this good news does not come to us as something new.

When one thinks of Black preaching, one normally thinks of traditional Black churches. Although this is an accurate assumption, Black preaching is rooted in the Black church experience, and it must not be presumed that the Black preaching style is inappropriate in African American Roman Catholic parishes. I am convinced that Black preaching is born out of the religious experience of Black people and is appropriate to the worship style of Black people of whatever Christian religious domination. In particular I argue that Black preaching is welcome in most African American Roman Catholic parishes. I maintain that not only is the Black preaching style appropriate within the context of the Roman Catholic liturgy, it typifies the recommendations for the effective proclamation of the gospel as proposed in *Fulfilled in Your Hearing*.

## Black Preaching and Cultural Adaptation
## in Roman Catholic Worship

Roman Catholic doctrine and theology are essential starting points in our discussion of the appropriateness of Black preaching in African American Catholic worship. Roman Catholic liturgy fundamentally expresses the unity of the Church. The African American Bishops remind us that African American Catholic liturgy expresses not only our African American cultural history but also our Catholic faith and unity.[29]

Cultural adaptation in the liturgy is not merely encouraged by the people of various cultures, but it also has a strong theological and doctrinal foundation in the teachings of the Roman Catholic Church. The *Constitution on Sacred Liturgy of* the Second Vatican Council formulated norms for adapting the liturgy to the temperament and traditions of various cultures. The document clearly states:

> Even in the liturgy the Church does not wish to impose a rigid uniformity in matters which do not involve the faith or the good of the whole community. Rather does she respect and foster the qualities and talents of the various races and nations. Anything in these people's way of life which is not indissolubly bound up with superstition and error she studies with sympathy, and, if possible, preserves intact. She sometimes even admits such things into the liturgy itself, provided they harmonize with its true and authentic spirit.[30]

Ultimately, in supporting cultural adaptation in Roman Catholic liturgy, the Second Vatican Council attempted to maintain the unity of the Roman Rite. "Provided that the substantial unity of the Roman Rite is preserved, provision shall be made for legitimate variations and adaptations to different groups, regions and peoples."[31] Moreover, the document on Sacred Liturgy makes provisions in the administration of the sacraments, sacramentals, processions, liturgical language, sacred music, and the arts.[32] Furthermore, in regard to cultural adaptation in worship, the African

---

[29] *What We Have Seen and Heard: A Pastoral Letter on Evangelization from the Black Bishops of the United States* (Cincinnati: St. Anthony Messenger Press, 1984), 31.

[30] *The Constitution on the Sacred Liturgy, Sacrasanctum Concilium,* in *Vatican Council II: The Conciliar and Post Conciliar Documents,* ed. Austin Flannery, OP (New York: Costello, 1975), no. 37.

[31] Ibid., no. 38.

[32] Ibid., no. 39.

American Catholic Bishops strongly emphasized that *all people* should be able to experience their own fulfillment when worshiping. Although the word *catholic* means *universal,* it does not mean that the Catholic Church must be uniform (particularly in regard to cultural expressions within worship). In *What We Have Seen and Heard,* the African American Catholic Bishops state, "Hence, we can legitimately speak of an African American cultural idiom or style in music, in preaching. . . . [Thus,] we encourage those in pastoral ministry to introduce the African American idiom into the expression of Roman liturgy."[33]

The call for African American Catholics to share with the Church their rich heritage has been important in promoting authentic cultural adaptation. Pope John Paul II in his historic meeting with African American Catholics in New Orleans on September 12, 1987, told them, "Your Black cultural heritage enriches the Church and makes her witness of universality more complete. In a real way the Church needs you, just as you need the Church, for you are part of the Church and the Church is part of you."[34] John Paul II later conveyed those same sentiments in an *Ad Limina* address made at the Vatican on June 6, 1998. The Holy Father declared that the multicultural reality of American society is a source of enrichment for the Church, but he acknowledged that it also presents challenges to pastoral action. John Paul II offers the following observation in regard to the importance of African American Catholics in the Church:

> The same should be said about the members of the African American community, who also are a vital presence in all your churches. Their love for the word of God is a special blessing to be treasured. While the United States has made great progress in ridding itself of racial prejudice, continuous efforts are needed to ensure that Black Catholics are fully involved in the Church's life.[35]

Above all, the call for a true African American cultural expression in the Catholic Church has resoundingly come from African American Catholics themselves. At the 1987 National Black Catholic Congress held in Washington, DC, delegates specifically spoke about their desire for effective

---

[33] *What We Have Seen and Heard,* 31.

[34] *The National Catholic Mentor* (Nashville), December 1987.

[35] John Paul II, "Ad Limina Address to the Bishops of the Provinces of Minnesota, North and South Dakota" (June 6, 1998), in *The Ad Limina Addresses of His Holiness Pope John Paul II to the Bishops of the United States* (February 1998–October 1998) (Washington, DC: United States Catholic Conference, 1998), 69.

preaching that addressed their spiritual, cultural, and pastoral needs and circumstances. In effect they were supporting not only the appropriateness but the necessity of good Black preaching in Roman Catholic liturgy. The *National Black Catholic Pastoral Plan,* in its directives on liturgy, proposed that "a conscious effort be made to infuse elements of Black culture into the Roman liturgy through effective preaching which speaks to the needs and aspirations of Black Catholics."[36] Cultural adaptation in the Roman Catholic liturgy is supported by Catholic doctrine, Catholic pastoral letters, a Black Catholic Pastoral Plan, and even from the mouth of the Pope himself. Indisputably, cultural adaptation is essential to the unity and life of the Catholic Church. African American Catholics have truly found a home in the Catholic Church. It is a home that allows members of its family to move all of their furniture in. In African American Catholic worship, it is truly right, just, and well that Black people totally bring themselves to the worship and praise of God. To *bring themselves* means to bring *all that they are and all that they offer.* It means bringing sorrows and joys, gifts, talents, and culture: song, dance, praise, prayers, healing silence, joyful shouting, hand clapping, foot stomping, and yes, powerfully inspiring Black preaching.

### Black Preaching and the African American Catholic Congregation

*Fulfilled in Your Hearing* recommends that the Catholic preacher make every effort to know the needs and concerns of the congregation, to inspire a total response to the proclaimed Word, and to urge the congregation to witness to the good news of Jesus Christ.[37] The bishops voiced their concern that preachers make every effort to meet the needs and concerns of the people. They write:

> Unless a preacher knows what a congregation needs, wants, or is able to hear, there is every possibility that the message offered in the homily will not meet the needs of the people who hear it. Only when preachers know what their congregations want to hear will they be able to communicate what a congregation needs to hear.[38]

---

[36]*The National Black Catholic Pastoral Plan,* Part VI: Liturgy, Section 1: "Liturgy and the Black Tradition" (Washington, DC: National Black Catholic Congress, 1987), 21.

[37]Bishops' Committee on Priestly Life and Ministry, *Fulfilled in Your Hearing: The Homily in the Sunday Assembly* (Washington, DC: United States Catholic Conference, 1982), 4.

[38]Ibid.

The Black preaching style and method presumes that the Black congregation needs and wants powerful proclamation. Many African American Catholics attend Sunday liturgy seeking strength and the spiritual nourishment that would sustain them throughout the week. The African American Catholic congregation attends Mass Sunday after Sunday because they are hungry for the Word of God and seek to be fed by God's Word. They hope to gain strength from the singing, from the praying and praising, from the fellowship, from the Eucharist and from the homily. The People of God have a right to good preaching, and they deserve to receive it.

African American Catholics by and large "go where they are fed." African American Catholics are less defined by parish loyalty and seek out vibrant preaching even if they must abandon their territorial parish. Many African Americans who have gained financial stability and have relocated to middle- and upper-middle-class suburban settings continue to travel great distances to attend predominantly African American Catholic parishes in the cities. This phenomenon applies not only to African American Catholics but to people of other races who are attending and actually joining African American Catholic parishes. Why? They, too, are hungry for moving preaching and vibrant liturgical celebrations, and the African American Catholic religious experience they encounter in these parishes is feeding them. It speaks to their basic human needs for community, freedom of expression, and most of all, a meaningful encounter with God.

Black preaching is rooted in the African American cultural experience, the experience of a people who have suffered pain, discrimination, and oppression. Therefore, when the Word is proclaimed in effective Black preaching, it is a Word that is indeed good news. Black preaching traditionally provides hope to a people who have felt the heavy burden of injustice. The good news for the Black congregation is that God loves us and is watching over us. The *Good News* proclaimed in Black preaching is a liberating Word.[39]

Moreover, Black preaching speaks to the particular spiritual, racial, social, and economic concerns of the African American congregation. African Americans come to worship with these burdens perhaps knowing that after the Mass or service their situation will be unchanged but feeling that they have found inner peace and consoling words of encouragement as they face their hardships. They come to church anxious about unemployment, the sickness of a loved one, neighborhood gangs, children on drugs, unfaithfulness in their marriage, or a neighbor who slanders the family name by gossip. These are only a few concerns that may be trou-

---

[39]Olin P. Moyd, *Redemption in Black Theology* (Valley Forge, PA: Judson Press, 1979), 104.

bling members of a Black congregation who come to receive good news.

In the context of Black preaching and worship, James H. Cone, African American systematic theologian, posits, "God is known primarily as the liberator of the poor and the downtrodden. God is the almighty sovereign One who is sometimes called a *heart fixer* and a *mind regulator.*"[40] Cone submits that within a Spirit-filled Black worship service the mighty power of God is manifested, and God's presence is felt by the congregation. During this powerful religious experience, a clear vision is given to the people that the evils of society must be changed. They are also given "the power and courage to help bring about that change."[41]

The assurance of God's presence with and concerns for the spiritual, racial, social, and economic needs of the poor and oppressed is at the heart of Black preaching. Cone asserts: "Black worship is a series of recitals of what God has done to bring the people out of harm, worry and danger." He states, "Through sermon, song, prayer, and testimony, the people tell their story of *'how they got over.'* God is that divine miracle who enables the people to survive amid wretched conditions. God is holy, personal, and all-powerful. God is everything the people need in order to triumph over terrible circumstances."[42]

When speaking of the African American community or even of a given Black congregation, one must be cautious not to overgeneralize. As with any race or nationality there is great diversity among African Americans. This diversity is seen with regard to socioeconomic, educational, and marital status. There is diversity in regard to men and women, old and young, the joyful and the bereaved, the fervent and the halfhearted, the strong and the weak. In particular, this diversity can be and indeed is represented within an African American Catholic parish. Yet I am convinced that there can be a clear point of unity in the midst of this obvious diversity.

Black preaching seeks a common ground among the African American congregation. The assembly has come together because its members have been baptized into the one Body of Christ and they share a common faith and culture. The recognition of common ground in no way negates the diversity of the assembly. Rather, it affirms the reality that through baptism the congregation shares a common faith. *Fulfilled in Your Hearing* explains *common faith* as "a common way that its members have of interpreting the world around them. For the Christian community, the world is seen and interpreted as the creation of a loving God."[43]

---

[40]James H. Cone, *Speaking the Truth* (Grand Rapids, MI: William B. Eerdmans, 1986), 139.
[41]Ibid.
[42]Ibid., 140.
[43]*Fulfilled in Your Hearing*, 6.

According to the US Catholic Bishops, the Catholic preacher "represents a given community by voicing its concerns, by naming demons, and thus enabling it to gain some understanding and control of the evil which afflicts it."[44] In other words, the preacher represents the Lord by offering the community another word—a word of healing and pardon, of acceptance and love. The bishops acknowledge that the people in the pews attend liturgy seeking meaning in their lives. True, they do find some meaning in family, friends, or even employment. Yet these fall short of providing the ultimate meaning sought by the People of God. The bishops maintain, "Without meaning we are ultimately unsatisfied. If we are able to hear a word which gives our lives another level of meaning, which interprets them in relation to God, then our response is to turn to this source of meaning in an attitude of praise and thanksgiving."[45]

Sunday after Sunday a given African American Catholic community comes together to await a word from the preacher that will give meaning to the lives of the community members and enable them to truly celebrate the Word and Eucharist. I am convinced that the Black preaching style provides the needed message in a manner that gives meaning to Black peoples' lives and gives them cause to celebrate fully the Word and Sacrament.

## The Black Preaching Style and Method

Unequivocally, preaching must be experienced, not explained. However, in this section I offer an explanation of what actually occurs during a Black preaching event. This section explores the various techniques and elements of the Black preaching rhetorical style, namely, call and response, storytelling, intonation, repetition, rhythm and rhyme, and song (musicality). I am convinced that these Black preaching techniques can be authentically adapted to a non–African American's style of preaching. The following is a brief explanation of some of the most common elements of the Black preaching style.

### Call and Response

Evans Crawford offers this concise example of the call and response technique in his book, *The Hum: Call and Response in African American Preaching*:

---

[44]Ibid., 7.
[45]Ibid.

Wyatt T. Walker, a noted pastor and preacher, tells of a revivalist preacher who established a pattern of call and response using the parable of the prodigal son. Under the title *The Wonderful Father,* he set the scene of a returning son and a waiting father at the edge of the porch in a chair. A week passed, "but the father kept on waiting." Two weeks passed, "but the father kept on waiting." Three weeks passed, "but the father kept on waiting." Once the refrain was established, the congregation picked it up and repeated it every time the preacher did. That's call and response.[46]

Black preaching is not a one-sided event in which the preacher preaches, and the congregation sits quietly listening. A key characteristic of the Black preaching style is that it evokes a total response to the proclaimed Word of God. The Black style, which includes the pattern of call and response, is deeply embedded in African American culture. Such responses require a participating audience. Mitchell argues, "If the Black preaching tradition is unique, then that uniqueness depends in part upon the uniqueness of the Black congregation which talks back to the preacher as a normal part of the pattern of worship."[47]

It should be noted here that whereas *Fulfilled in Your Hearing* recommends a joyous response to preaching that points to God's goodness in our lives, the response is by and large an internal feeling of gratitude. However, Black preaching evokes a total response that goes beyond an internal feeling to an overt, emotional response. Black preaching appeals to both the head and the heart, the intellect and the emotions. Critics have made a grave mistake considering Black preaching to be merely a thoughtless, emotional process. It is true that Black worshipers want to be stirred; they want to have an emotional experience. But they also want to be stretched, enlightened, renewed, or helped. "They want the cream of the Black pulpit; they want the kind of preaching that is highly relevant in content and charismatic delivery. When such content and imaginative delivery grips a congregation, the ensuing dialogue between preacher and people is the epitome of creative worship."[48]

During the preaching, responses given may be overtly or covertly emotional, verbal or nonverbal. Perhaps the most obvious and widespread manifestation of the freedom of religious expression is the custom of

---

[46]Evans E. Crawford, *The Hum: Call and Response in African American Preaching* (Nashville: Abingdon Press, 1995), 56.

[47]Henry H. Mitchell, *Black Preaching* (New York: Harper and Row, 1979), 95.

[48]Ibid., 98.

responding to the preaching with *Amen!* or other emotional verbal expressions (e.g., *Preach it; that's right; yes, Lord; sure, you're right*). Mitchell posits that the spectrum of responses to good preaching is almost endless. He states, "The Black worshiper does not acknowledge the Word delivered by the preacher at the end of the service; he talks back during the preaching."[49]

Traditionally, the verbal emotional responses elicited by Black preaching are a way of letting preachers know that they are on the right track and that what they say rings true to the Spirit's presence in their midst. For James Cone, "An *Amen* involves the people in the proclamation and commits them to the divine truth they hear proclaimed. It means that the people recognize that what is said is not just the preacher's ideas but God's claim, which God lays upon the people."[50]

Furthermore, when a person hears Bible truth preached within his or her own cognitive grasp and clearly to one's contemporary needs, it is verily impossible *not* to make an audible response. Audible responses are not only an overt sign of agreement with what the preacher is saying, but, further, they are an urging, a coaxing, an encouragement to the preacher to help him or her sustain the ministry of proclaiming God's holy Word.

Another emotional response to Black preaching is the nonverbal response. In essence its function is the same as the overt response, namely, to show agreement and to visibly confirm the proclamation of the preacher. The nonverbal response may simply be expressed by a person nodding his or her head in agreement, the congregation clapping their hands, or a catharsis of tears of joy or sorrow from the congregation.

Although the nodding of heads and the hand clapping are fairly self-explanatory, mystique surrounds the response of tears. When someone cries helplessly in response to an experience of powerful proclamation, African Americans usually say that person was truly *touched* by the Word of God. To be *touched* by the Word means that something was heard that spoke to the life situation of that individual. Something said may have convicted a person into realizing that they *had better make a change in their life and get on the path of righteousness.* Perhaps something said in the sermon or homily gave a person hope and the ability to realize that they are special and loved by God. Maybe something is said that gives a person an added lift as he or she strives to walk their Christian journey. African American elders also equipped with words of wisdom, describe this catharsis of tears for whatever reason, as being *God's way of trying*

---

[49]Ibid., 44.
[50]Cone, *Speaking the Truth*, 24–25.

*to tell you something.* They would say, *he preached that sermon just for you this morning.*

### Storytelling

Unquestionably, storytelling is a hallmark of Black preaching. The preacher must tell the story using a method that is an end in itself, even though he or she may intersperse anecdotes to sustain the obvious relevance of the action in the story. Throughout the story, a good storyteller must be so motivated as to give the impression that he or she had seen it happen. Likewise, the storyteller must also play all the roles and make the story live. The storyteller must communicate the story so that the congregation feels as if they too are at the scene of the action.

Although storytelling actively engages the emotions, it should not be understood as being merely entertainment. A preacher, like the writer of a play, has a message to convey. Mitchell states, "No matter how charming the story or how captivated the audience, the preacher must take care of business and lead the hearer to do something about the challenge of the Word of God."[51] The story in Black preaching is told to pull the congregation into the preaching event. It serves to help people identify with the proclamation, to see themselves in the Word and to be challenged by the Word. Storytelling is a practical reminder or a first-time challenge to put into practice the message of the gospel.

The Black storytelling style also interprets the biblical story in the Black idiom and transforms the biblical story into the Black biblical story. *Telling the story* is the essence of Black preaching. Cone argues that storytelling from a Black perspective means "proclaiming with appropriate rhythm and passion the connection between the Bible and the history of Black people. The preacher must be able to tell God's story so that the people will experience its liberating presence in their midst."[52] Quite often in the Black community, someone is heard asking whether the reverend told the story. It is so important that Black people hear the old, old, biblical story told in a way that speaks to them in their life and living.

### Intonation

Intonation, which involves the use of a chant-like musical tone, is a very common characteristic of Black preaching.[53] According to Mitchell,

---

[51]Mitchell, *Black Preaching,* 133.
[52]Cone, *Speaking the Truth,* 24.
[53]Mitchell, *Black Preaching,* 165.

intonation vividly expresses Black identity. It is rooted in the African custom of sung public address. Besides serving as an identity signal in Black preaching, intonation also serves to enhance the sermon climax.[54]

Today the intonation technique is not often used by many preachers, Black or otherwise. Perhaps the reason is that one needs to know how to sing, how to carry a note and pitch, and to do well. Intonation is reaching a climactic point where the preacher becomes so caught up in the revelation of the good news of the Word that he or she moves from preaching the Word to chanting or singing the message. However, more and more African American churches no longer require intonation for a religiously climactic experience. In fact, many preachers use climactic material rather than moving into a chant. Sometimes preachers will use old, well-worn climax clichés. Preachers using material-based climactic endings tend to incorporate solid content from their message, while maintaining power and momentum in their preaching.

## Repetition

According to Mitchell, "Repetition simply refers to the restatement of texts, aphorisms and other significant words and phrases for emphasis, memory, impact and effect."[55] Repetition is present not only within the call and response rhetorical elements but also within the general course of the sermon. Mitchell observes that repetition is seen by the Black church mainly as an indication of the worthiness of the dialogue and its context. It is believed that such repetitive material may be retained by the hearer well after the sermon has ended because of the vividness of its impact.

Increasingly, preachers using the Black preaching style have adopted this technique by inspiring the congregation to interact among themselves. For instance, a preacher may instruct the congregation to turn to a neighbor and say, "The Lord is blessing you right now." The congregation does as instructed by repeating after the preacher. Inevitably, the preacher continues the repetitive process by instructing the congregation to turn to the neighbor on the other side and say, "And I know that I am truly blessed!" This technique engages the congregation in a more meaningful way. The listeners become preachers of the Word to those around them within the congregation. In essence this is in-house preparation for their commission to go forth and preach to all the nations.

To illustrate how this particular technique of the Black preaching style

---

[54]Ibid.
[55]Mitchell, *Black Preaching*, 93.

is used in the context of an African American Catholic homily, I turn to Rev. John T. Judie, an African American priest from Louisville, Kentucky. The following excerpt is transcribed from Judie's homily titled *Turning and Re-turning to God* (Luke 11:1–13, date unknown):

> Our first step to being renewed is our turning and returning to the God who made us. And the starting point of everything we do in life needs to be turning to God in prayer. If there's anything at all that we as followers of Jesus, as church-going folk need to do, it's to know how to bow our heads, bend our knees and turn to the Father in prayer. You see, Jesus was a praying man. He was:
>     —a teacher and a preacher but, most of all, he was a praying man!
>     —a walking man and a talking man but, most of all, he was a praying man!
>     —a confronting man and a forgiving man but, most of all, he was a praying man!

It is very clear that the repetition technique in Judie's homily is both memorable and effective. A congregation hearing this homily will definitely leave the liturgy knowing that Jesus was a "praying man."

### Rhythm and Rhyme

Rhythm refers to the pacing and movement of the preached sermon. This includes intonation, volume, and pitch. The sermon or homily develops a certain pattern that invites the congregation to "pick up the beat" and move with the preacher. Mitchell, in general, underplays this element of the Black style. He concludes, "While rhythm is vitally important in Black music, it is, to say the least, unimportant in Black preaching."[56] However, I adamantly disagree with Mitchell's assertion that rhythm is not particularly important. Rhythm enhances the movement of one's preaching. The congregation is kept attentive to the preaching when there are variances in the rate, pitch, and intonations of the preacher's voice.

Rhyme refers to the matching of words with similar sounds to enable the congregation to remember important points of the preached Word. It also serves to hold the congregation's attention and to entertain. If good preaching were like cooking a good meal, I would compare the rhyme technique of Black preaching to that needed spice that makes the dish taste

---

[56]Mitchell, *Black Preaching*, 167.

just right. Rhyme is the spice of Black preaching that gives the message vigor and life. Rhyme grabs the attention and permits the congregation to laugh, smile, and, most important, to remember what was said. For instance, here are a few phrases used by some Black Catholic preachers who use rhyme most effectively: "The saints and the ain'ts"; "Sashay if you may, but you won't get in that way"; "The Lord gives us healin' for the dealin'"; "When God starts to bless, the devil begins to mess"; "Sometimes you feel tore up from the floor up"; "When your money is funny and your change is strange"; and "May God bless you with a double dose of the Holy Ghost!"

## Song (Musicality)

Finally, I address the element of song in the Black preaching style. The use of singing is a distinguishing mark of good Black preaching. It can be used by the preacher either working up to a climactic point where he or she begins to sing the message (like intonation) or by the preacher singing an appropriate spiritual or gospel song relevant to the message within the context of the preaching.

Song is a very important ingredient in African American worship. Most Black people believe that the Spirit does not descend without a song. Song opens the hearts of the people for the coming of God's Spirit. Cone says, "That is why most church services are opened with a song and why most preachers would not attempt to preach without having the congregation sing a *special* song in order to prepare the people for God's Word. Song not only prepares the people for the Spirit but also intensifies the power of the Spirit's presence with the people."[57]

Many European American priests preaching in African American Catholic parishes have noted that this technique of introducing a song either at the beginning or at the end of their homily not only opens the people to the Word but also makes the preacher feel free and relaxed to preach God's Word. For many white preachers preaching in African American Catholic settings, the gift of song (if they can sing) is possibly the easiest of the Black preaching techniques to incorporate in their preaching.

This chapter has addressed the very core of the Black preaching style by journeying back to its origins during the evil days of slavery. This preaching style conceived in oppression has for generations been a source of strength for not only African Americans but for all of God's children.

---

[57]Cone, *Speaking the Truth*, 25.

Through this exploration of the language, methodology, and techniques of the Black preaching style, I demonstrated that it is a unique experience of survival and spiritual prosperity. African Americans have formulated a genuine preaching style to *tell the story* among themselves and others. Today, as seen in the growing number of "mega churches" throughout our nation, many non–African Americans are preaching in the Black idiom. Why? Because it satisfies the soul.

3

# Will It Preach? Homily Preparation, Development, and Delivery

I am disturbed whenever I hear a priest say on a Saturday afternoon, "I'd better try to pull something together to preach about for the Vigil Mass in a few hours." Seriously? The People of God deserve so much more than just a few hours of "pulling something together to preach." Most likely the priest would simply read a few homily helps and that would be the extent of his homily preparation. Unfortunately, this kind of cursory preparation for preaching is customary in many Catholic parishes. Priests offer lame excuses of being too busy with administrative responsibilities, dealing with maintenance repairs, hospital visits, and the deluge of demands made by the diocese. And yet preaching reveals so much about the preacher. The substance of a homily holds before a congregation a priest's prayer life, spirituality, and relationship with God. The state of homily preparation also conveys the priest's care and concern, or lack thereof, for his parishioners. Thus, homily preparation must be a priority for the preacher called to preach.

The vast majority of parishioners in a parish will see and hear from their priest for only sixty minutes one day a week in the context of a eucharistic liturgy. And of that sixty minutes at most European American parishes they may receive a seven- to twelve-minute homily that feels unconsidered and boring due to a lack of homily preparation, development, and delivery.

In the context of many African American parish liturgies, the priest or deacon has not "broken open the Word" if they have preached less than twenty minutes. Typically, Black Catholics want their priest or deacon to pray over, live with, "make plain," inspire, motivate, and relate God's word to their current situations. If they have not come prepared and ready to deliver, they have just rambled off some words, as well intended as they might be, but essentially, they have not preached.

## The Purpose of the Homily

Within the context of the eucharistic liturgy the homily is a liturgical act directed to faith. Preaching functions to bring people who have never heard the gospel to an acceptance of Jesus Christ and to those who have already accepted Jesus Christ to a deeper understanding of faith. Roman Catholics who are baptized believers and who are members of the Body of Christ view the homily as preaching to inform, inspire, motivate, and celebrate their life of faith. As a liturgical act, the homily actually forms part of the liturgy. Situated in the Liturgy of the Word of the eucharistic liturgy, the homily flows from the proclamation of the Hebrew and Christian scriptural texts of the Roman Lectionary. The homily also serves to transition to the celebration of the Liturgy of the Eucharist. The liturgical reforms of the Second Vatican Council (1962–1965) promulgated a renewed form of preaching at the Roman Catholic Mass. Prior to Vatican II preaching at eucharistic liturgies was mostly catechetical and doctrinal in nature. Preaching then was concerned mainly with God's salvation of souls. Scriptural texts were employed to reinforce what the priest wanted to teach. For instance, the parables of Jesus were often used as allegories to teach about sanctifying grace rather than preached as analogies about the Reign of God. In fact, pre–Second Vatican Council preaching at Catholic liturgies were called "sermons" because they were topical or instructional talks that were not necessarily based on biblical texts. The term "homily" indicated that the renewal of Roman Catholic liturgical preaching emphasized an interpretation of the lectionary based on scriptural texts.

Any examination of liturgical preaching and the purpose of the homily should heed the wise counsel and recommendations found in the 1965 Second Vatican Council's *Dogmatic Constitution on Divine Revelation (Dei Verbum)*, the United States Conference of Catholic Bishops' Committee on Priestly Life and Ministry's 1982 document, *Fulfilled in Your Hearing: The Homily in the Sunday Assembly (FIYH)*, the 2008 Synod of Bishops' XII ordinary general assembly on *The Word of God in the Life and Mission of the Church (Instrumentum Laboris)*, and the 2012 document *Preaching the Mystery of Faith: The Sunday Homily* developed by the United States Conference of Catholic Bishops Committee on Clergy, Consecrated Life, and Vocations. All of these documents offer salient and complementary insights on the purpose of the homily.

The *Constitution on Divine Revelation* quotes St. Augustine, "It must not happen that anyone become 'an empty preacher of the Word of God to others, not being a hearer of the Word in his own heart,' when he ought to be sharing the boundless riches of the divine Word with the faithful committed to his care, especially in the sacred liturgy."[1]

*Fulfilled in Your Hearing (FIYH)* says that "a homily presupposes faith. The liturgical gathering is not primarily an educational assembly. Rather the homily is preached in order that a community of believers who have gathered to celebrate the liturgy may do so more deeply and more fully— more faithfully—and thus be formed for Christian witness to the world."[2]

*The Word of God in the Life and Mission of the Church* holds that "the Spirit guides the presider in the prophetic task of understanding, proclaiming and adequately explaining the word of God to the assembly and, in a parallel way, invoking a just and worthy reception of the Word by the gathered community."[3] *Preaching the Mystery of Faith* insists that "an increasingly important objective of the Sunday homily in our day is to stir the hearts of our people to deepen their knowledge of the faith, to renew their living the faith in the world and participation in the Church and her sacraments."[4]

As seen in these four statements, the purpose of a homily in relation to the liturgical assembly presupposes faith and the importance of growing in knowledge of God's word. The homily requires inspired intentional witnessing to Christ and his gospel message and entering fully into the celebration of God's word and the sacramental life of the Church.

## Four Functions of the Homily in an African American Catholic Liturgical Context: Information, Inspiration, Motivation, and Celebration

Assessing the integral elements of a liturgical homily from an African American Catholic perspective is both constructive and extremely valuable to the Black preaching style. Preaching a number of years in African American Catholic parishes has enabled me to understand what makes a homily effective. An effective preacher essentially must engage the congregation's imagination by crafting and delivering a homily that provides

---

[1]Pope Paul VI, *The Dogmatic Constitution on Divine Revelation [Dei Verbum]* (November 18, 1965), no. 25.

[2]Bishops' Committee on Priestly Life and Ministry, *Fulfilled in Your Hearing: The Homily in the Sunday Assembly* (Washington, DC: United States Catholic Conference, 1982), 17–18.

[3]Synod of Bishops. XII Ordinary General Assembly, *The Word of God in the Life and Mission of the Church (Instrumentum Laboris)* (Vatican City, 2008), 34.

[4]Bishops' Committee on Clergy, Consecrated Life, and Vocations, *Preaching the Mystery of Faith: The Sunday Homily* (Washington, DC: United States Conference of Catholic Bishops, 2012), 4.

information, inspiration, motivation, and celebration. In the following, the function of these components is explored in depth for preaching in African American Catholic settings.

## Information

Given the African American Christian community's affinity with the word of God, it is important when crafting the homily not to simply take the text at face value or reiterate only what the biblical text says. Effective use of the Black preaching style demands a thorough exegesis of the text. Though the preacher is not expected to preach strictly from exegetical research, exegetical understanding and insight serve as a launching pad into something or someplace much more meaningful. This "more meaningful" moment of the homily for the preacher and the congregation is grounded in interpretation. James Henry Harris understands the sermon (homily) as "a poetic creation, an amalgamation of interpretation and imagination culminating in the spoken word."[5] Therefore, the various facets or ingredients of a homily must be interpreted, first by the preacher, and then when preached also interpreted by the listening community.

The expectation of those in the African American Catholic community is to have their imaginations piqued with information: they want to be edified with something that they didn't know, or they want to be drawn in with something that they had never thought about. The preacher is called upon to go behind the scriptural text, to dig deep for a symbol, a ritual, a word, the meaning of a person's name, the meaning of a town's name, the significance of a certain day, a number, an article of clothing, or some other inanimate object. The insights garnered from going behind the scriptural text will provide new information for listeners that not only informs but engages the listening imagination.

## Inspiration

The term *inspiration* is often relegated to a form of homiletic delivery. For example, a person may be deemed an inspiring preacher—and yet the work of crafting a homily also functions to inspire. Creating an inspiring homily that stimulates both the intellect and the emotions is found in the ability to connect in a personal and relevant way with the assembly. Often the inclusion of real-life stories, childhood memories, some moving or evocative current event, some belief or core value that is life-changing will enhance a homily in ways that deeply resonate with the congregation.

---

[5]James Henry Harris, *The Word Made Plain: The Power and Promise of Preaching* (Minneapolis: Fortress Press, 2004), 51.

When an assembly gathers for worship, it is more than a rare treat to be the beneficiaries of an inspiring homily; it is oftentimes an urgent need. A parishioner once told me, "I need for God to inspire you, so that you can inspire me!" Another parishioner informed me, "There is pain in the pews, and we need a word from God that heals the pain or at least helps us deal with the pain." A preacher never knows what kind of week the congregation has had, what kind of problems they are facing. and what kind of issues they are confronting. Coming up with a homily that is healing is a tall order. In an African American liturgical context, the people want and need to be inspired by the homily. They have lived through a week filled with bad news; they come to church to hear the kerygma, the "Good News"—good news that is inspiring.

*Motivation*

The general understanding of the word *motivation* is that it means the reason or reasons that one has for acting or behaving in a particular way. The very nature of preaching is persuasion—the ability to influence the actions or beliefs of others. Through the homily the preacher seeks to influence the assembly's beliefs, actions, attitudes, and opinions, not only about the scriptural texts but about the Christian life, the Church, and needed changes in their own lives or in society. In the traditional Black church or Protestant experience of preaching the preacher spoke with authority and urged his congregation to believe in a certain idea or value as well as to do something that needed to be done. This was most evident during the Civil Rights movement when Black preachers from their pulpits urged their congregants to boycott certain businesses because of their racist practices or to register to vote and to actually vote for social, political, and economic change. Besides these reasons, motivation is the impetus to instill faith and to promote a deeper relationship with Jesus among the assembly. The preacher, much like a lawyer in a courtroom, stands before the gathered faith community to spur people on to have an unwavering faith in the gospel. During the preaching event, motivation is accomplished not by insincere coercion or manipulation but rather by the genuine conviction of the preacher. In other words, people are not motivated to do or to believe what is not evidenced in the life of the preacher.

In crafting a homily, the preacher has to ask and answer some fundamental questions: What is the central message that I want to convey? What do I want my congregants to believe having heard my homily? As a result of my homily what do I want my congregants to do? What do I want my fellow believers to feel and to be able to identify after listening to my homily? I appreciate getting the view from the pew to observe the effects of the homily on the congregation. One Sunday morning while attending Mass at an African American Catholic parish after a Black priest finished his homily, a Black middle-aged lady sitting behind me said, "So what?" Thinking she was being humorous, I turned around to look at her and she wasn't smiling. Her expression, "So what?" was perhaps an indication that she had heard the twenty-minute homily and was in a quandary about what she was supposed to do, feel, or believe. The homily simply did not motivate her. Pinpointing your motivation is vitally important when crafting a homily.

*Celebration*

Experiencing a celebration within a homily might seem quite novel or even considered out of place in Catholic worship. The paradox is that the Catholic homilist is instructed by the liturgical documents to move from the preaching of the Word to the celebration of the Eucharist and yet the words of the crafted homily and the manner in which the preacher delivers the homily do not feel the least bit celebratory. I address the role of celebration here in the context of a written homily, and later in the book as a manner of delivering the conclusion of a homily, and finally as a component integral to the formulation of an African American Catholic theology of preaching.

Henry H. Mitchell has written extensively on celebration as a homiletical method in the Black preaching style. And although he did not "invent" this manner of summation and conclusion of a sermon or homily, he most definitely retrieved this method, signifying the creative genius of the Black preacher. Some Protestant congregations would judge a spirited conclusion of a sermon out of place, unnecessary, and overly emotive. I dare say that most Catholic congregations would feel uncomfortable to say the least with a rousing boisterous ending of a homily. Clearly, the purpose of celebration is widely misunderstood.

Various Protestant homileticians have sought to give meaning to the manner of concluding a sermon. Let's examine a few. Mitchell conjectures that "the celebration expresses gladness about what God has done and is doing in the same area in which it is the purpose to engender growth. The affirmation celebrated must be the very same affirmation as that taught and experienced in the main body of the sermon."[6] Mitchell insists that in crafting a sermon or homily the celebration should be consistently connected to the biblical text. For the preacher to end the homily from

---

[6]Henry H. Mitchell, *Celebration and Experience in Preaching* (Nashville: Abingdon Press, 1990), 66.

some unrelated or even well-known and inspirational biblical text would be unacceptable. Frank A. Thomas agrees with Mitchell that the climactic utterance known as celebration has a specific function. "Celebration in the final stage of the sermon functions as the joyful and ecstatic reinforcement of the truth already taught and delivered in the main body of the sermon."[7]

Many African American Catholic congregations could wholeheartedly embrace a stirring conclusion of a homily as long as it serves to help them remember the central message of the homily. The challenge before the preacher using a celebratory closing when crafting a homily for an African American Catholic congregation is not only to remain faithful to the biblical text but to be creative in writing the climactic conclusion. It must not be irrelevant, redundant, predictable, or worse yet, forgettable. Remember, the purpose of celebration in a homily highlights the goodness and faithfulness of God; therefore, the preacher must utilize good imagery, anecdotes, or illustrations that ecstatically reinforce and celebrate an unforgettable message.

### Appreciating the Lectionary

The advent of Vatican Council II ushered in some profound and revolutionary statements about a return to the biblical proclamation of the Church:

Sacred scripture is of the greatest importance in the celebration of the liturgy.[8]

The sermon, moreover, should draw its content mainly from scriptural and liturgical sources.[9]

The treasures of the Bible are to be opened up more lavishly, so that a richer fare may be provided for the faithful at the table of God's word. In this way a more suitable part of the sacred scriptures will be read to the people in the course of a prescribed number of years.[10]

---

[7]Frank A. Thomas, *They Like to Never Quit Praisin' God: The Role of Celebration in Preaching* (Cleveland: Pilgrim Press, 1997), 85.

[8]Pope Paul VI, *The Constitution on the Sacred Liturgy [Sacrosanctum Concilium]* (December 4, 1963), no. 24.

[9]Ibid., no. 35.

[10]Ibid., no. 51.

Before the Second Vatican Council there was a one-year cycle of read-ings (epistles and gospels) that were part of the *Missale Romanum* (Ro-man Missal) of 1570.[11] The revised *Lectionary for Mass* was revised and promulgated in 1969 as a result of the Council's mandate for a "richer fare" of the Bible; thus, the formulation of a three-year cycle of scriptural readings.

The lectionary is defined as an "orderly sequence of selections from Scripture to be read aloud at public worship by a religious community."[12] The *Lectionary for Mass* is composed of a two-year cycle of daily scripture readings and a three-year cycle of readings (Years A, B, C) for Sundays of the liturgical year. The readings include a scripture text from the Old Testament, a Psalm (preferably sung), a New Testament scripture, and a gospel text. After the third year, the cycle repeats itself. The gift of the lec-tionary as a liturgical resource for hearing and studying the Word of God and for preaching should be appreciated. Preachers from other religious traditions often have to think about which biblical text that they will use as the source of their preaching Sunday after Sunday. That is not the case for preachers of the Catholic Church. The lectionary is a scriptural guide throughout the liturgical year. Besides the liturgical rituals of the Catholic liturgy, the lectionary scriptural texts also demonstrate the universality of the Catholic Church because the same scripture texts are proclaimed and preached on throughout the world.

However, some Catholic preachers have found the lectionary to be lim-iting. Comments such as "I preached on that gospel text three years ago" are often heard. I disagree with the assessment that the lectionary limits the Catholic preacher. In fact, the lectionary offers the preacher various possibilities for preaching. What becomes problematic is that the preacher tries to address too much in a limited amount of time during the homily. Technically there are four scripture texts provided by the lectionary each Sunday. We often forget about the psalm being a written scripture text because many times the cantor will sing it during the liturgy. Preachers try to do too much by trying to "say a little" about each scripture text during the homily. We've heard preachers predictably say, "In the first reading, and in the second reading, etc." Trying to "say a little" in my estimation does a disservice to both the sacred scriptures and the homily. It is impossible to justly address each scriptural passage and to deliver a

---

[11] Robert P. Waznak, *An Introduction to the Homily* (Collegeville, MN: Liturgical Press, 1998), 73.

[12] John Reumann, "A History of Lectionaries: From the Synagogue at Nazareth to Post-Vatican II," *Interpretation* (April 1977), 116.

succinct and well-developed homily. Since there is a three-year cycle, the Catholic preacher could use only one of the four possible scripture texts on a given Sunday and then come back to the others in later years. Here is where Protestant preachers can teach Catholic preachers an important lesson: that less is more. Many Protestant preachers base their sermons on a single scriptural text and even a single verse. From that one passage or verse, they are able to deliver an informative, inspiring, and motivating sermon. I have developed the practice of using only one scriptural text as the foundation of my homily. People appreciate a well-developed single-scripture-based homily, opposed to rambling and not making clear connections from a few scriptural texts.

### Creating a Preaching Notebook

Where does a preacher find ideas, illustrations, stories, and inspiration to undergird and support the biblical foundations of a homily? Actually, inspiration can be found in daily life. I was encouraged by a former preaching professor to create a preaching notebook. It serves as a reservoir for anecdotes, ideas, stories, quotes, poems, current events in newspapers, and illustrations that can be used for future homilies. Organizing a preaching notebook is at the discretion of the preacher. Some preachers choose to organize their notebooks by themes and topics, by categories, by biblical references, or the liturgical year. However the notebook is organized, it is a valuable source of inspiration and saves the preacher time in trying to search for homily illustrations. Whether a preacher is African American or not and is preaching to a primarily African American congregation, the best way to find illustrations for a preaching notebook is to engage those in the community, listen to their stories, ask pertinent life questions, learn from their cultural sayings, and especially garner the wisdom of the elders. Preachers: gather these precious, insightful treasures, write them in your preacher's notebook, and watch them bring new life to the homiletic moment and captivate your listeners.

### Homily Preparation within a Week

Procrastination is an enemy of the preacher. Procrastination tricks the preacher into believing that time is on his or her side. Why rush to craft a homily; it's only the middle of the week, and besides there are more important tasks to attend to. Every preacher has been in this place of procrastination when having to prepare for a Sunday homily. Ideally, a preacher needs a week to prepare and a craft an effective homily. Many homilists prefer to jot down a few phrases or list a few points of an outline. While preaching notes and outlines are certainly acceptable for delivering a homily, I have found more drawbacks than benefits to using this option. Black preachers in traditional Black churches almost always have a manuscript before them in the pulpit. I submit that Catholic preachers of African American congregations should begin with crafting a homily because of the expectation to fully develop what David Buttrick termed moves or shifts in the homily. Black preachers likewise refer to these moves or shifts as "making points" to carry the sermon from beginning to end. Outlines and notes do not allow the preacher to fully develop thoughts in the homily. A few notes on a notecard likewise do not allow the preacher to expand his or her "preaching vocabulary." When speaking, a person typically uses a limited number of words—crafting a homily enables the preacher not only to expand his or her vocabulary but to formulate thoughts, develop points, and provide fluid images and illustrations. Here I propose a six-day exercise/plan of homily preparation:

- Day One: *Pray with the Scripture Text.* The preacher discerns the one scriptural text that will be used as the foundation of his or her preaching. The preacher then takes on a posture of prayer with the scriptural text. Prayerfully meditate on the scriptural passage and slowly read it aloud (*lectio divina*). While praying, be attentive to the presence of God and be present to the scriptural text. While reading the passage, be aware of words or phrases that stand out or resonate. There will be temptations to analyze or think about what to preach about, but remain focused only on the words and phrases of the text. Perhaps repeat this exercise at least three times on this first day.

- Day Two: *Converse with the Scripture Passage.* The preacher has remained focused on the scripture passage for a day. Now the words and phrases that resonated are written and reflected upon. Next the preacher begins to talk to the scriptural text. It may help to do so aloud. It is advised to begin with the words or phrases that captured one's attention. Ask the scripture passage: What do they mean and why are they important? If there are specific names of persons or places, ask the meaning of the names. If there is a historical context, a ritual, a religious festival or observance, or an event in the biblical narrative, seek its meaning. If specific numbers or a certain day of the week is mentioned, ask its significance. Perhaps there are various nationalities or ethnicities in the text; ask about their cultural and religious beliefs. Take note of biblical persons from Ethiopia, Egypt, Canaan (Syro-phoenicia), Cush, Niger, Cyrene, Alexandria; these persons are of African descent and will have cultural significance when preaching to African Americans. Write down the questions and ponderings that were asked of the scriptural text. They have been revealed and may have significance in the crafting of the homily.

- Day Three: *Consult Biblical Commentaries.* On this third day it is time to consult with biblical commentaries in order to exegete the scriptural text. Exegesis for the preaching endeavor is to gain a deeper understanding of the meaning of words, phrases, events, specific people, cultures, religious beliefs and observations, and historical significance. It is also important to note to whom the biblical text was written, because there were specific religious and cultural beliefs held by ethnic and religious groups, certain laws observed, and issues communities faced. The preacher does not preach the exegesis but allows it to inform the crafting of the homily. The homily is to be an inspired biblical proclamation not an uninspired history lesson. Most of the commonly known Catholic and Protestant biblical commentaries would be useful for exegeting a biblical text. I also suggest *Stony the Road We Trod* (1991) edited by Cain Hope Felder and *True to Our Native Land: An African American New Testament Commentary* (2007) edited by Brian K. Blount, Cain Hope Felder, Clarice J. Martin, and Emerson B. Powery.

- Day Four: *Consider Life Experiences, Stories, Current Events.* Making momentous and relevant connections between the biblical text and lived experiences are essential to crafting a homily. Here is where the preacher can utilize his or her preaching notebook. When using a personal life experience, it is important that the preacher's personal situation is general enough that others can identify and resonate with it. An incident too farfetched may perhaps draw too much attention to the story itself or to the preacher personally and miss leading back to the scriptural passage. Most, if not all, of the biblical narratives are about human experiences; not much is new today that didn't happen thousands of years ago. Preachers find ways to link what happened in the distant past with the current events of today. Preachers should be keenly aware of what is currently happening in the African American community today both locally and nationally. African Americans are community-oriented, and something that affects someone within their race deeply touches them.

- Day Five: *Crafting the Homily | Practicing the Homily.* This fifth day brings the preacher to reviewing the work of the past few days: from praying and conversing with the scriptural text to consulting commentaries and making life applications by way of stories or current events. The preacher is ready to write the homily using all the gathered information and resources. It is important that the homily have a sound structure, meaning a clear introduction, body, and conclusion. I will elaborate more on the homily structure when addressing homily development. The homily should be written from the perspective of a sinner speaking to fellow sinners. The personal pronoun "we" should always be used rather than "you." The assembly must be assured that the preaching is not preaching *at them* but *with them.* The homily is written to be performed and not merely read; therefore, it should not be written like an insipid research paper.

  Once the homily has been sufficiently written, it must be thoroughly proofread to eliminate any writing errors because the preacher will preach the precise words on the printed page. Then it is time to practice the homily. Practicing the homily should never become obsolete. The adage "practice makes perfect" is true for preaching. Practicing the homily allows the preacher to have a dress rehearsal, if you will, of the preached homily. In practicing the homily, the preacher can hear the words, make adjustments to pitch, rate, volume, breathing, cadences, and rhythm. Practicing the homily also enables the preacher to embody the written manuscript with the addition of facial expressions and purposeful movements and gestures. Finally, I highly advise, at the beginning of homily preparation, that the preacher pause to pray, totally dependent upon God, before delivering the homily to a congregation anxiously awaiting some good news.

- Day Six: *Proclaiming the Homily.* How the homily is delivered is based in part on how familiar the preacher is with the written homily. Even with a manuscript, the preacher should have practiced giving the homily so that there is a sense of ease. A preacher almost never loses some nervousness; and this is certainly all right. When preaching, the preacher should always have good eye contact with the congregation. It is important that the assembly knows that the preacher is with them and a part of them. Facial expressions and gestures enliven the written words of the homily in preaching. The preacher shouldn't be stoic when preaching. It is vital to be aware of the assembly. Through nonverbal communication the listeners inform the preacher whether or not they understand what is being preached. They tell the preacher when they are bored or it is time to move on to another point or to end the homily by coughing, fidgeting, looking at their phones, or shifting in their pews. Conversely, the preacher is most definitely connecting when the assembly is looking at the preacher, and he is keeping their undivided attention. Finally, know when to end. I find that this is most problematic when the preacher has not written a manuscript and the preacher doesn't know how to bring the homily to a logical and hopefully an inspiring conclusion.

## Structuring the Homily

All effective communication must be clear, well organized, and logical. Preaching is no exception to this rule. Without order and direction, the preacher is simply rambling, spouting off unrelated random thoughts, and not making a connection with his or her listeners. Worst yet, the preacher becomes repetitious and is not making sense! Homily preparation prevents the homilist from making blunders. It is advisable to craft a manuscript that has a definite introduction, middle, and conclusion. Sacred rhetoric for many African American congregations is not merely a "talk" but an artistic oratorical experience marked by eloquence and compelling persuasion carrying listeners on an inspirational journey. An unfaltering homiletical structure will assure the arrival at the desired metaphorical destination.

### Narrative Preaching in the African American Tradition

Preaching in the African American tradition is fundamentally narrative preaching. It draws on the stories of scripture and requires the preacher to know the story and be capable of telling the story. The Black preaching style subscribes to a narrative theology rooted in the Incarnation. The Black community resonates with an incarnate Christ who enfleshes both our humanity and our culture. Henry Mitchell advocates understanding the incarnational nature of Black preaching by acknowledging what it is not. It is "not a corpus of material to be scientifically analyzed. It could be argued that the Incarnation is described best as God's effort to reconcile humanity by way of a lived-out *story*, seen and heard and felt."[13] Mitchell contends that for African Americans doctrines or theories about God do not communicate as well as knowing that God sent Jesus into the world to share in and to redeem our humanity. "The Word still reaches us best as story, picture, and song."[14]

Structuring the homily inherently demands organization. The preacher must consciously organize the exegetical context, illustrative materials and stories, local and world events, and life-applications—essentially the preaching material—so that the thoughts flow smoothly and logically. Transitional sentences serve as a bridge from one idea or one paragraph to the next idea or paragraph and move the homily along in a logical, sequential way. Deductive, inductive, or narrative homily designs require methodological and commonsense transitions.

Whether the homily or sermon is based on a story or another type of biblical literature, there will be an integral plot that has a narrative quality. David G. Buttrick[15] developed a homiletical method of plotting a sermon according to progressions called "moves." He believed that "sermons are a movement of language from one idea to another, each idea being shaped in a bundle of words. Thus, when we preach; we speak in formed modules of language arranged in some patterned sequence."[16] Buttrick structured the plot by selecting and sequencing various parts of the sermon to work together to achieve a particular goal. The plot is composed of moves—small segments of the sermon, typically no longer than four minutes each. Therefore, a sermon or homily would be twenty minutes in length consisting of an introduction, four to six moves, and a conclusion. Buttrick devised three standard plots that form sermons.[17] The first plot is "the immediacy mode," in which the sermon focuses on the immediate actions of the biblical text, especially a narrative text. A preacher would not merely retell the biblical story but relate the ancient narrative to assist the congregation in making pertinent connections to their present situation. The next is the "reflective mode" where the plot emanates from the movement of the preacher's reflection. Essentially the

---

[13]Mitchell, *Celebration and Experience in Preaching*, 87.

[14]Ibid.

[15]David G. Buttrick (1927–2017) was an ordained Protestant minister (Presbyterian and then the United Church of Christ). Among his teaching positions he was a professor of homiletics at a Roman Catholic seminary. He also served on the National Conference of Catholic Bishops' ad hoc committee on the homily.

[16]David Buttrick, *Homiletic: Moves and Structures* (Minneapolis: Fortress Press, 1987), 23.

[17]David Buttrick, "Sermon as Plot and Moves," in *Patterns of Preaching: A Sermon Sampler*, ed. Ronald J. Allen (St. Louis, MO: Chalice Press, 1998), 87–88.

sermon consists of moments flowing from the preacher's personal contemplation of the biblical text. Finally, there is the "praxis mode." In this mode the attention is on a specific topic rather than a biblical passage. The plot is composed of theological inquiries that lead the listeners to a meaningful Christian understanding of a specific topic or situation.

Although there are other homiletical options, some preachers using the Black preaching style are drawn to Eugene L. Lowry's method known as the "Lowry loop" or "preaching from oops to yeah." Lowry's homiletical method, promoted in his book *Homiletical Plot*, has five stages for developing the narrative:

(1) upsetting the equilibrium, (2) analyzing the discrepancy, (3) disclosing the clue to resolution, (4) experiencing the gospel, and (5) anticipating the consequences.[18]

Lowry posits that "because a sermon is an *event-in-time*—existing in time, not space—a process not a collection of parts, it is helpful to think of sequence rather than structure."[19]

Lowry understands the sermon to be a drama, a play, events happening in time. The sermonic plot flows through five moments that involve a question or disturbance captivating the congregation's attention. The sermon imaginatively lures the congregation into the "drama" and carries them from one life event to another. The sermon leads to a response to the question or ambiguity that ultimately settles the issue. It is an effective preaching method in the Black preaching tradition because it engages the emotions and sensibilities of the congregation pulling them into the sermonic drama that parallels the "drama" of their lives. The congregation can resonate with this biblical narrative because they *live* the story.

Buttrick, who was influenced by the Black homiletic tradition, believed of the Black preaching style that "all things considered, it is the finest preaching in America today."[20] Drawing from the wisdom of both Mitchell and Buttrick, preaching professor Frank A. Thomas agrees that within the Black preaching tradition, the sermon instinctively moves from the presentation of a problematic situation or complication to a gospel assurance, to the celebration of the resolution. This unique homiletic method is known as "preaching from problem through gospel assurance

---

[18]Eugene L. Lowry, *The Homiletical Plot: The Sermon as Narrative Art Form*, expanded ed. (Louisville: Westminster John Knox Press, 2001), 26.

[19]Ibid.

[20]Buttrick, *Homiletic*, 469.

to celebration." Thomas explains that in the beginning of the sermon, the preacher identifies and elaborates a problem that disrupts and complicates the tranquility of the congregation.[21] This complication could be a national crisis, a civic conundrum, or a dilemma within the local parish. The problem might present a difficulty to one's faith, a theological or doctrinal quandary, or a difficult issue raised by a biblical text. The preacher expounds on the problem to illustrate how the congregation is implicated or affected by the problem. The vexing issue stirs the listeners' cognitive, emotional, and spiritual sensibilities. The sermon may need to help the congregation indicate the causes of the problem and or its ramifications.

The sermon also moves to the gospel assurance stage. At this point the sermon shifts from the problematic to the providential: the assurance that God's care and protection are manifested in times of trouble. The sermon offers a path to hope and the promise of deliverance. The preacher reminds the congregation that God's universal and unconditional love is ever-present. The gospel assurance is the certainty that no one is excluded from God's mercy. The preacher also uses the opportunity to help the community cope with and overcome future problems; to use the problematic experience in the biblical text or in reality as a source of strength to weather future calamities. The sermon extols God as One who offers love and wills justice. The preacher offers exegetical interpretation, teachings, and traditions of the Church, examples from the lives of holy women and men both ancient and contemporary, Christian practices and other biblical passages—all in service to speaking to both the spirit and mind of the congregation. At times the movement to resolution may not be expedient—painful memories and life events take time to heal. The place of resolution may require that individuals within the congregation or the congregation as a whole have to change. The gospel assurance is not the holy oil to make everything all right or make people feel good. Healing is a process that may demand contrition, making amends, and repentance. Personal and communal transformation does not usually occur by the end of a sermon, but hopefully the preacher has illuminated for the congregation a possible way forward to resolution. While the function of celebration will be explained when addressing the closing of a homily, suffice it to say that celebration is intertwined with resolution in that it facilitates the experience of the assurance of grace.

---

[21]Frank A. Thomas, "From Problem through Gospel Assurance to Celebration," in *Patterns of Preaching: A Sermon Sampler*, ed. Ronald J. Allen (St. Louis, MO: Chalice Press), 43.

## Appreciating African American Literature as a Resource for Preaching

If one wishes to preach to Black people, then that preacher should come to an appreciation of the cogency of words written by Black authors within Black literature and, when it is appropriate, to use them when preaching. As a Black person growing up and devouring the tantalizing, delightful, and stirring words of Black writers, I quite honestly took their sentence structures, use of adjectives and adverbs, phraseologies, idioms, and sounds for granted. I recall having a white, former college English literature professor as a priest in my home parish. Inevitably, at some point in his homily, typically at his introduction or conclusion, he cited a paragraph of prose of a Black writer or a verse or the entirety of a poem by a Black poet. At times there was a clear connection to his homily, but many times there was not.

At the time, I recall thinking that the priest was going to his "default" or comfort zone—literature. But later I realized that he was connecting to his mostly Black congregation through the unique and very familiar words of Black people. Black phraseology, cadence, dialects, descriptors, and idioms are not only familiar but when appropriately used they make satisfying connections with Black congregations. It says to them that Black words—English words used by Black people—are valued by and valuable to the preacher and can convey salient messages better than the words the preacher may use.

Those called to preach to Black congregations should mine the treasure trove of Black literary authors such as W. E. B. Du Bois, Zora Neal Hurston, Langston Hughes, James Baldwin, Ralph Ellison, Claude McKay, Alice Walker, Ernest Gaines, Maya Angelou, Toni Morrison, Audre Lorde, Suzan Lori-Parks, Colston Whitehead, Channing Godfrey Peoples, Ta-Nehisi Coates, and Amanda Gorman. Incidentally, yet importantly, McKay, Morrison, Gaines, Parks, Godfrey Peoples, and Gorman are Black Catholic writers, playwrights, and poets. Read Black writers' words aloud, hear how they sound, comprehend their meaning, feel their enunciation on your lips, and resonate with their import—the power and conviction of these "Black words." This savoring of Black literature enables the preacher to enter into and encounter the literary, yet real, lived experiences of Black people and enhance his or her preaching.

### Homily Introduction: Capturing and Keeping Their Attention

Beginning a homily can be a daunting task for the preacher. Conventional wisdom suggests that when beginning a homily, it is the obligation of the preacher to conjure up ways to engage the congregation—to capture and keep their attention. This expectation is also true of the Black preaching style. In many Black Protestant churches, the sermon is the "main event" of the worship experience, and the introduction of the sermon is a distinctive part of the structure of a sermon. However, within the Catholic eucharistic liturgy, the homily does not stand alone. The homily is an integral part of the liturgy as a whole—and should not be viewed as a separate entity. In most cases, the presiding celebrant of the Mass is also the homilist. In theory and in ritual, the homily flows within the overall context of the liturgy. The late bishop of the Diocese of Saginaw, Ken Untener offered a unique perspective regarding an introduction to a homily in his book *Preaching Better: Practical Suggestions for Homilists*: "Go right to the middle [of the homily]. Our reluctance to do that may stem from the fear that we won't have anything left to say. We feel we have to hold back on the heart of our homily and lead into it gradually."[22] Criticisms of the introductions to homilies in Catholic parishes include: "He rambles on in the beginning; just get to the point. He is so predictable; he always starts with a story or a dry joke. My pastor's homily inevitably begin with the words, 'In today's readings . . .' I don't need a retelling of the gospel passage, I just heard it!"[23]

Another justifiable critique of introductions of homilies is the lack of connection with the biblical text and heart of the homily. Arbitrary introductory statements distract from centering in on the core thought of the homily. These unrelated introductions of homilies are confusing. Untener believed that "a good measure of a beginning statement of a homily is whether or not the material could easily fit later in the homily. If not, it is probably unnecessary verbiage."[24]

Incorporating an introduction in a homily using the Black preaching style is essential, even within the context of Mass. It is inherent in the nature of Black homiletics. The introduction is crucial to the performance of the homily. Most preachers using the Black preaching style are aware that the introduction must begin low, meaning that it gives the listeners the ability to tune into the preacher's voice to become familiar and comfortable with its tonality. The introduction must also start slow, giving the preacher ample time to set the scene, to lay out the situation of the text, to establish the "itinerary" of the homiletical journey. The slow pace does

---

[22]Ken Untener, *Preaching Better: Practical Suggestions for Homilists* (Mahwah, NJ: Paulist Press, 1999), 22.

[23]I have heard these comments throughout my years of ministry.

[24]Untener, 24.

not mean unnecessarily prolonging the introduction but rather enabling the preacher to sufficiently establish the focus of the homily.

Within the African American preaching tradition there are a variety of strategies for creating an introduction. Here are some of the most common ways to begin a homily: Give a title to the homily. The title can be in the form of a statement, a question, or a proposition. For instance, a title may be "When God Disrupts Your Agenda," "What Will You Do with What You Have?" or "Forgiving What You Can't Forget." The preacher might begin a homily by telling a brief story, giving an illustration, citing a quotation, reciting a poem, speaking or singing the verses or refrain of a Spiritual, relaying a personal or communal experience all relating to the biblical text or focus of the homily. The preacher may highlight an issue in the world or local community requiring justice or resolution. While there are many strategies to begin a homily, the introduction sets forth the plan, purpose, and promise of the homily.

### The Heart of the Homily: Carrying Them on a Journey

The structure of the middle part of the homily is often referred to using anatomical language, the legs, the body, or the heart of the homily. This section of the homily gives life to the homiletical message. Just as life is a journey, the middle or heart of the homily is a significant division or point that takes listeners on a metaphorical journey through various "ports of call."

This heart of the homily needs to consider how the listener hears and receives the preached message. The topic of the message, the literary text, the logical progression of the unfolding thought, appropriate illustrations, use of life experiences, and the timing and position of each sequence—are all vital to the organization and arrangement of the homily. Properly tending to the arrangement of the homily helps the preacher to be clear and concise and to be understood by those who are listening. Whether or not listeners are engaged and attentive to the homily will depend on how effective the preacher is in making points and illustrations that are powerful. Transitions in the message must be timely, and all movement must provide a clear goal or purpose.

### Homily Conclusion: Inviting Them to Celebrate

Introductions and conclusions of the homily are often problematic for many Catholic preachers. Just as some preachers ramble on in the beginning, many do not know how to bring preaching to a close. The conclusion of a homily is not the time to bring in an additional point or a new thought or idea. The whole homily needs to be carefully predetermined and sequenced.

Within the context of the Catholic eucharistic liturgy the homily is not an ending in itself but a segue from the Liturgy of the Word to the Liturgy of the Eucharist. Typically, the final words or closing of the homily lead the listeners to the celebration of the Eucharist. Without contrivance or manipulation, the homily should not only lead *to* the celebration of the Eucharist but *be* a celebration of the good news proclaimed. The Black preaching style helps Catholic preachers achieve this objective.

A celebrative moment is employed when the sermon or homily slowly builds and ascends to its highest point of celebration. Perhaps it is best expressed in the familiar saying of the African American preaching tradition: "Go slow, rise high, strike fire, and sit down!" Henry Mitchell rediscovered the art of celebration as an essential aspect of the Black preaching style, and Frank A. Thomas has further lifted up the purpose of celebration in both the structure and delivery of a sermon. In the celebration phase, the sermon exalts God's power and presence that brings about the resolution.[25] At this point the sermon moves to celebrate the mighty actions of God—to recount and rejoice in "what God has done, is doing, and will do that makes the assurance possible."[26] The point of celebration culminates in an ecstatic, climactic fusion of sermon, preacher, and congregation uninhibitedly rejoicing in the goodness of God. In the Black preaching tradition, celebration is the logical and appropriate conclusion of a sermon. The preacher has methodically guided the community by way of the biblical text through sermonic oration fraught with complications, dilemmas, uncertainties, tensions, and suspense, to a place of introspection, personal and communal examination, contrition, repentance, and resolution leading to gospel assurance and celebration. In the Black preaching tradition, the preacher, on behalf of the congregation, accepts the role and responsibility to know the story and has experienced the story and is able to tell the story, while discerning the congregation's spiritual needs and facilitating the place of celebration in the sermon.

An integral part of celebration in the Black preaching style is what Frank A. Thomas identifies as experiential preaching, meaning "the ability of the preacher to stir identification, emotion, and interest through sense

---

[25]Thomas, "From Problem through Gospel Assurance to Celebration," 44.
[26]Ibid.

appeal."[27] He holds that it is difficult to have an experience of something without thinking about it. However, experiences also evoke emotions, feelings. In other words, the preacher's sermon appeals to the congregation's senses, not in the abstract, but in vivid and tangible ways. The listeners are not just hearing a sermon but also seeing and feeling it. Thomas states:

> If we want people to experience rather than solely intellectualize the good news, then we must construct sermons that help people to see, taste, hear, touch, and feel the gospel. When we say that a sermon is boring or lifeless, at least some of what we mean is that it appealed to few if any of our senses. Without our senses being stirred, we do not have a means of identification, and if there is no identification, there is no release of emotion that sustains interest. And if our interest is not sustained, how will we respond to the reversals and challenge to change demanded by the gospel?[28]

Celebration ordinarily belongs at the conclusion of a sermon or homily—though for some—Black experts in homiletics, not exclusively so. In his study of many African American sermons, Olin Moyd observed that a number of African American sermons reveal that the preachers become ecstatic or celebratory at various times interspersed throughout, with the greater intensity at the end.[29]

Richard Eslinger in *The Web of Preaching* has affirmed the celebratory vocation of the preacher: "The preacher stands before the people as the conscious celebrator. If that calling is to be fulfilled, the sermon will come to a crescendo of celebration."[30] Thomas enlists the image of baptismal waters to vividly illustrate both the experience of celebration in the sermon and the function of the preacher as the "conscious celebrator":

> Therefore, the preacher is the first into the waters of celebration, and invites the congregation to wade in as well. Based upon the preacher's experiential invitation, several accept, and celebration becomes a contagion that spreads until we find many members of the congregation in the waters. Celebration usually will not occur if the preacher/designer/catalyst does not celebrate and wade in first.

---

[27]Thomas, *They Like to Never Quit Praisin' God*, 37.
[28]Ibid.
[29]Olin P. Moyd, *The Sacred Art: Preaching and Theology in the African American Tradition* (Valley Forge, PA: Judson Press, 1995), 108–109.
[30]Richard L. Eslinger, *The Web of Preaching: New Options in Homiletic Method* (Nashville: Abingdon Press, 2002), 134.

As we stated earlier, if the preacher does not experience celebration in the preparation and delivery of the sermon, then in all likelihood the people will not experience celebration either.[31]

## Delivering the Homily

Delivering the sermon entails basic knowledge of communication and the preacher's use of voice and diction to transmit the message. In the midst of singular definitions of "good" preaching, the study of communication is an essential tool for sound delivery of the good news. The content of the sermon may be excellent, the content fully understood, the exegesis may lead biblical scholars to cheer, but a weak delivery can overshadow all the preliminaries.[32]

The above quote is the sage wisdom of homiletics professor Teresa L. Fry Brown on the importance of delivering a sermon or homily well. Although the techniques of the Black preaching style are adequately addressed in the preceding chapter of the book, some critical elements of delivering a homily are covered here. For example, it is vital that a preacher be comfortable with his or her voice in communicating the good news. To deliver the Word of God efficiently, many qualities of oral speech are to be considered in the preaching moment, including controlled breathing, speaking from the diaphragm (vocal control), voice projection, tonality, pronunciation, rate, pitch, clarity, energy, and pausing. When preaching to a Black congregation in the call and response dynamic, it is crucial to know the appropriate times to pause. If the congregation gives the preacher a sustained applause in approval of a pertinent point made or if the congregation offers verbal feedback, the preacher should not move through the congregation's response but pause to wait for its completion.

A frequent misconception of the Black preaching style is that the preacher must be loud for the sake of loudness. While being energetic is a vital aspect, shouting at the congregation for no apparent homiletic effect is inappropriate. The Black preaching style employs varying vocal ranges throughout the preaching moment consistent with the mood, emotion, and movement of the homily or sermon text.

When practicing the homily, it is important for the preacher to have

---

[31]Thomas, *They Like to Never Quit Praisin' God*, 48.

[32]Teresa L. Fry Brown, *Delivering the Sermon: Voice, Body, and Animation in Proclamation* (Minneapolis: Fortress Press, 2008), 2.

others listen and critique how the homily sounds. Constructive criticism from others informs the preacher how the message is received and what corrective measures may be needed.

## Finding and Owning Your Voice

Every preacher is unique, and each person called to the preaching vocation must come to this ministry confident in who they are. Some preachers seek to imitate their favorite preacher, a televangelist, or some well-known preacher instead of being as God uniquely created them. In an age of imitation, impersonation, and emulation, listeners simply want to witness authenticity in the pulpit, not a replication of someone else. A preacher must find and cultivate his or her own authentic voice. One's distinctive preaching voice is shaped by one's gender, ethnic culture, geographic location, education, societal culture, church or denominational culture, and lived and religious experiences. These personal attributes determine how a preacher sounds when preaching but also convey all of their cultural, educational, and religious influences. In essence, while the congregation sees and hears a single person, they are also witnessing the many people and perspectives that have formed that particular preacher. Therefore, in owning his or her voice the preacher is acknowledging God's unique creation. Owning one's voice does not negate a preacher's ability to appreciate and incorporate the tenets of the Black preaching style.

## Claiming Your Preaching Presence

The physical presence of a preacher speaks to the congregation even before a word is barely uttered. The preacher's presence informs the congregation whether the preacher comes to the pulpit confident or insecure, well prepared to preach or ill prepared to deliver a homily. There are those preachers, Protestant or Catholic, male or female, white, Black, or Hispanic, whose distinctive preaching voices and presence command the congregation's attention. Think of Rev. Dr. Martin Luther King Jr., Rev. Dr. Gardner C. Taylor, Bishop Gilbert Earl Patterson, Archbishop Fulton Sheen, Father John Kavanaugh, SJ, Sister Thea Bowman, FSPA, and St. Oscar Romero. Their characteristic preaching styles, voices, and presence are still easily identified and remembered long after their deaths.

At times a preacher is unaware of the message that his or her body language conveys. Teresa Fry Brown asserts, "Presence is sometimes viewed as the quality of self-assurance and effectiveness that allows the preacher to achieve rapport with the congregation. Authentic preaching presence is absent caricature or stereotype. The mannerisms, idiosyncrasies, and at times, eccentricities of the preacher enhance the message and open communication with the congregation."[33] The preacher must be conscious of his or her authentic preaching presence and use it fully in proclaiming God's word. Fundamentally this is why teachers of preaching require their students to video-record their homilies. Preachers are not always cognizant of their body movements, facial expressions, eye contact, hand gestures, stance, or posture when preaching. Video-recording and viewing one's preaching help the preacher, novice or veteran, to be aware of his or her preaching presence. Additionally, the video serves to provide critical feedback affirming or correcting facets of one's preaching presence. A preacher's presence has the power to positively promote the message or negatively distract from it. Thus, the importance of preachers being "self-aware" during the preaching moment.

---

[33]Ibid., 60.

# 4

## The Black Preaching Style
## as An Effective Means
## of Inculturated Evangelization

This chapter defines evangelization and its meaning and its impact on Roman Catholicism and the African American community. I believe most African Americans will be drawn to the Catholic faith primarily through the proclamation of the gospel in a style and language that speaks to their lived experience. Here, I concretely demonstrate the need for non–African American priests and deacons to learn to use the Black preaching style effectively to evangelize African Americans into the Catholic faith. There is a desperate need for non–African Americans ministering in the African American community to fully immerse themselves in this particular ethnic group.

"The Word became flesh and dwelt among us." I contend that the Word preached in African American Catholic settings must be a word that becomes "Black" flesh. Indigenization and inculturation are the sine qua non requisites for evangelization. Any other approach will prove superficial and ineffective.

The Gospel of Jesus Christ and the faith that accompanies it have always been proclaimed and experienced in cultural trappings. They do not exist as an abstract core per se. This chapter emphasizes the importance of the inculturation process in evangelizing African Americans. I provide operative definitions of evangelization and inculturation. It is vital to this discussion to gain a clear understanding of a uniquely Catholic approach to evangelization. Likewise, it is equally important to explore the Catholic identity of African Americans. Finally, at the heart of this chapter is the role that Black preaching plays in effective inculturated evangelization of African Americans to Catholicism. To this end, I demonstrate proven ways of how the Black preaching style has contributed to the tremendous growth of African American Catholic parishes.

## What Is Evangelization?

The proclamation of the good news of Jesus Christ is both the privilege and the vocation of the whole Church. All the faithful, by virtue of their baptism, are invited to participate in this grace-filled work, as individuals and as a community of faith. The good news of the gospel not only transforms those who hear it, but it must also transform those who preach it. "The person who has been evangelized," Pope Paul VI wrote, "goes on to evangelize others."[1] This transforming gospel, however, goes much further than personal conversion. The gospel message means the transformation, through holiness, of the heart of society.

Evangelization is an authorized work. The risen Lord commanded the Church to be engaged in this task. That command is recorded in Matthew 28:18–20, the passage usually referred to as the "Great Commission." There is a parallel passage found in Luke 24:44–49 and still another one in the longer ending of Mark 16:14–19.

Bearing authority from God, Jesus had come evangelizing. His synagogue sermon in Nazareth was based on Isaiah 61:1–4, and Jesus used that "Servant Song" to explain the focus and scope of his ministry. But having died and risen, he met with his disciples and addressed them in his messianic role with these words: "All authority in heaven and on earth has been given to me" (Matthew 28:18). It was a preparatory statement before issuing this command: "Go therefore and make disciples of all nations, baptizing them in the name of the Father and of the Son and of the Holy Spirit, teaching them to observe all that I have commanded you" (Matthew 28:19–20).

This was an authorizing command—authorized because of the nature of the assignment and commanded because of the importance attached to it. In referring to his received authority, Jesus was assuring the disciples that they were being given an authorization to handle their work of announcing, sharing, convincing, baptizing, and teaching. The right to call the entire world to repentance and faith in Jesus as Savior rests on a divine authority found in Jesus himself.

The one who first proclaimed the good news had become the central figure in what was to be proclaimed as good news. According to James Earl Massey, "This was a God-purposed result and only God-authorized persons would have the right or understanding to talk about it in depth

---

[1] Pope Paul VI, *Evangelii Nuntiandi,* apostolic exhortation (December 8, 1975), no. 24.

with anyone else. The authorizing word about who backed them allowed the disciples to do their work with confidence."[2]

The very term *evangelization* speaks of movement or doing something. This might explain why some Catholics have trouble appropriating the word for their own sense of mission. The word "evangelization" challenges us to break out of the stagnation or complacency into which we all can easily fall as disciples of the Lord. As we reclaim evangelization as our central mission, as Pope Paul VI encouraged us to do, we must be involved in two simultaneous processes: the ongoing evangelization and conversion of ourselves as a Church and the movement into the world to share the good news.[3]

Pope Paul VI explained why both are necessary: "The Church . . . begins by being evangelized herself by constant conversion and renewal, in order to evangelize the world with credibility."[4] He continued, "Evangelizing means bringing the good news into all strata of humanity, and through its influence transforming humanity from within and making it new."[5]

The term *evangelization* denotes and connotes movement or dynamism. Our evangelizing Church is called to be countercultural, continuing the work of the Old Testament prophets and the saving mission of Jesus. Israel gradually came to see itself as God's chosen people and a "light for the nations." Moreover, Jesus has sent his Church into the world. We who are the Church must not allow ourselves to be paralyzed by focusing too much on individual or private salvation. Again, believers are to remember Pope Paul's challenging understanding of evangelization: the transformation of humanity and the whole world from within.

I can reasonably infer that a major hindrance to the work of evangelization is that our spiritual leadership can become "active non-participants." I find that bishops, priests, deacons, religious, and lay ecclesial ministers (those who have both professional credentials and careers in ministry) need to be cognizant of what Pope Paul VI described as a real obstacle to evangelization—"Lack of fervor, manifested in fatigue, disenchantment, lack of interest, and, above all, lack of joy and hope."[6] Many times this is the reason that there are so many empty pews in our Catholic parishes. The uninspired monotony of the liturgy lacks the spark to ignite the spiritual

---

[2]James Earl Massey, "Culture But Without Color," *Evangelizing Blacks*, ed. Glenn C. Smith (Wheaton, IL: Tyndale House, 1988), 139.

[3]Kenneth Boyack, CSP, ed., *Catholic Evangelization Today: A New Pentecost for the United States* (New York: Paulist Press, 1987), 1.

[4]*Evangelii Nuntiandi*, no. 15.

[5]*Evangelii Nuntiandi*, no. 18.

[6]*Evangelii Nuntiandi*, no. 80.

fire within them. Consequently, they do not develop the thirst or yearning and choose to remain at home and lose all interest in attending Mass.

Pope Paul VI reminded us that evangelization is essentially a work of *love*. That love manifests itself with our continually giving our hearts to the Lord and, in turn, giving our hearts and experience of Jesus to one another.[7]

I maintain that to evangelize is to become instrumental in facilitating and continuing God's self-revelation to our world. Christians believe that Jesus is the apex, the fullness of God's self-disclosure. In evangelizing, we proclaim the Word of God, Jesus, to the modem world. Therefore, in order to evangelize with a sense of integrity and to partake in this ministry of revelation one must do much more than pass on doctrine or tradition, memorize passages from scripture, or convey transitory peak religious experiences.[8]

As the late Joseph Cardinal Bernardin once said, "To evangelize is to touch someone's heart, mind, and imagination with the risen Lord. That encounter becomes so significant that the person begins to reinterpret and redirect his or her whole life around Jesus."[9] I concur with Bernardin's assertion, for to evangelize is to help another person pay attention to, celebrate, and live in terms of the living God, revealed fully by Jesus, and present in our human experiences. This notion will become clearer in our discussion of inculturated evangelization.

## A Catholic Approach to Evangelization

The Church exists to evangelize, to proclaim the good news of the Word-made-flesh. "The pilgrim Church is missionary by her very nature," Vatican II tells us. "For it is from the mission of the Son and the mission of the Holy Spirit that she takes her origin."[10] Thus, Pope Paul VI points out in *Evangelii Nuntiandi*: "Having been born consequently out of being sent, the Church in her turn is sent by Jesus. . . . She prolongs and continues him. And it is above all his mission and his condition of being an evangelizer that she is called upon to continue."[11]

It seems that the Catholic approach to evangelization tends to put the cart before the horse. Catholics speak of Jesus establishing the Church

---

[7]Boyack, *Catholic Evangelization Today*, 2.
[8]Ibid.
[9]Joseph Bernardin, preface to *Catholic Evangelization Today*, 3.
[10]*Ad Gentes [Decree on the Missionary Activity of the Church]* (December 7, 1965), no. 2.
[11]*Evangelii Nuntiandi*, no. 15.

and giving it the mission of evangelization and a number of other important tasks and ministries. But *Evangelii Nuntiandi,* returning to the evidence of Sacred Scripture, tells us matter of factly that this is not the way that it happened: "The Church is born of the evangelizing activity of Jesus and the Twelve."[12] It is the mission of evangelization which has the Church, not the Church which has the mission. In other words, every task and every ministry within the Church serves this continuing mission. All ministries, whether in missionary extension or pastoral care, in outreach to the unchurched and inactive Catholic, in substance abuse counseling, in feeding the hungry in soup kitchens, in catechesis, in preaching, or in teaching—all ministries converge to serve the one "primary and essential mission" of evangelization.[13]

I contend that ministry schooled properly in the art of evangelization takes on a new dynamism and a new purpose and focus. However, many Catholic parishes have a tendency to slip into a maintenance mentality. Catholic parishes can easily provide a comfortable pew where parishioners come to worship and receive the sacraments and return to their homes unchallenged, uninspired, and unchanged. In light of Sacred Scripture and the teachings of the Church, a maintenance mentality is simply unacceptable. Ministry within our Catholic parishes demands a fervor and commitment to spread the good news of Jesus in ways that are truly life-giving. Clergy, religious, and laity alike are encouraged to live out their baptismal calling by being bold witnesses to the power of Jesus Christ within a sin-sick world. We, as Church must minister and evangelize from a position of strength and authority to change our temporal circumstances. If we do not, our preaching, teaching, and service to others will be in vain.

Only when we begin to realize that God calls us together to be Church (*Ecclesia*), can we live our baptismal call. God gathers us together in communion and fellowship as members of Christ's body (*koinonia*) for the purpose of mission and service; God calls us to bear witness to God's hidden plan (see Col. 1:26); then we are really and truly the Church. Vatican II describes the Church "as the universal sacrament of salvation,[14] simultaneously *manifesting* and exercising the mystery of God's love for humanity" (emphasis mine).[15] Everything is not contained in the command to go and teach. There is also the prayer that "they may be one" as the Father and the Son are one "so that the world may believe" (John

---

[12]*Evangelii Nuntiandi,* no. 15.

[13]*Evangelii Nuntiandi,* no. 29.

[14]Pope Paul VI, *Lumen Gentium [The Dogmatic Constitution on the Church]* (November 21, 1964), no. 48.

[15]Pope Paul VI, *Gaudium et Spes [The Pastoral Constitution on the Church in the Modern World]* (December 7, 1965), no. 45.

17:21–23). The Church's fundamental task is simultaneously both to be evangelized and to evangelize, both to become and to share the news.[16]

## Pope Francis on Preaching and Evangelization

### A Preaching Pope

As the evening hours of Rome unfolded on Wednesday, March 13, 2013, and the consistent light rainy weather saturated the teeming crowd gathered at St. Peter's Square, people anxiously awaited the words of the French cardinal, Jean-Louis Tauran announcing from the balcony of St. Peter's Basilica the name of the new pope. The words in Latin finally came, "*Annuntio vobis Gaudium magnum, habemus papam!*"[17] ("I announce a great joy to you: We have a pope!") reverberated across Vatican City's inclement sky. Tens of thousands of Romans, pilgrims, and tourists from around the globe rejoiced at the news with thunderous applause. Tauran, only when the crowd became silent, continued, "The most eminent and most reverend Lord, Lord Jorge Mario Bergoglio, cardinal of the Holy Roman Church, has taken the name Francis." While the announcement was perfunctory, the name was unfamiliar and left a quizzical murmur over the crowd. "Bergoglio, who is this Cardinal Bergoglio?" This prelate apparently from Argentina with an Italian surname was unknown to the vast crowd. Not only was the new pontiff unknown, the salutation he uttered was also most unusual. With a warm smile on his face, he approached the microphone and greeted them, "Fratelli e sorelle, buona sera!"[18] (Brothers and sisters, good evening!) The new Argentinian Bishop of Rome touched the hearts of the people as a familiar and cherished friend. The throng enthusiastically shouted back to their new Holy Father, "Buona sera!"

The very first words of his pontificate indicated that he would bring something entirely different to his papal ministry. Beyond his words were his engaging gestures, warm personality, and sense of humor. "You know that it was the duty of the conclave to give Rome a bishop. It seems that my brother cardinals have gone to the ends of the earth to get one . . . but here we are. . . ." Pope Francis prayed with the people and then said in parting:

---

[16]*Evangelii Nuntiandi*, no. 15.

[17]Gerard O'Connell, *The Election of Pope Francis: An Inside Account of the Conclave that Changed History* (Maryknoll, NY: Orbis Books, 2019), 234.

[18]Ibid.

Let us always pray for one another. Let us pray for the whole world, that there may be a great spirit of fraternity. It is my hope for you that this journey of the church, which we will start today, and in which my cardinal vicar, here present, will assist me, will be fruitful for the evangelization of this most beautiful city.[19]

Even the traditional blessing by the new pope over the city of Rome and the world (*Urbi et Orbi*) was done in an unconventional manner. Francis told the assemblage, "And now I would like to give the blessing, but first—first I ask a favor of you: before the bishop blesses his people, I ask you to pray to the Lord that he will bless me: the prayer of the people asking the blessing for their bishop. Let us make, in silence, this prayer: your prayer over me." Francis humbly bowed his head as the people silently prayed over him and for him.

In this first encounter with the new pope there are notable elements that must be considered characterizing Francis's future ministry both in style and substance. He never refers to himself as "pope," "pontiff," or "Holy Father." He calls himself "bishop." His personality conveys warmth, friendliness, comfortability, and compassion. His disposition is one of humility, sincerity, and being a prayerful person. His message is one of unity, love, hope, and trust. Quite intentionally included in Francis's inaugural message is the word *evangelization*, a word highlighting the mission of the church to preach good news and to make disciples of Jesus Christ throughout the world. Although Pope Francis did not elaborate on it at that precise moment, he left this clue that his pontificate would be eminently committed to the ministry of preaching and evangelization.

This Argentinian Jesuit chosen to lead the estimated 1.2-billion-member Roman Catholic Church was known for his simple lifestyle, traveling Buenos Aires by city bus, and for his closeness with the people, especially the poor. Remaining true to himself would certainly disrupt the customary functioning of the Vatican. His first moments as supreme pontiff were indicative of something that had never been seen before: he chose the name "Francis," honoring St. Francis of Assisi, apostle to the poor (a name never chosen by previous popes). He declined the red papal shoes and continued to wear his black well-worn shoes that walked the impoverished streets of Buenos Aires. He declined the new papal pectoral cross and opted to continue to wear the pectoral cross that he had long worn as an archbishop. He accompanied his brother cardinals back on the

---

[19]Ibid., 238.

bus to Santa Marthae, where he paid his hotel bill and where he would make his permanent domicile. "If actions speak louder than words," the world was embarking on a journey with Pope Francis that would amaze and elate some while confusing and frustrating others.

## To Those on the Peripheries: A Pastoral Preaching Pope

*I am convinced of one thing: the great changes in history were real-ized when reality was seen not from the center but rather from the periphery. It is a hermeneutical question: reality is understood only if it is looked at from the periphery, and not when our viewpoint is equidistant from everything.*[20]

—Pope Francis: Address to Superior Generals<br>of Religious Communities

From the very beginning of his pontificate Pope Francis consistently emphasized the vital importance of preaching and evangelization to the life of the Church. The Holy Spirit and the cardinal electors blessed the Church with a "preaching pope." On most days Pope Francis presides and preaches at the fifty-seat chapel of Domus Sanctae Marthae. Although the space is small and cramped, it is expected that Francis will deliver a word that will fill not only the room but the hearts and minds of his listeners. It was immediately noted by reporters and attendees alike, that rather than preaching from a well-crafted manuscript, the Holy Father's style is to reflect closely on the scriptures and concisely relate the daily scriptural texts to either the liturgical season or feast day, but always to human and lived circumstances and to do so unscripted. Dominican Father and homiletics professor Gregory Heille notes:

His daily homilies are unguarded, transparent, and often prophetic.[21] . . . Pope Francis is a day-to-day icon of "to teach, to delight, to per-suade." What we observe him doing each day in his Santa Marthae worshipping community plays out likewise in our experience of daily churches and chapels around the world. Day by day, faith communi-ties are sustained as the church by Christ in word and sacrament. And day-by-day, we in turn as Body of Christ sustain our families,

---

[20]Antonio Spadaro, "Wake Up the World: Conversations with Pope Francis about Religious Life," trans. Donald Maldari, SJ, *La Civiltà Cattolica* 165, no. 1 (2014): 3.

[21]Gregory Heille, OP, *The Preaching of Pope Francis: Missionary Discipleship and the Ministry of the Word* (Collegeville, MN: Liturgical Press, 2015), 5.

our work places, and our world. We, too, are, as Pope Francis tells us, missionary disciples and evangelists. We, too are called to teach, to delight, and to persuade.[22]

In the infancy of his papacy, an unambiguous indicator of his singular focus on preaching and evangelization was most evident in two significant homilies that Pope Francis preached on the occasions of the Chrism Mass and at Pentecost.

An excerpt of Pope Francis's 2013 Chrism Mass homily:

A good priest can be recognized by the way his people are anointed: this is a clear proof. When our people are anointed with the oil of gladness, it is obvious: for example, when they leave Mass looking as if they have heard good news. Our people like to hear the Gospel preached with "unction"; they like it when the Gospel we preach touches their daily lives, when it runs down like the oil of Aaron to the edges of reality, when it brings light to moments of extreme darkness, to the "outskirts" where people of faith are most exposed to the onslaught of those who want to tear down their faith. People thank us because they feel that we have prayed over the realities of their everyday lives, their troubles, their joys, their burdens and their hopes. And when they feel that the fragrance of the Anointed One, of Christ, has come to them through us, they feel encouraged to entrust to us everything they want to bring before the Lord: "Pray for me, Father, because I have this problem"; "Bless me Father"; "Pray for me"—these words are the sign that the anointing has flowed down to the edges of the robe, for it has turned into a prayer of supplication, the supplication of the People of God. When we have this relationship with God and with his people, and grace passes through us, then we are priests, mediators between God and men. What I want to emphasize is that we need constantly to stir up God's grace and perceive in every request, even those requests that are inconvenient and at times purely material or downright banal—but only apparently so—the desire of our people to be anointed with fragrant oil, since they know that we have it.[23]

Without question, Pope Francis's Chrism Mass homily demanded that those preaching in the Roman Catholic Church must be anointed

---

[22]Ibid.,7.

[23]Pope Francis, Chrism Mass homily, St. Peter's Basilica, Vatican City, Holy Thursday, March 28, 2013, https://www.vatican.va/content/francesco/en/homilies/2013/documents/papa-francesco_20130328_messa-crismale.html.

preachers of good news. He is saying that effective preachers will have an undeniably joyful effect on the people hearing and experiencing good news through the preached Word. The Bishop of Rome clearly told priests throughout the world that people want and depend on anointed preaching that enables them to contend with the bad news that they experience in their daily lives. They appreciate preachers who have not only prayed over the scripture texts but have also prayed over the lives and the issues of those to whom they are called to preach. Pope Francis used carefully chosen phrases to express the need and urgency of anointed preaching like "the edges of reality," "moments of extreme darkness," "to the 'outskirts' where people of faith are most exposed to the onslaught of those who want to tear down their faith." The Holy Father in essence is conveying to priests globally that they must have a deep relationship with God through prayer and with God's people through close contact, no matter how inconvenient, and bring them grace—that desired anointed fragrant oil.

Within months of the stirring Chrism Mass homily, Pope Francis celebrated the solemnity of Pentecost—the birthday of the Church—with yet another homily that elucidates the foci of his papacy.

An excerpt of Pope Francis's 2013 Pentecost homily:

A final point. The older theologians used to say that the soul is a kind of sailboat, the Holy Spirit is the wind which fills its sails and drives it forward, and the gusts of wind are the gifts of the Spirit. Lacking his impulse and his grace, we do not go forward. The Holy Spirit draws us into the mystery of the living God and saves us from the threat of a Church which is gnostic and self-referential, closed in on herself; he impels us to open the doors and go forth to proclaim and bear witness to the good news of the Gospel, to communicate the joy of faith, the encounter with Christ. The Holy Spirit is the soul of mission. The events that took place in Jerusalem almost two thousand years ago, are not something far removed from us; they are events which affect us and become a lived experience in each of us. The Pentecost of the Upper Room in Jerusalem is the beginning, a beginning which endures. The Holy Spirit is the supreme gift of the risen Christ to his apostles, yet he wants that gift to reach everyone. As we heard in the Gospel, Jesus says: "I will ask the Father, and he will give you another Advocate to remain with you forever" (John 14:16). It is the Paraclete Spirit, the "Comforter," who grants us the courage to take to the streets of the world, bringing the Gospel! The Holy Spirit makes us look to the horizon and drive us to the very outskirts of existence in order to proclaim life in Jesus Christ. Let us ask ourselves: do we tend to stay closed in on ourselves, on our group, or do we let the Holy Spirit open us to mission? Today let us remember these three words: newness, harmony and mission.[24]

In the vein of a Black Protestant preacher, Pope Francis's Pentecost homily sought to make three points. In the "Black Church" the preacher calls this a three-point sermon. Pope Francis reiterated three important words in his Pentecost homily that he distinctly wanted his listeners to remember: newness, harmony, and mission. In the context of his homily, he noted that "newness" might be frightening because it moves us out of our security and comfort zones. He informed his listeners that throughout salvation history that whenever God was revealed, something new occurred. Pope Francis emphasized that God's newness requires trust and actually brings us fulfillment. He challenges the Church to be open to the "surprises of God" and to be open to allow the Holy Spirit "to be the soul and guide of our lives in every decision." Essentially, this new pope is homiletically and literally inviting the Church to allow the Holy Spirit to move her to new places and to new people that desperately need the Church's witness. Second, the pope said that the Holy Spirit creates harmony. The very nature of the Holy Spirit implies unity but not uniformity, a unity that always leads to harmony. Pope Francis preached, "When we are the ones who want to build unity in accordance with our human plans, we end up creating uniformity, standardization. But if instead we let ourselves be guided by the Spirit, richness, variety and diversity never become a source of conflict, because he impels us to experience variety within the communion of the Church."[25] On Pentecost Sunday, the pope wanted the world to know that he was leading the Church to value and celebrate its rich diversity and to live harmoniously in it.

Finally, the new pontiff proclaimed that the Church was also missionary by nature with a mission to move outside of its enclaves—to move out and to joyfully witness to and celebrate the Gospel of Jesus Christ. Pope Francis preached, "The Holy Spirit is the soul of mission. The events that took place in Jerusalem almost two thousand years ago are not something far removed from us; they are events which affect us and become a lived experience in each of us."[26] Emphatically, he urged his listeners to recognize the Holy Spirit still living in them and moving them beyond the

---

[24]Pope Francis, Homily for the Solemnity of Pentecost, St. Peter's Basilica, Vatican City, Sunday, May 19, 2013, http://www.vatican.va/content/francesco/en/homilies/2013/documents/papa-francesco_20130519_omelia-pentecoste.html.

[25]Ibid.

[26]Ibid.

familiarity and comfort of their surroundings and to go out—out to the outskirts—out to peripheries and proclaim the good news.

Prior to his election as Bishop of Rome, Pope Francis had an affinity for those who were poor, neglected, marginalized, and oppressed. This existential affinity was not merely a theological disposition for Francis but his empirical, lived reality as a vowed Jesuit and from his episcopal ministry among his people living in poverty in Buenos Aires. The pope is indisputably a pastoral preacher who appreciates preaching to "ordinary folk," people who manage their lives from day to day, those who struggle against poverty and oppression, and those on the peripheries who have little hope or influence. For Francis, those living on the peripheries of life should not be viewed as poor in spirit; on the contrary, these are people who are rich in faith and are dependent on God. When Pope Francis goes to the slums, to the prisons, to the peripheries to celebrate Mass and preach, he is not only evangelizing and bringing good news to the poor, but also being evangelized and receiving good news from the poor. He sees the poor as having something that all Christians need: faith and fortitude. His view of the poor was made more apparent on the Feast of St. Francis of Assisi when he visited Assisi, the hometown of Francis, the saint's name he now bore and whose life he sought to emulate, and urged other Christians to do likewise. At Assisi Francis said, "It is unthinkable that a Christian—a true Christian—. . . would want to go down the path of worldliness." He told those gathered to listen to him, "[It] is a homicidal attitude. Spiritual worldliness kills! It kills the soul! It kills the person! It kills the church!" He admonished the crowd to disentangle themselves from unnecessary luxury and wealth. Pope Francis averred, "We would become like Christians in a pastry shop," admiring the beautiful cakes but never receiving true sustenance.[27]

## The Joy of the Gospel | *Evangelii Gaudium*

In November 2013, on the Solemnity of Christ the King, signifying the end of the liturgical year, Pope Francis presented the Church universal in general and the Catholic Church's homiletical lexicon in particular with a significant gift. The publication of the apostolic exhortation *Evangelii Gaudium*, The Joy of the Gospel, was the first encyclical composed by

---

[27]Pope Francis, "Meeting with the Poor Assisted by Caritas" (Assisi, Italy, October 4, 2013), http://www.vatican.va/content/francesco/en/speeches/2013/october/documents/papa-frances-co_20131004_poveri-assisi.html.

Francis himself. Pope Francis formulates his apostolic exhortation around a broad array of important topics including care for the elderly, the poor, economic disparities, wealth distribution, and sexual human trafficking. *Evangelii Gaudium* was unlike previous documents. Missing were the usual lofty or pious aspirations advocating for the world to become a better place. No, this apostolic exhortation was candid, courageous, and pragmatic. The pope was intentional in the conversational matter in which he wrote, indicating that he wanted everyone to understand this important message to the world. The pope proposed a radical and unwavering review of the church and the role of Christians in society.

Quite curiously in the five-chapter document, there appears in the third chapter a poignant commentary on the proclamation of the gospel. Although the preceding two chapters argued for progressive ecclesial transformation for mission and radical social and economic reforms, Pope Francis pivots to the prospects of the entire People of God. Pope Francis wants the Church to proclaim the gospel, become missionary disciples, and understand the purpose of the liturgical homily. He challenges those called to preach to properly prepare to preach, evangelize, and to gain a deeper understanding of the kerygma. In customary fashion, the inclusion and placement of these topics by Francis were deliberate. Sensing that the trajectory of his apostolic exhortation might be questioned, Pope Francis writes in the opening paragraph of chapter 3: "After having considered some of the challenges of the present, I would now like to speak of the task which bears upon us in every age and place, for 'there can be no true evangelization without the explicit proclamation of Jesus as Lord' and without the 'primacy of the proclamation of Jesus Christ in all evangelizing work.'"[28]

Indubitably, Pope Francis is clear that the work of the Church is evangelization and that it is a mission that is inclusive of everyone. He wrote that "Jesus did not tell the apostles to form exclusive and elite groups. He said, 'Go and make disciples of all nations' (Mt. 28:19)."[29] The Bishop of Rome directly said that even those who feel distanced from or alienated in any way from the Church are being called respectfully and lovingly by the Lord Jesus to be a part of the People of God. The work of the Church and the message of the gospel are ones of mercy, welcome, love, forgiveness, and encouragement.[30] Francis's message, while seemingly simple, was a strong challenge to a church that has not always been one of welcome, mercy, and forgiveness.

---

[28]Pope Francis, *Evangelii Gaudium*, apostolic exhortation (November 24, 2013), no. 110.
[29]*Evangelii Gaudium*, no. 113.
[30]*Evangelii Gaudium*, no. 114.

Likewise, Francis's apostolic exhortation urges a respect and appreciation of the various cultures of the Church emphasizing that Christianity is not and never has been one cultural expression. A ubiquitous theme in Francis's writings and preaching is that cultural diversity enriches the Church and informs the way that the gospel is preached, understood, and lived. *The Joy of the Gospel* is emphatic that "[w]e would not do justice to the logic of the incarnation if we thought of Christianity as monocultural or monotonous. While it is true that some cultures have been closely associated with the preaching of the gospel and the development of Christian thought, the revealed message is not identified with any of them; its content is transcultural."[31] Diversity is not a threat to the Church but on the contrary a cherished gift that boldly enables the Church to preach the gospel to *all* nations.

The pope introduces the concept of "missionary disciples" in his chapter on preaching and evangelization. In defining this concept, Francis states, "Every Christian is a missionary to the extent that he or she has encountered the love of God in Christ Jesus: we no longer say that we are 'disciples' and 'missionaries,' but rather that we are always 'missionary disciples.'"[32] Francis argued that we are missionary disciples who have uniquely been touched and thus changed by a sacred encounter with the Lord Jesus Christ. It is not a singular encounter but many and varied encounters in which the People of God come to experience the love and joy of the risen Redeemer in their daily lives, in their interactions with others, and in their prayer and worship experiences. They feel that they must not keep these encounters to themselves but share them, proclaim them—evangelize. In the words of Francis:

> All of us are called to offer others an explicit witness to the saving love of the Lord, who despite our imperfections offers us his closeness, his word and his strength, and gives meaning to our lives. In your heart you know that it is not the same to live without him; what you have come to realize, what has helped you to live and given you hope, is what you also need to communicate to others.[33]

This statement is at the heart—the nexus—of evangelization. To the pope's clarion call, I say, let the Church say, "Amen" and go evangelize!

To those who preach in liturgical settings, Francis calls for a renewed

---

[31]*Evangelii Gaudium*, no. 117.
[32]*Evangelii Gaudium*, no. 120.
[33]*Evangelii Gaudium*, no. 121.

confidence in the knowledge that it is God who uses the preacher to powerfully convey God's message to the people in need of a word from the
Lord. The pope forthrightly said that the homily serves as a touchstone to
determine whether a preacher is close to his congregation and can communicate with them. This candid assessment illustrates the importance
of the homily and the role of the preacher within the eucharistic liturgy.
According to Francis the homily is not a time for meditation, catechesis,
or entertainment. The homily serves as an ongoing dialogue between God
and God's people about the great work of salvation and the reaffirmation
of God's covenant. The preacher's challenge is to know the congregation
so well that he knows that the desire for God is alive and ardent or once
loving has become sullen. If the congregation's desire for God is dim or
arid, the preacher is called to renew the flame of faith by reminding the
congregants of God's salvation and covenant. For Francis the liturgical
preaching moment should "guide the assembly, and the preacher, to a
life-changing communion with Christ and the Eucharist."[34]

Francis understands that a properly prayed-over and well-prepared
homily greatly benefits the spiritual life of God's people. He is also cognizant of the harm that unprepared homilies cause those seeking a transformative encounter with God through the preached word. This preaching
pope without hesitation states, "Preparation for preaching is so important
a task a prolonged time of study, prayer, reflection and pastoral creativity
should be devoted to it."[35] Conversely, the lack of preaching preparation
results in uninspired, uncreative, unintellectual, unrelatable, and irrelevant
homilies, something that has unfortunately become universally normative.
Francis makes this unflinching indictment of the "unprepared preacher":
"A preacher who does not prepare is not 'spiritual'; he is dishonest and
irresponsible with the gifts he has received."[36]

### Sunday of the Word of God

On September 30, 2019, the Feast of St. Jerome, Pope Francis intentionally used the occasion of the 1600th anniversary of his death to publish
an Apostolic Letter, *Aperuit Illis*, and to institute the Third Sunday in
Ordinary Time as the Sunday of the Word of God. St. Jerome was born
in Stridon, Dalmatia, in c. 347; he died in Bethlehem, Palestine, in 419.

---

[34]*Evangelii Gaudium*, no. 138.
[35]*Evangelii Gaudium*, no. 145.
[36]*Evangelii Gaudium*, no. 145.

Jerome was a monastic monk and biblical translator who is credited with translating much of the Bible into Latin, the Vulgate or common version. St. Jerome famously said, "Ignorance of the Scripture is ignorance of Christ."[37] Pope Francis wanted this special day of the liturgical calendar to be devoted to the celebration, study, and dissemination of the Word of God.[38]

Pope Francis titled his apostolic letter *Aperuit Illis* from the words of the Gospel of Luke 24:45, in which the Evangelist recalls how Jesus appeared after the Resurrection to his disciples on the road to Emmaus, and how "[h]e opened their minds to understand the Scriptures." Francis's apostolic letter most importantly is a response to the requests of the People of God to honor and celebrate the prominence of sacred scripture within the Catholic faith. He asserts, "It is now common for the Christian community to set aside moments to reflect on the great importance of the word of God for everyday living. The various local Churches have undertaken a wealth of initiatives to make the sacred scripture more accessible to believers, to increase their gratitude for so great a gift, and to help them to strive daily to embody and bear witness to its teachings."[39] Although the pontiff gives latitude in the ways for local faith communities to celebrate the Sunday of the Word of God, he suggests that in the Eucharistic celebration the sacred text be enthroned and that it is particularly appropriate to highlight the proclamation of the word of the Lord and to emphasize its importance in the homily. He also pastorally suggests that this special Sunday would be an ideal time to commission readers and to offer lector training in parishes. The pope offers the idea of giving out Bibles and teaching parishioners how to study and pray with the scripture. He also encourages adopting the practice of *lectio divina* in parishes.[40]

The pope concludes his apostolic letter by making two salient points. First, Francis is concerned that in reading and studying Sacred Scripture without the guidance of the Holy Spirit there lies the risk of remaining limited only to a fundamentalist understanding of the written text. He argues that it is the Holy Spirit who "makes sacred Scripture the living word of God, experienced and handed down in the faith of His holy people."[41] Second, Francis is mindful that the Church has celebrated an

---

[37] Quotation of St. Jerome, https://catholicexchange.com/ignorance-of-scripture-is-ignorance-of-christ-3.

[38] Vatican News, "Pope Establishes Sunday of the Word of God," published September 30, 2019, accessed February 24, 2020.

[39] Pope Francis, *Aperuit Illis*, apostolic letter (September 30, 2019), no. 2.

[40] *Aperuit Illis*, no. 3.

[41] *Aperuit Illis*, no. 9.

Extraordinary Jubilee Year of Mercy (2016) and that the Church is now challenged to listen to Sacred Scripture and then to practice mercy. Francis contends, "God's Word has the power to open our eyes and to enable us to renounce a stifling and barren individualism and instead to embark on a new path of sharing and solidarity."[42] God's Word moves us from selfishness to a greater empathy for others. Scripture also reminds us that as beneficiaries of God's mercy we must be merciful to others (Luke 6:36).

Not only does Pope Francis asks the Church to highlight the word of God in the homily on the Sunday of the Word of God, but he demonstrates how it is done. Preaching from Mark 1:14–20 (the making fishers of men text) on the Third Sunday of Ordinary Time (January 24, 2021), Francis preaches:

> Yet the word of God also has particular power, that is, it can touch each person directly. The disciples would never forget the words they heard that day on the shore of the lake, by their boats, in the company of their family members and fellow workers: words that marked their lives forever. Jesus said to them: "Follow me, I will make you become fishers of men" (v. 17). He did not appeal to them using lofty words and ideas, but spoke to their lives. He told fishermen that they were to be fishers of men. If he had told them: "Follow me, I will make you Apostles, you will be sent into the world to preach the Gospel in the power of the Spirit; you will be killed, but you will become saints," we can be sure that Peter and Andrew would have answered: "Thanks, but we'll stick to our nets and our boats!" But Jesus spoke to them in terms of their own livelihood: "You are fishermen, and you will become fishers of men." Struck by those words, they come to realize that lowering their nets for fish was too little, whereas putting out into the deep in response to the word of Jesus was the secret of true joy. The Lord does the same with us: he looks for us where we are, he loves us as we are, and he patiently walks by our side. As he did with those fishermen, he waits for us on the shore of our life. With his word, he wants to change us, to invite us to live fuller lives and to put out into the deep together with him.[43]

---

[42]*Aperuit Illis*, no. 13.

[43]Pope Francis, Homily on The Sunday of the Word of God (January 24, 2021), St. Peter's Basilica. The Holy Father was ill that day, so his prepared homily was read by Archbishop Rino Fisichella, http://www.vatican.va/content/francesco/en/homilies/2021/documents/papa-francesco_20210124_omelia-domenicadellaparoladidio.html.

## What Is Inculturation?

Inculturation is the theological term that refers to the ongoing developing process by which the Church "establishes itself among diverse cultures in a manner that is both meaningful and appropriate to those cultures."[44] Inculturation is a process that begins with the first proclamation of the gospel and moves to a point of integration with the lived human experiences of a particular culture.

In order to authentically continue the work of inculturation it is necessary that the gospel penetrate a particular culture and that a particular culture penetrate the gospel. The best illustration of this process of inculturation is found in the incarnation event. The Church's theology of the incarnation emphasizes the significance of the fact and the process by which God communicated with the world in a unique way. God entered human history and became active in human history in a special way in the person of Jesus Christ. Jesus, in his preaching, teaching, and miracles of healing used the language, customs, symbols, stories, and worldview of those with whom he walked in order to communicate to them the good news of God's presence and action in human history, and the inauguration of the coming of the kingdom of God).[45]

Authentic inculturation must start with the worldview and values of a particular culture. Any discussion of effective evangelization of African Americans must commence within the context of this particular culture. The good news cannot be authentically proclaimed in isolation. The acknowledgment of culture is vital to the work of evangelization. In fact, culture is the starting point of any effective efforts of preaching the gospel. Again, Pope Paul VI wrote:

> All this could be expressed in the following words: what matters is to evangelize man's culture and cultures (not in a purely decorative way as it were by applying a thin veneer, but in a vital way, in depth and right to their very roots), in the wide and rich sense which these terms have in *Gaudium et Spes*, always taking the person as one's starting point and always coming back to the relationships of people among themselves and with God.[46]

---

[44]Jamie T. Phelps, OP, "The Theology and Process of Inculturation: A Theology of Hope for African American Catholics in the United States," *New Theology Review* 7, no.1 (1994): 7–8.

[45]Peter Schineller, *A Handbook on Inculturation* (New York: Paulist Press, 1990), 24.

[46]*Evangelii Nuntiandi*, no. 20.

The gospel, and therefore evangelization, is certainly not identical with culture, and they are independent in regard to all cultures. Nevertheless, the Kingdom which the gospel proclaims is lived by people who are profoundly linked to a culture, and the building up of the Kingdom cannot avoid borrowing the elements of human culture or cultures. Though independent of cultures, the gospel and evangelization are not necessarily incompatible with them; rather, they are capable of permeating them all without becoming subject to any one of them.

Aylward Shorter, in *Toward a Theology of Inculturation,* describes inculturation as "an on-going dialogue between faith and culture or cultures. More fully, it is the creative and dynamic relationship between the Christian message and a culture or cultures."[47] I concur with Shorter's operative definition and assert that Christianity is enriched by a particular culture. Inculturation also entails an ongoing process of *reciprocal* and *critical* interaction and assimilation between them. Note the two words emphasized. Both parties in dialogue are open to learn and to change through the process of dialogue.

According to cultural anthropologist Father Gerald A. Arbuckle, inculturation does not have the same meaning as cultural adaptation. Arbuckle argues that the term "cultural adaptation" is a pejorative phrase closely associated with a dated theology and the missionary experiences of a Eurocentric church.[48] Adaptation meant the uncritical submission of cultures to the dominant Eurocentric way of thinking and praying, with the admission that these cultures might have some customs that could be useful in liturgy or in explaining theology. It connotes a one-way manipulation of cultures, not an openness to receive on the part of both parties in dialogue.

The process of inculturation is radically different from adaptation—paternalistic manipulation. The living faith community is the primary agent of inculturation, not the evangelizer. Gerald A. Arbuckle maintains that it is not the theological or liturgical elite alone who "somehow create inculturation in their ecclesiastical laboratories or libraries and then communicate it to the people. Remote elitists do not touch the hearts of the people being evangelized and evangelizing."[49] John Paul II was sensitive to this. Inculturation, he wrote, "presupposes a long and courageous process

---

[47]Aylward Shorter, *Toward a Theology of Inculturation* (Maryknoll, NY: Orbis Books, 1988), 11.

[48]Gerald A. Arbuckle, SM, "Inculturation and Evangelization: Realism or Romanticism?" in *Anthropologists, Missionaries and Cultural Change* (Williamsburg, VA: Studies in Third World Societies, 1985), 25.

[49]Ibid.

. . . in order that the Gospel may penetrate the soul of living cultures."[50]

When a particular culture embodies the Christian message, it carries the gospel joyfully to the people. The message of Jesus becomes personal—it means something of great importance to their cultural condition. Those who have encountered God's gift of grace generally become active in continuing the mission of Jesus. Within the African American experience, once something is deemed "good news," it does not remain a secret; it must be told. African American Catholics seek not only to be evangelized but to evangelize. They have their faith story to tell and their cultural gifts to share with the universal Church. Sister Thea Bowman, FSPA, an African American Catholic teacher and evangelist, issued a manifesto to the Roman Catholic bishops of the United States, "naming and claiming" her right as a baptized Christian to evangelize the Church. Thea Bowman uttered her prophetic comments to those who would exercise defining power over her Black brothers and sisters. Using the Black preaching style at its best, the "speech" Sister Thea gave to the bishops was *a call to conversion*—which is the first step toward *justice*. Sister Thea said:

> I bring myself, my Black self, all that I am, all that I have, all that I hope to become. I bring my whole history, my traditions, my experience, my culture, my African American song and dance and gesture and movement and teaching and preaching and healing and responsibility as gift to the Church.[51]

## Inculturation and Evangelization

Telling the Gospel of Jesus Christ from the perspective of a particular culture is known as *inculturated evangelization*. In the context of the African American community, evangelization will be increasingly effective as the agents of evangelization engage with the processes of inculturation. Those engaged in preaching, mission, and ministry within the African American community must discover the "soul" of that community. They must discover African American culture at both its practical and symbolic levels. I maintain that merely having good intentions is not enough for ministry within the African American community. Those willing to preach

---

[50]John Paul II, *The Church Is a Creator of Culture* (Melbourne: Australian Catholic Theological Society, 1983), 6.

[51]Thea Bowman, FSPA, in *Sister Thea Bowman, Shooting Star: Selected Writings and Speeches,* ed. Celestine Cepress, FSPA (Winona, MN: St. Mary's Press, 1993), 32.

and serve in this community must examine their conscience and make attitude adjustments.

Sidney Mintz and Richard Price contend that there are three major attitudes that hinder inculturated evangelization of African Americans to the Catholic faith:

> The first attitude is the belief that African Americans either have no distinct language, and therefore no distinct culture, and thus should adopt the culture of the particular dominant group within the local church or parish. Second, that the culture of the African American is so different and bereft of positive value that one cannot appropriate it within a Catholic Christian milieu. Third, that African American culture is simply a variation of a generalized American culture that can be addressed by adapting material symbols characteristic of current efforts of African Americans to rediscover their cultural and religious roots in Africa.[52]

None of these attitudes is correct or helpful in the process of inculturation within the African American Catholic community because each represents a false notion about African American culture. African American culture is a distinct, dynamic culture, born of the commingling of the diverse cultures of slaves and free persons of African descent, as well as immigrant and native cultures within the historical context of the United States. Those ministering among African Americans must realize that this race is not monolithic. Although there is much commonality within this culture, there is also diversity. Therefore, non–African Americans seeking to preach, minister, or evangelize can never be an "expert" on this race. Each day they minister amid new revelations of the African American culture. Even as ministers or preachers, they are nonetheless still students of this particular culture.

### From Parish-Centered to Metro-Centered Evangelization

Pastoral strategy in the Black community has primarily found its focus in pastoral ministry within the parish context. The parish church is seen primarily as a community of believers. Though many are attracted to the Church by the Catholic religious and lay persons engaged in works of

---

[52]Sidney Mintz and Richard Price, *The Birth of African American Culture: An Anthropological Perspective* (Boston: Beacon Press, 1976), 67.

charity, education, health service, and justice, they first encounter the faith family as a community assembled for worship. The worshiping community that expresses the heart's longing and relieves the heart's burden is a key aspect of evangelization within the Black community. The national plan for evangelization says:

> The parish is the most fitting location for carrying out these goals because the parish is where most Catholics experience the Church. It has on the local level, the same commitments as the universal Church, with the celebration of God's word and Eucharist as its center of worship. Evangelization inevitably involves the parish community for, ultimately, we are inviting people to our Eucharist, to the table of the Lord.[53]

This emphasis on the parish represents a shift in the primary locus for the evangelizing ministry of the Church. Most of the converts in the last half of the twentieth century have come through Catholic education. Today, however, students in Catholic schools with predominantly Black populations are overwhelmingly non-Catholic. Catholic schools in the Black community that served the Black Catholic faithful and those unchurched or Protestant Christians interested in a Catholic education have become alternative private schools. Parents enroll their children in these schools not for evangelization but as a viable alternative to public education. Those staffing Catholic schools in the Black community usually see their educational institution solely as a ministry of service to the Black community, not as an institutional medium for evangelization. In many schools there is little evidence of a Catholic presence, much less an attempt to evangelize. In a few isolated cases, students have inquired about the Catholic faith as a result of hearing a dynamic Black priest preach at the weekly school liturgy or at a school retreat. Such attitudes signal a contemporary crisis, since in the past Catholic schools were the most effective medium for evangelization throughout the African Diaspora. Precious Blood Father Clarence Williams, lecturer on African American Catholic evangelization, says:

> Many Blacks did convert, due to the priests' and nuns' evangelization programs and the baptism of Black children who attended Catholic

---

[53]*Here I Am, Send Me: A Conference Response to the Evangelization of African Americans and The National Black Catholic Pastoral Plan* (Washington, DC: National Conference of Catholic Bishops, 1990), 12.

schools. In 1940 Church statistics showed 300,000 Black Catholics. By 1970, due to conversions, there were a reported 800,000 Black Catholics in a period of three decades. In 1981 2 percent of the American Catholic population is Black; and Black Catholics make up approximately 5 percent of the Black population in the country.[54]

Today there are more than forty million Americans of African ancestry. By an imperfect count, two million of these are members of the Catholic Church.[55] Most of these Catholic Christians were educated in Catholic schools. There has been no significant growth in recent years. Some would say that there is an ever-growing exodus of African Americans from the Catholic faith. The number of African American priests, sisters, and brothers is declining as well. There are five active Black bishops out of over three hundred bishops serving the United States.[56]

Although the statistics are dismal, they reflect a crucial reality: the need for Catholic evangelization among African Americans. Millions of Black Americans over thirty-five years of age are members of other Christian traditions, particularly the Baptist and African Methodist Episcopal Churches. Nearly half of the total African American population, or almost twenty million, are under thirty years of age.[57] Many of those under thirty, especially those who live in large cities, are not members of any faith tradition. There is a great number of African Americans that the Church has an opportunity to evangelize.

My focus on the parish as the center for pastoral evangelization is reinforced by the changed environment of the Catholic Church in the African American community. There must be a reexamination of who the people are who make up the African American Catholic parish. Many of the programs in which African American parishes are involved still work from an implicit model of the neighborhood parish when in reality Black Catholic parishes are more and more metro parishes. Many, and in some cases most, parishioners are not coming from the immediate neighborhood but from throughout the metropolitan area, including the suburbs. As African American Catholics have progressed economically, they, like their European American counterparts, have moved away from their parish neighborhoods. Unlike whites, however, they return each Sunday

---

[54]Clarence Williams, CPpS, *The Black Man and the Catholic Church* (Detroit: Academy of the Afro-World Community, 1981), 20.

[55]Ibid.

[56]Edward K. Braxton, "The View from the Barbershop: The Church and African American Culture," *America* 178, no. 4 (1998): 18.

[57]Ibid.

to their parish. Parish territorial boundaries established by the diocese mean little to African American Catholics who base their membership on relationships and spiritual nourishment, rather than boundaries. "Metro parishes" are the norm across the nation among African American Catholics. Many of the larger predominantly African American parishes have high percentages of parishioners who do not live within the parish boundary. St. Charles Borromeo Church in Harlem, New York; St. Sabina Church and St. Katharine Drexel Church in Chicago; St. Augustine Church and St. Teresa of Avila Church in Washington, DC; St. Martin de Porres Church and St. Cyprian Church in Philadelphia; St. Peter Claver Church, St. Joseph the Worker Church, St. Raymond, and St. Leo Church in New Orleans; Our Lady of Lourdes Church in Atlanta; St. Brigid Church in Los Angeles; St. Columba Church in Oakland; and St. Alphonsus "Rock" Church in St. Louis—all are large African American Catholic parishes well known for their far-reaching ministries and metropolitan attraction.

Like many Black Protestant churches, Catholic parochial membership is far-flung and socially diverse. Unlike Black Protestant churches, many Spirit-filled African American Catholic parishes are drawing large numbers of European Americans to their worship. This would seem to be a strange phenomenon given that only since the Civil Rights Movement of the 1960s were African American Catholics welcomed at white parishes. Still, the welcome was not always a warm welcome. There are many reasons why European American Catholics feel welcome at African American parishes. First, African Americans are a forgiving and innately spiritual people. Their spirit is one of seeking unity and oneness with God and with God's creation. For African Americans Sunday morning Mass or worship is not done out of obligation, but rather out of a desire to worship God and to gather as a community of believers. Mass or worship provides needed support as the members struggle to walk their Christian journey. Second, there is a sense of spiritual freedom that I do not believe exists in many predominantly white parishes. Within the context of a Black worship experience or an African American Catholic parish, there is a deliberate "calling down of the Holy Spirit." Through worship, song, praise, ritual, preaching, and celebration of the Eucharist, African Americans invite the presence of the Holy Spirit into the liturgical event. That event is a "happening" that says, "Holy Spirit welcome to this place!" Where the Spirit of the Lord dwells, there is liberty—there is freedom of emotion and expression. Many whites attest to feeling peace and joy as a result of their Black worship experience. Finally, non–African Americans are drawn to African American Catholic parishes because they are places of celebration. The African American Catholic parish is a place where the congregation, as a general rule, fully participates in worship. The congregants enjoy the moving singing and the Spirit-filled preaching. Worshipers feel invited to sing along with the swaying and hand-clapping gospel choir. The Black preaching style draws them into the telling of the story and empowers them to go forth and tell the story to others.

### Black Preaching and Inculturated Evangelization

*In Spirit and Truth: Black Catholic Reflections on the Order of Mass,* by the United States Bishops' Committee on Liturgy, cites the "deepening of one's faith" as an essential element of good preaching in African American worship. It states:

> The homily is preached to an assembly of believers. Its primary purpose is to deepen and enrich the meaning of the sacred texts and to allow the assembly to celebrate more faithfully the liturgy and give Christian witness to the world. The purpose of the homily is not to offer such elementary catechesis so as to move the assembly from initial unbelief to belief. Rather, the homily is an application of the Scripture readings and the meaning of the solemnity or feast to everyday Christian living and continued conversion.[58]

This conversion inspired by proclamation is not solely personal. On a communal level, the proclamation of the gospel calls the community to be transformed and to go out and spread the Good News in word and deed. Effective preaching calls the community to the work and witness of evangelization. In the Black community an idiomatic reference to the spread of the gospel is, "Just can't keep it to myself; I got to tell someone else!"

In spreading the good news of the gospel, the Black congregation proclaims it as it receives it: just as they are. Black preaching conveys the gospel in a Black context, meaning that it is relevant to that Black situation and religious experience, and thus the hearers witness to the gospel through their Black cultural heritage. Father Giles Conwill, preacher and cultural anthropologist, observes that the gospel and the faith that accompanies it have always been proclaimed and experienced in cultural trappings. Conwill holds, "They do not exist as an abstract core in and of

---

[58]Bishops' Committee on the Liturgy, National Conference of Catholic Bishops, Wilton D. Gregory, ed., *In Spirit and Truth: Black Catholic Reflections on the Order of Mass* (Washington, DC: United States Catholic Conference, 1988), 15.

themselves. Authentic and mature evangelization will be promoted only when this equation is realized: Evangelization = Gospel + Inculturation + Indigenization."[59] He notes that this is the way that the Word will be effectively heard and thus produces the effect of spreading the Good News among African American Catholics.

The future for evangelization in the African American community will not come from new programs or new strategies. African Americans will not seek to enter the Catholic Church by way of clearly defined and implemented Rite of Christian Initiation for Adults (R.C.I.A.) sessions. I maintain that African Americans will be drawn to Catholicism through the preaching of God's Word in a manner that speaks to their spiritual and cultural condition. Outreach programs, food pantries, social events, and bingo are not what evangelizes. The powerful preaching of the gospel is what calls people to conversion and ultimately to Christ and the Church. While such an objective seems so achievable, it simply is not happening in many of our Catholic parishes. The Word is not being preached in a prophetic manner with the purpose of evangelization. One wonders if Catholic clergy thoroughly understand their mission, ministry, and identity as preachers.

In many other Christian traditions, when the preacher has finished preaching there is an invitation or call to discipleship offered to the congregation. This invitation is an opportunity for those who have heard the Word of God to respond to it. If preaching is intrinsically for evangelization—bringing souls to Christ—then this invitation is vital. The opportunity to "come to Christ" or to join a particular congregation is also referred to in Protestant worship services as the period of "opening the doors" of the church. Usually after preaching a powerful message, the preacher ends his or her sermon simply with the words, "The doors of the church are opened."

Realizing that there are no opportunities in our Roman Catholic liturgy to come to Christ in a visible way, I believe that Catholic ministers, clergy, religious, and the laity must explore ways of welcoming souls to Christ and to the Catholic faith. African Americans appreciate the urgency of responding to the Word of God. They also appreciate the invitation to respond in the presence of a supportive Christian community. They are aware that one is not invited to walk the Christian journey alone. "Opening the doors of the church" involves making a public confession of Jesus Christ as one's Lord and Savior. There is a time of prayer for

---

[59]Giles A. Conwill, "The Word Becomes Black Flesh: A Program for Reaching the American Black," in *Evangelizing Blacks,* ed. Glenn C. Smith (Wheaton, IL: Tyndale House, 1988), 45.

the individual. The congregation stands and applauds the individual for making this important step in his or her life. The person choosing Christ and that particular church is given a "prayer warrior," who has the responsibility of praying for the individual and walking with him or her during a period of instruction.

One can readily see parallels between the Roman Catholic Rite of Christian Initiation of Adults (RCIA) and the process of "opening the doors of the church." However, the RCIA process does not begin necessarily as a response to the Word of God immediately after the homily at Mass. Usually one joins the RCIA process at the invitation of a Catholic friend or spouse, or due to the work and the presence of the Catholic Church in a particular neighborhood, or as a response to an announcement in the parish bulletin. Many African Americans join the Roman Catholic Church for those stated reasons as well. However, a growing majority of African Americans are evangelized by Spirit-filled liturgies and preaching. I submit that an opportunity to respond to the Word of God should be a prominent if not requisite component of the Mass, especially in predominantly African American parishes.[60] This is clearly a valid time of inculturation in the liturgy. It is a proven means of inculturated evangelization. Roman Catholicism must be open to learn from other Christian traditions if it is to welcome African Americans into the life of the Church. However, I contend that if preachers in African American Catholic parishes were confident and personally convicted by their own preaching, they would be comfortable in offering an invitation to discipleship. That invitation validates the sermon or homily and in essence defines the purpose of preaching.

### Mission, Ministry, and Identity of the Preacher

It is not superfluous to emphasize the importance and necessity of preaching. "And how are they to believe in him whom they have heard? And how are they to hear without a preacher? . . . So, faith comes from what is heard and what is heard comes by the preaching of Christ" (Romans 10:14,17). This law once laid down by the Apostle Paul maintains its full force today.

---

[60]I have found in my preaching ministry this suggestion of "opening the doors of the church" to be an effective means of evangelization. African Americans welcome opportunities to make a visible commitment to God's Word, to Jesus Christ, and the faith community they are joining. At St. Alphonsus Liguori "Rock" Church in St. Louis, Missouri, I have witnessed over one hundred people join the parish and the Catholic Church as a direct result of this invitation immediately after the homily during liturgy.

Pope Paul VI was clear about the evangelistic nature of Catholic preaching. Paul VI wrote:

> Preaching, the verbal proclamation of a message, is indeed always indispensable. We are well aware that modern man [and woman are] sated by talk; he [and she] are obviously often tired of listening and, what is worse, impervious to words. We are also aware that many psychologists and sociologists express the view that modern man [and woman] has passed beyond the civilization of the word, which is now ineffective and useless, and that today [they live] in the civilization of the image. These facts should certainly impel us to employ, for the purpose of transmitting the Gospel message, the modern means which this civilization has produced. Very positive efforts have in fact already been made in this sphere. We cannot but praise them and encourage their further development. The fatigue produced these days by so much empty talk and the relevance of many other forms of communication must not, however, diminish the permanent power of the word or cause a loss of confidence in it. The word remains ever relevant, especially when it is the bearer of the power of God. This is why Saint Paul's axiom, "Faith comes from what is heard" [cf. 1 Cor 2:1–5] also retains its relevance: it is the Word that is heard which leads to belief.[61]

The voice of the preacher becomes the voice of the Eternal. The audacious assignment is to speak for God and about God to the people of God. The preacher is one called out as proclaimer. The preacher is like student to teacher. The teacher instructs the student to "stand up and repeat after me." When the preacher stands up to preach, Jesus says, "Repeat after me."

At preaching time, the personal significance of the preacher fades into the background in light of the divine message. Preachers assure others of their destiny, even as they realize they are not masters of their own destiny. They preach with authority but are under orders from a greater authority. They give the Word but are just the servants of that Word. Their title of honor is often ridiculed by some hearers, as well as by outside detractors. But the whole counsel of God, revealed in the proclamation, gives the masses the strength to endure, the courage to struggle against dehumanizing forces, and the power to transcend the human-caused trials and tribulations in countless otherwise hopeless situations.

---

[61] *Evangelii Nuntiandi*, no. 42.

In African American worship there is much inspiration. The preaching is oratorical and replete with artistic beauty. But the intrinsic efficacy in Black preaching of the whole counsel of God is the revelation that comes on the wings of the inspiration and celebration. The calling is to reveal God's plan of redemption. The mission of the preacher is to be the bearer of the gospel—the Good News of redemption. According to Olin P. Moyd, theologian and pastor, "In the African American theological preaching tradition, there is the message of reproach (chastisement for wrongdoing) and threat (the pronouncement of judgment). But the preaching always included a message of exhortation and promise—guidance and hope."[62] So the idea of "How beautiful upon the mountains are the feet of the one bringing good news, announcing peace, bearing good news, announcing salvation, saying to Zion, 'Your God is King!' " (cf. Isaiah 52:7) is of utmost importance. The beauty here, as understood by the preacher and congregation in an African American setting, has nothing to do with the physical feet of the messenger, but rather it is an expression of gladness in the coming of the one who preaches good news.

Clergy preaching in African American Catholic settings are not only ambassadors for God on a general mission in the world. They are also ambassadors to a particular people with a particular message of redemption that transcends the meaning of redemption in the larger Christian community. The message is anchored in practical theology. The message is a reflection on the gospel in the light of faith becoming action in the cause of social justice. The preacher is a special person with a special calling, with a special message of hope to a special people from the underside of life in America. Black preaching never turns away from the social ills of the Black community. Black preaching confronts and condemns the injustices that plague the world, as well as the local Black community. The preached Word is a word of hope in the midst of despair and oppression.

In the final analysis, African Americans want to hear about Jesus Christ. Effective Catholic evangelists and preachers must not only have a deep, personal relationship with Jesus Christ, they must be comfortable bearing witness to that relationship. The Catholic community is blessed with the sublime gift of the sacramental presence of Christ in the Eucharist and this can be at the heart of catechesis. However, care must be taken not to use forms of sacramental language that seem to distance the faithful from the encounter with Christ. There is a perception at large that suggests that while other Christian traditions know the Lord "for themselves,"

---

[62]Olin P. Moyd, *The Sacred Art: Preaching and Theology in the African American Tradition* (Valley Forge, PA: Judson Press, 1995), 57.

Catholics have a highly abstract and theoretical sense of Christ's presence in the sacraments, but not in their lives. African American people, who are often regular scripture readers, want to know how they can grow closer to Jesus Christ and experience the mystery of his life, death, and resurrection.

I contend that the Church must hand on its tradition. Although efforts to assist prospective members to the Church in the appropriation of African American consciousness are of great value, assisting them in experiencing and learning the breadth and depth of the Catholic tradition in all its richness must not be neglected. More harm than good is done by inviting people to participate in the Rite of Christian Initiation of Adults and baptizing them at the Easter Vigil if these candidates for Baptism or full communion really do not understand the basic teachings and practices of the Church. If no one has explained to them the ways in which the Catholic tradition differs from what they previously knew to be the meaning of salvation, the structure of the Church, and other questions, they may well drift away when they learn of these differences if they are confused by them. In handing on the tradition, attention must be paid to what the Second Vatican Council called the "hierarchy of truths." Potential new Catholics can be easily bewildered if a catechist seems to suggest that popular devotions and sacramentals are more important than scripture and the sacraments. Handing on the tradition must be vital and dynamic. Handing on the tradition should never be confused with traditionalism.

Lastly, effective preachers and evangelists need to become familiar with African American Catholic resources. It is not enough for individual ministers, parishes, or communities to know where outstanding resources for African American evangelization can be found. There is a pressing need for an ongoing national networking so that from Los Angeles to New York, from New Orleans to Memphis, from St. Louis to Seattle, there can be a beneficial sharing of effective evangelization resources. The Secretariat for Cultural Diversity in the Church, the National Black Catholic Congress, the Institute for Black Catholic Studies at Xavier University in New Orleans, the Sankofa Institute for African American Pastoral Leadership at Oblate School of Theology in San Antonio, and individual parishes are already making valuable contributions to this goal. Yet more must be done.

## The Catholic Church: Acknowledging a Racist Past and Forging a Hopeful Future

Before concluding this chapter regarding inculturated evangelization, I must be explicit about the shortage and decline of African American

Catholics. History records that little effort was given to the work of evangelization by the Catholic Church among Blacks. However, immediately after the Civil War some bishops continued to work for the evangelization and ministry of the Blacks in their dioceses. A bishop like Martin J. Spalding, archbishop of Baltimore (1864–1872), went even further. While in Rome in 1867, Spalding sought help from the Congregation of the Propaganda of the Faith in obtaining from Pope Pius IX a mandate that certain religious orders—notably the Jesuits, Dominicans, Redemptorists, and Vincentians—cooperate with the bishops in evangelizing African Americans in the United States.[63] The Congregation accepted the idea that the pope should send a letter to the American bishops on this matter. It seems, however, that such a letter was never sent, nor was any pressure brought to bear on the religious orders.[64]

Nevertheless, Archbishop Spalding called a provincial council of his suffragan bishops in 1868. This was the Tenth Provincial Council of Baltimore, which met the last week of April 1869. In keeping with his deep concern for Blacks, Spalding included the question of the African American apostolate in the topics for discussion. One of the recommendations made was the establishment of separate churches for Blacks. Moreover, it was urged that missions be held for the Black Catholic people, that special instructions be organized for them, and that separate parish organizations and confraternities be organized. Finally, there was the suggestion that richer dioceses should take up special collections to further the African American apostolate in the poorer dioceses of the province.[65] This special collection was the precursor to the current annual national Catholic collection for Blacks and Native Americans. Although the recommendations made by Spalding and the other bishops were commendable and were eventually implemented, they were still separatist and did not meet the unique cultural and spiritual needs of African Americans.

A century after Spalding's Tenth Provincial Council in Baltimore discussing the pastoral needs of African American Catholics, another important meeting occurred. This time the meeting was not of the hierarchy but of self-determined and articulate Black Catholic priests and religious Brothers. Motivated by the Civil Rights Movement and the recent assassination of the Rev. Dr. Martin Luther King Jr., Black priests and religious men formed the National Black Catholic Clergy Caucus (NBCCC) on

---

[63]Cyprian Davis, OSB, *The History of Black Catholics in the United States* (New York: Crossroad, 1990), 122.

[64]Ibid.

[65]Ibid.

April 18, 1968. They organized themselves out of an urgent concern for the racism of the Catholic Church as well as for a call for greater leadership and responsibilities for Black priests and religious within the Church. Most important for this study is the demand made by the NBCCC that white priests learn how to minister to the Black Catholic community from Black priests, religious, and laity.

In a published statement, the National Black Catholic Clergy Caucus accused the Catholic Church in the United States as being primarily "a white racist institution that has addressed itself primarily to white society and is definitely a part of that society."[66] They also stated that the Church cannot effectively lead the Black Catholic community if it is not willing to listen and learn from its African American children. The National Black Catholic Clergy Caucus asserted: "Within the ghetto, the role of the Church is no longer that of spokesman and leader. Apart from a more direct spiritual role, the Church's part must now be that of supporter and learner. This is a role that white priests in the Black community have not been accustomed to playing and are not psychologically prepared to play."[67] And in their nine-point list of demands to the Catholic Church was a demand for "dioceses to provide centers of training for white priests intending to serve and survive in Black communities."[68]

The acknowledgment of a history of blatant racism and the abuse that many African Americans have endured as members of the Roman Catholic Church causes one to wonder why they remained faithful to the Church. Additionally, it is equally puzzling that African Americans continue to join the Catholic faith. Fortunately, the Second Vatican Council challenged Catholics to read the signs of the times and apply the gospel of Christ directly to their historical situations. This is precisely what the bishops of the United States did on November 14, 1979, when they published *Brothers and Sisters to Us: A Pastoral Letter on Racism in Our Day*.

The first words of the letter are:

Racism is an evil which endures in our society and in our Church. Despite apparent advances and even significant changes in the last two decades, the reality of racism remains. In large part it is only the external appearances which have changed. How great is that sin of racism which weakens the Church's witness as the universal sign

---

[66]National Black Catholic Clergy Caucus, "A Statement of the Black Catholic Clergy Caucus," *Black Theology: A Documentary History, 1966–1979*, ed. James H. Cone and Gayraud S. Wilmore (Maryknoll, NY: Orbis Books, 1979), 322.

[67]Ibid.

[68]Ibid., 324.

of unity among all peoples. How great the scandal given by racist Catholics who would make the Body of Christ, the Church, a sign of racial oppression! Yet all too often the Church in our country has been for many a "white Church," a racist institution.[69]

First, pastoral evangelists in the African American Catholic community, Black or white, must be aware of the Catholic Church's role in slavery and its present support, consciously and unconsciously, of racism. Racism in the Catholic Church has been and continues to be the greatest obstacle to African American evangelization in the United States and throughout the world. A pastoral evangelist must be prepared to answer the questions posed by the African American community about the Church's stance.

In 1992 Pope John Paul II acknowledged this necessity when he spoke at Goree Island, from the place where one hundred thousand captured Africans were sent to slave plantations in the New World. He spoke candidly and apologetically to people of African descent about the role the Catholic Church played in the greatest atrocity in Western civilization, the economic exploitation of Africa's chattel slaves.

> Goree, which symbolizes the coming of the gospel of freedom, also, alas, symbolizes the shocking transgression of people who reduced other people to slavery, their brothers and sisters for whom this Gospel of freedom is intended. . . . This island, it could be said, remains engraved in the memory and on the hearts of the entire Black diaspora.[70]

Racism flows from personal attitudes and actions into the human world around us; it becomes a social evil. Our social institutions and structures are affected. Racism affects families and schools, public institutions and governmental programs, large corporations and small businesses, and our own church communities. I contend that all Christian believers and all responsible members of our society are obligated to do our part to eradicate racism from this society—from the whole and from each of its component parts.

The former bishop of the Diocese of Columbus, Ohio, Bishop James Griffin in a pastoral letter on racism released on May 4, 1997, called for zero tolerance of racist comments or activity within his diocese. He called

---

[69]*Brothers and Sisters to Us: A Pastoral Letter on Racism in Our Day* (Washington, DC: United States Catholic Conference, 1979), 8.

[70]Catholic International, "Goree Island—Twin Symbol: Excerpts from Pope John Paul II's Address on Goree Island," *Catholic International*, February 1992, 357.

on his diocese to rid itself of fear and ignorance and to embrace all God's children. Bishop Griffin wrote:

> As a church, we must examine and confront the subtle forms of racism of which we are guilty. The Catholic Church in the United States is an overwhelmingly white church. As the Bishops' Committee on Black Catholics stated, "History reveals that racism has played a powerful role in discouraging African Americans from the Catholic Church as a spiritual home." It is therefore vitally important that predominantly white parishes learn to worship and live as open invitations to all races. We need to change our hospitality habits in order to become a true gathering of believers. We must face the challenge of liberating ourselves from the bonds of racism. Racism, as sin, harms not only the victim but the sinner too. We are held bound by our prejudices and our fears of letting go of control and power. Perhaps racism does not register as a "sin" in "my parish"—but it can be present. We must name and confess our prejudices in order to be freed from them. How does your parish welcome the stranger and celebrate diversity?[71]

African American suspicion and disdain of Catholicism is understandable, and it is continually fueled by the reality of Catholic expressions of racism. In 1989, when Yusef K. Hawkins, a Black sixteen-year-old, was murdered in Bensonhurst, an Italian neighborhood in Brooklyn, New York, the racism of the Catholic Church was implicated. One guest editorial in the *National Catholic Reporter,* reprinted from the *Amsterdam News* (the Black newspaper of Harlem, New York), read:

> It can be said of these New York Italians that they are Catholic Christians—by birth, by culture, by allegiance. . . . This country's bishops in the 19th century never condemned slavery. The Catholic Church was sinfully slow to desegregate and late and reluctant to push for desegregation in American society as a whole. This does not mean that all Catholics did nothing. There were outstanding examples of courageous priests, brothers, sisters, laity and bishops. However, our church did not practice what it preached where racial equality was concerned. To hear many of today's Hispanic and African American Catholics tell it, we still do not practice what we preach.[72]

---

[71]James Griffin, "Racism: A Tarnished Reflection of Ourselves," *Origins* 27, no. 2 (May 29, 1997): 19.
[72]*National Catholic Reporter,* September 23, 1989, 14.

A sad history of blatant racism is unquestionably a major obstacle in the evangelization efforts of drawing African Americans to the Catholic faith. Can African Americans trust Catholicism to defend, welcome, and protect them? Can the Catholic Church truly be a spiritual home for them and offer a hope of salvation? "Unless the Catholic Church can witness to racial reconciliation and reparation, it is not a sign of good news, but a bulwark of institutional racism and a menacing sign of terror to many in this nation."[73] Sister Jamie Phelps, OP, adds, "Tragically, despite [the US bishops' condemnation of racism], institutional racism—like slavery—is still generally condoned by silence and neutrality in the public, political, and ecclesial arenas of contemporary life."[74]

The topics of discussion in this chapter have included evangelization; a Catholic approach to evangelization; inculturation; inculturated evangelization; the mission, ministry, and identity of the preacher; and racism as a hindrance to effective evangelization. These subjects can never be exhausted. Effective preaching calls the congregation to witness to the power of the proclaimed Word in their lives and to spread the Good News to others. Preaching in the African American style, in effect, aims at provoking the members of the congregation into a continual conversion to God and the Gospel. Moreover, this personal conversion must lead African Americans to the work of witnessing and evangelizing to the goodness of Jesus Christ.

I have offered evidence that the Black preaching style is highly developed and structured to achieve the aims of evangelization. Beyond the style, however, is the substance. In that regard, this chapter also highlighted procedural and substantive elements of the Black Church that are initial components of the evangelization mechanism. The most significant of the tools—the call to discipleship—is an underutilized mechanism in the Catholic Church. Its proven effectiveness in the Protestant Church and its place as an outreach tool to Black preachers and those who use this style make it another of the critical contributions that can derive from the utilization of the Black preaching style.

---

[73]Ibid.

[74]Jamie T. Phelps, OP, "Caught between Thunder and Lightning: A Historical and Theological Critique of the Episcopal Response to Slavery," in *Many Rains Ago: A Historical and Theological Reflection on the Role of the Episcopate in the Evangelization of African American Catholics* (Washington, DC: United States Catholic Conference, 1990), 30.

# 5

# Whom Shall I Send?

*Then I heard the voice of the Lord saying, "Whom shall I send?*
*Who will go for us?" "Here I am," I said; "send me!"*
—Isaiah 6:8

## Who *Can* and Who *Should* Preach? Seeking a Way Forward

By the sacramental and sanctifying grace received through the waters and anointing of baptism, as duly initiated disciples and members of the Body of Christ, Catholic Christians along with other baptized Christians should see it as their calling to proclaim the "good news" to all whom they encounter. Baptism enables Christians to witness to Jesus and to the kingdom of God. And to witness means to announce, to proclaim, to testify, to make known, to preach.

In recent history there has been much debate about the nature of preaching and who is specifically qualified to proclaim the "good news," what is the context of the proclamation, and when and where does it happen. Before taking a deep dive into these perennial ponderings, I suggest that the effects of Christian baptism in relation to gospel proclamation be explored. Patricia A. Parachini, in her book *Lay Preaching: State of the Question*, states:

Proclaiming the gospel (preaching) is effected in many ways throughout our lives as Christian believers, especially in words and works of reconciliation, healing, and justice. We preach through the witness of our life, through teaching, through ordinary conversation and personal testimony to God's love, as well as through a more formal proclamation in worship. Preaching is the call of all the baptized.[1]

---

[1] Patricia A. Parachini, *Lay Preaching: State of the Question* (Collegeville, MN: Liturgical Press, 1999), 5.

To clarify terms within the Roman Catholic tradition, I define "lay preaching" as various forms of preaching by baptized Christians who are not ordained deacons, priests, or bishops. The term "lay preaching" is also designated for women and men in religious congregations. Although religious women and men are not in either sense "cleric" or "lay," it is the way that they are referred to in the canons germane to lay preaching of the 1983 Revised Code of Canon Law. In order to shed light on certain delimitations and capacities of lay preaching within the context of the Eucharistic liturgy, it is important to know the canons regarding those persons who can preach, are granted faculties to preach, and permissions needed to preach:

- Canon 764 states, "With due regard for the prescriptions of can. 765, presbyters [ordained priests] and deacons possess the faculty to preach everywhere, to be exercised with at least the presumed consent of the rector of the church, unless that faculty has been restricted or taken away by the competent ordinary or unless express permission is required by particular law."[2] "Bishops have a right to preach everywhere, including the churches and oratories of religious institutes of pontifical right, unless the bishop of the place has expressly denied it in particular cases. (Can. 763; see also cans. 762, 768–772)."[3]

- Canon 767 states, "Among the forms of preaching the homily is preeminent; it is a part of the liturgy itself and is reserved to a priest or to a deacon; in the homily the mysteries of faith and the norms of Christian living are to be expounded from the sacred text throughout the course of the liturgical year."[4]

- "There must be a homily when people are gathered at Masses on Sunday and holy days and should not be omitted except for a serious reason. If people are gathered for weekday liturgies, a homily is highly encouraged, most especially during the seasons of Advent, Lent, and special feast days."[5]

- "The pastor or rector of the church is responsible for implementing the norms for preaching homilies and to see that they are zealously observed. (Can. 767)."[6]

---

[2] *Code of Canon Law: Latin-English Edition* (Washington, DC: Canon Law Society of America, 1983), Canon 764.

[3] John M. Huels, *The Pastoral Companion: A Canon Law Handbook for Catholic Ministry* (Chicago: Franciscan Herald Press, 1986), 77.

[4] Canon 767.

[5] Huels, *Pastoral Companion*, 78.

[6] Ibid.

## A Canonical Rationale for Lay Preaching

There is one canon in the Revised Code of Canon Law that addresses the circumstances whereby a lay person may be permitted to preach in a church or oratory. Canon 766 states, "Lay persons can be permitted to preach in a church or oratory if it is necessary in certain circumstances or if it is useful in particular cases according to the prescriptions of the conference of bishops and with due regard to can. 767.1."[7] Besides Canon 766, some have made a broad interpretation for lay preaching found in Canon 759 under the heading of "The Ministry of the Divine Word." Canon 759 states, "In virtue of their baptism and confirmation lay members of the Christian faithful are witnesses to the gospel message by word and by example of a Christian life; they can also be called upon to cooperate with the bishop and presbyters in the exercise of the ministry of the word."[8]

Although there will be some reluctance to view an interpretation of Canon 759 as supporting lay preaching to be a "far stretch," and some people are more comfortable with viewing it as an invitation solely to proclaiming the word at liturgies, I find fluidity in considering Canon 759. There are documents of the Second Vatican Council and beyond that both value and support the laity in being responsible for spreading the gospel of Jesus Christ (e.g., *Apostolicum Actuositatem* 6; *Evangelii Nuntiandi* 70; *Evangelii Gaudium* 14).

In the United States there is an ever-growing interest in liturgical preaching among many lay women and men who are not ordained to the diaconate, priesthood, or episcopacy. Likewise, there have also been occasions where circumstances have deemed lay preaching useful in liturgical settings. Parachini highlights five increasingly common circumstances that have precipitated the benefit of lay preaching: (1) "a significant number of laity have had the opportunity for continuing education in Scripture, theology, liturgical studies, and spirituality"; (2) "more laity have been presiding in liturgical services in their local communities of worship"; (3) "laypersons have been invited to greater involvement in renewed ministries of evangelization and retreat work"; (4) "certain gatherings by their very nature seem to call for preaching by a member of the group itself (e.g., religious orders of women or men with no ordained members)"; (5) "in many instances where laypersons have been preaching, the call to lay

---

[7] Canon 766.
[8] Canon 759.

preaching has been encouraged and affirmed by their local communities of faith."[9] Certainly, the continual decline in vocations to the priesthood has necessitated the need for formed lay ecclesial ministers to offer communion services in the absence of a cleric where the lay ministers offer a reflection on the scripture text. There are several dioceses in the United States that must depend on lay ecclesial ministers for parochial administration and in many cases to offer communion services in the absence of a priest. In some dioceses it is commonplace to have a lay ecclesial minister to "run the parish" while perhaps one priest is the designated sacramental minister for several parishes.

Once I was asked to drive three hours to a small rural parish that has a permanent deacon who serves as the administrator of the parish, but the priest-sacramental minister had been sick for over a month and the community wanted the celebration of eucharistic liturgies. The community was customed to having their eucharistic liturgies celebrated in English, Spanish, and Vietnamese. I felt bad that I was fluent only in English and did not speak Spanish or Vietnamese. The deacon was from a Spanish-speaking country and was fluent in Spanish, so he preached at the two Masses in Spanish, and I celebrated the Mass in English. Naturally I preached at the one Mass in English, and for the Mass in Vietnamese, the music minister told me to celebrate the Mass in English and that the congregation would respond in Vietnamese and that he would simultaneously translate my homily in Vietnamese. The people were so grateful that a priest was present to celebrate their liturgies, and yet I felt disappointed that I was not equipped to celebrate using their God-language. Especially during the Vietnamese Mass, it would have been most useful to have a lay person preaching in the language of the people.

Although there are scriptural, historical, and theological arguments that can be made supporting lay preaching, it wasn't until 2001 that the United States Conference of Catholic Bishops (USCCB) affirming Canon 766 of the Code of Canon Law regarding lay preaching issued a complementary norm on this matter. Interestingly, this complementary norm was promulgated by the only African American bishop serving as president of the USCCB, then Bishop Wilton D. Gregory of the Diocese of Belleville. Not only would a Black bishop approve and sign this complementary norm allowing lay people to preach in churches and oratories under certain conditions but one with a doctorate in sacred liturgy—someone who has the knowledge and appreciation of liturgical norms. The following is the complementary norm issued by the USCCB:

---

[9]Parachini, *Lay Preaching*, 7.

On November 14, 2001, the Latin Church members of the United States Conference of Catholic Bishops approved complementary legislation for canon 766 of the Code of Canon Law for the dioceses of the Latin Church of the United States.

The action was granted *recognitio* by the Congregation for Bishops in accord with article 82 of the Apostolic Constitution *Pastor Bonus* and issued by decree of the Congregation for Bishops signed by His Eminence Cardinal Giovanni Battista Re, Prefect, and His Excellency Most Reverend Franciscus Monterisi, Secretary, and dated November 27, 2001.

**Complementary Norm:** Preaching the Word of God is among the principal duties of those who have received the sacrament of orders (c. 762–764). The lay faithful can be called to cooperate in the exercise of the Ministry of the Word (c. 759). In accord with canon 766 the National Conference of Catholic Bishops hereby decrees that the lay faithful may be permitted to exercise this ministry in churches and oratories, with due regard for the following provisions:

If necessity requires it in certain circumstances or it seems useful in particular cases, the diocesan bishop can admit lay faithful to preach, to offer spiritual conferences or give instructions in churches, oratories or other sacred places within his diocese, when he judges it to be to the spiritual advantage of the faithful.

In order to assist the diocesan bishop in making an appropriate pastoral decision (Interdicasterial Instruction, Ecclesiae de Mysterio, Article 2 §3), the following circumstances and cases are illustrative: the absence or shortage of clergy, particular language requirements, or the demonstrated expertise or experience of the lay faithful concerned.

The lay faithful who are to be admitted to preach in a church or oratory must be orthodox in faith, and well-qualified, both by the witness of their lives as Christians and by a preparation for preaching appropriate to the circumstances.

The diocesan bishop will determine the appropriate situations in accord with canon 772, §1. In providing for preaching by the lay faithful the diocesan bishop may never dispense from the norm which reserves the homily to the sacred ministers (c. 767, §1; cfr. Pontifical Commission for the Authentic Interpretation of the Code of Canon Law, 26 May 1987, in AAS 79 [1987], 1249). Preaching by the lay faithful may not take place within the Celebration of the Eucharist at the moment reserved for the homily.

As President of the United States Conference of Catholic Bishops, I hereby decree that the effective date of this decree for all the dioceses of the Latin Church in the United States will be January 15, 2002. Given at the offices of the United States Conference of Catholic Bishops in Washington, DC, on December 13, 2001.[10]

> Most Reverend Wilton D. Gregory
> Bishop of Belleville
> President, USCCB
>
> Reverend Monsignor William P. Fay
> General Secretary

In the complementary norms there are certain conditions that must be considered when a pastor is requesting permission for a lay person to preach. "The lay faithful who are to be admitted to preach in a church or oratory must be orthodox in faith, and well-qualified, both by the witness of their lives as Christians and by preparation for preaching appropriate to the circumstances." I do not believe that these conditions are unreasonable or overbearing. I firmly believe that lay preachers should be well qualified and have the necessary preparation to preach, just as ordained clerics should be. In actuality there are many lay people and religious women and men who have earned degrees and have been prepared for reflecting on the gospel. There just have not been sufficient opportunities for them to preach. This complementary norm would suggest that there would be certain "circumstances" in which it would be advantageous for a lay person to preach. In other words, it would not be the norm that lay persons would preach on any given Sunday.

This calls into question those certain circumstances that would call for lay preaching. Parish faith communities are unique and have different needs. However, I would like to suggest certain circumstances that having a qualified non-ordained preacher would greatly benefit a parish congregation. Presuming that the lay preacher is qualified, I would think that Catechetical Sunday would be a day that a director of religious education could offer a reflection; a father or mother could give reflections on parenthood in light of the scriptural texts on Father's or Mother's Day or the Feast of the Holy Family. Almost certainly a lay person would be best to preach at a children's Mass if a priest could not relate to a young audience (cf. Directory for Masses with Children). Perhaps a spirit-filled and talented orator could offer a reflection on Pentecost. In my estima-

---

[10]https://www.usccb.org/beliefs-and-teachings/what-we-believe/canon-law/complementary-norms/canon-766-lay-preaching.

tion, a non-ordained person would be best qualified to offer a personal and consoling message at funerals, especially if the priest or deacon didn't know the deceased person. It would be both pastoral and logical that qualified non-ordained preachers would offer reflections at the profession liturgies of religious, most especially religious women. Beyond my few suggestions, I am sure that there would be more unique opportunities for lay preaching based on the needs or circumstances of a particular worshiping community.

Although the spirit of the Second Vatican Council, the postconciliar documents, the 1983 Code of Canon Law, and the 2001 complementary norm for lay preaching approved by the Catholic bishops of the United States all offer various levels of consent and affirmation for lay preaching, unfortunately lay preaching at Catholic parishes remains an exception to the rule and arbitrary at best. I suspect that in certain (arch)dioceses, pastors are reluctant to present qualified and prepared lay people to preach at eucharistic liturgies at which their preaching would be advantageous in the fear that bishops would decline their request. Pastors fear that lay preaching is not a value for many bishops and want to prevent the laity from feeling rejected by the leader of the local church when they simply wanted to share their gift and "calling" for breaking open the word of God for their fellow parishioners. Unfortunately, many Catholics sitting in pews in parishes across the country remain ignorant of the fact that lay preaching is even a possibility. Sadly, people (and parishes) continue to be ruined for lack of knowledge (Hosea 4:6).

## Lay Preaching within the African American Catholic Community

To fully understand and appreciate the need and evolution of lay preaching in the African American Catholic community today, it is imperative to revisit American slavery. Diana Hayes observes that the Bible was not accessible to enslaved Roman Catholics or to enslaved Protestants, and even if it were, the Catholic Bible was written in Latin, a language that was mostly foreign to Black Catholics who could read.[11] They did not have their own indigenous ordained priests to preach, teach, and offer the sacraments to them. Fortunately, they remembered and shared the biblical stories among themselves. With this sacred memory, enslaved Black Catholics recalled and cherished within their hearts the biblical

---

[11]Diana L. Hayes, *Forged in the Fiery Furnace: African American Spirituality* (Maryknoll, NY: Orbis Books, 2012), 59.

stories of salvation and freedom from oppression. Many slaves, however, most especially in Louisiana where there was French and Spanish colonization, became literate because they "were house servants, craftsmen, skilled laborers, teachers."[12] Not only did these French and Spanish male colonizers share their Catholicism, they also shared their beds with young Black women whom they took as concubines. Thus, a great many slaves were biracial resulting from these liaisons. It is interesting to note that most of these French and Spanish slave owners readily acknowledged their mulatto offspring, and by doing so also admitted their paternity and their children's humanity. In most cases they gave their children their surnames and insisted on their baptisms into the Roman Catholic faith, therefore creating what became known as "the free people of color" (*gens libres de couleur*), especially in and around the city of New Orleans.[13]

Diana L. Hayes offers further enlightenment regarding these Catholic free people of color:

> They formed an independent group of faith-filled Catholics of color who worshiped alongside their white brothers and sisters and participated in society, albeit at a lower level. They helped to form a Black Catholic spirituality rooted in the Latin mass and, in the popular Catholicism of the people, a culture that encouraged syncretism of Catholic beliefs with still-present African traditions, especially Yoruba. The result was the emergence in the Caribbean and Latin America of distinct Afro-Catholic religions (Vodoun, Santería, and Candomblé) that also existed in the lower South, especially after the Haitian revolution (1791–1804).[14]

Black Protestant churches were heavily influenced by Methodist and Baptist denominations[15] and in some instances had moved away from Anglican congregations due in part to their staid and rigid religious expressions. Evangelical Christians promoted an inward feeling that gave way to freely expressing one's emotions in worship. "The emotionalism and plain doctrine of revivalist preaching appealed to the masses, including slaves."[16] As mentioned in certain parts of the country, Black Catholic slaves and free people of color made adaptations with the Latin Mass to allow for emotive freedom in cultural religious expressions, but it is not

[12]Ibid.
[13]Ibid.
[14]Ibid., 59–60.
[15]Ibid., 59.
[16]Albert S. Raboteau, *Slave Religion* (Oxford: Oxford University Press, 1978), 148.

known if Black Catholic slaves were drawn to Protestant revival preaching at this time. Protestant revivalist preachers were traveling on horseback holding tent revivals that were enthralling the masses.

Somewhat equivalent to Protestant revival preaching was the Catholic parish mission that was becoming more and more common in white Catholic parishes in the nineteenth century. However, Catholic missionaries such as the Jesuits, Passionists, Redemptorists, and Paulists made concerted efforts to travel on horseback to plantations during slavery and to Black Catholic parishes after slavery to hold parish missions. Although the parish missions did not evoke any spontaneous outward and audible religious expressions, the preaching of these Catholic missionaries was no less dramatic and evoked an internal sense of conversion. The Redemptorists most especially with their fire and brimstone preaching dramatically conjectured images of the fires of hell to move the people to remorseful tears, to the confessional, and to conversion by amending their sinful lives. This explicit extraordinary preaching on various themes outside of Mass became a source of revivalism and renewal for the Black Catholic faithful both then and now.

## Is There a Word from the Lord?
## Opportunities for African American Catholic Lay Preaching

*"Oh no, I don't preach! I witness. I testify. I share the Good News of the Lord Jesus Christ. The priests can preach. You know women don't preach in the Catholic Church."*[17]

—Sister Thea Bowman, FSPA

The quote above by Sister Thea Bowman, FSPA, who is now on the path of sainthood, was from her 1987 interview with veteran CBS news reporter Mike Wallace for *60 Minutes*. Sister Thea was humorously making the point that she does something different from preaching as a Catholic religious woman—she witnessed and testified. She went on to say in the broadcast that if she couldn't preach in the church, she could preach on the bus, on the train, in the classroom, or in the school yard. In her estimation, the church was not the singular place where preaching happens. Deeply rooted in the understanding of Black spirituality is that *any place* and *every place* are places for prayer and testifying and preaching about the goodness of God!

---

[17]Excerpt from Sister Thea Bowman's interview with Mike Wallace for a 1987 *60 Minutes* telecast, CBS News, New York.

Although admittedly biased, I believe that Black people are a preaching people because our spirituality is biblically based and our captivity and incessant struggles in America have caused us to wholly depend on God and to tell of God's benevolence, protection, provision, and mercy. Non-sacramentally ordained Black Catholics are perennially heard "preaching" in their households. Most Black Catholics would attest that the first preachers they heard growing up were not the priests in church but their mothers and grandmothers expounding on "sermon topics" such as trusting God, believing that God could make a way out of no way, knowing that God was an ever-present help in time of trouble, that God would never leave you or forsake you, or living right because you'll have to give an account on Judgment Day. These "sermons" were used in Black households to chastise and to challenge as well as to encourage and praise. I vividly recall my mother's chastisement sermons, and even though I had heard enough, I knew that I better not try to walk away until the sermon had ended and the benediction given. Sister Thea conveyed this lay preaching phenomenon in the Black community best when she said, "The Word of God became incarnate. We are called to preach that word day by day by day—in our homes, in our families, in our neighborhood—to bear witness, to testify, to shout it from the rooftops, with our lives."[18]

Within the African American Catholic community, I submit that there are several occasions when it would be most appropriate for qualified lay people to offer a reflection during the liturgy, namely, Mother's Day, Father's Day, Grandparents' Day celebrating the elders in the community, a Sunday during Black Catholic History Month in November, and the Feast of the Holy Family that coincides with the African American celebration of Kwanzaa (December 26–January 1) that lifts up the seven Nguzo Saba principles and values for the African American community to strive to incorporate in their daily lives.

There are also beneficial occasions outside of the Eucharistic liturgy when qualified lay Black Catholics could preach. Perhaps lay preachers could be called upon to preach at a parish retreat, revival, or parish mission. As a pastor, I invited parishioners who were deeply spiritual and had a strong connection with the word of God to offer reflections during our weekly Lenten prayer services. We called the prayer services, "Sweet Hour of Prayer," and the congregation eagerly anticipated, supported, and prayed for their fellow parishioners who were called to witness to their

---

[18]An excerpt from Sister Thea Bowman's "Women's Day" undated speech at Saint Clement Pope Church is from her handwritten notes for that speech, Franciscan Sisters of Perpetual Adoration archives, La Crosse, WI.

Christian discipleship and reflect on the scripture texts. Their particular parish mission statement was "To preach, teach, and joyfully live the Word of God." And they were very intentional in fulfilling their parish's mission.

For one elderly parishioner, the annual "Sweet Hour of Prayer" was too limited for her to completely share good news. The parishioners affectionately dubbed her "Mother Julia Jones." She was a unique non-ordained lay preacher. She was a convert to Catholicism who had been reared in a Catholic orphanage staffed by a religious order of sisters in Mississippi. Mother Julia migrated as a young lady to St. Louis where she worked as a housekeeper for wealthy white families. She possessed a unique mixture of traditional Catholicism and spirited Pentecostalism. For her there was no dissonance or conflict in her commingled spiritualities. She came to church post–Vatican II with a veil covering her head, her rosary beads in her hand, while shouting "Hallelujah, praise the Lord!" She was the first in our congregation to shout "Amen" and "Say it, Father" while the priest preached his homily. Her outbursts during Mass were at first unsettling for our traditional Black Catholic parish but eventually her spirit-filled exuberance became contagious, and many other parishioners joined Mother Julia in shouting and praising the Lord during Mass. On many occasions Mother Julia could be found after Mass in the church parking lot giving an "addendum" to the morning's homily. She was a woman who deeply loved God and studied God's word and offered her weekly spiritual reflections to anyone who would listen to her. This spirit-filled elderly lady was literally the catalyst for the spiritual revival and renewal of an inner-city Black Catholic parish in St. Louis. Mother Julia would shout, "Lord Jesus, I'm not ashamed to be a witness for you!"

### Preaching without Words:
### African American Catholic Witness of Holiness

Mother Julia was certainly a Black Catholic woman who boldly and exuberantly proclaimed good news—an expression of her holiness of life. She wasn't apologetic about her holy boldness—her exultant witness to Jesus and all that he had done for her. In his apostolic exhortation *Gaudete et Exsultate* (Rejoice and Be Glad), Pope Francis states that "Holiness is also *parrhesia:* it is boldness, an impulse to evangelize and to leave a mark in this world."[19] He further asserts that boldness and apostolic courage are

---

[19]Pope Francis, *Gaudete et Exsultate (Be Glad and Rejoice), On the Call to Holiness in Today's World,* apostolic exhortation (March 19, 2018), no. 129.

an essential part of our mission as Christians. Pope Francis understands parrhesia as "a seal of the Spirit; it testifies to the authenticity of our preaching. It is a joyful assurance that leads us to glory in the Gospel we proclaim. It is an unshakeable trust in the faithful Witness who gives us the certainty that nothing can 'separate us from the love of God' (Romans 8:39)."[20] Mother Julia lived to be over a hundred years old and never ceased to testify to the goodness of God, the faithfulness of Jesus, the One she often called, "Mary's baby," and her joy in being Catholic. She unquestionably was possessed by parrhesia; she was sealed by the Holy Spirit.

In my life and ministry there have been many others who have exemplified very holy lives. It is important that those called to preach to African American Catholic communities be aware of the people and their signs of holiness around them. The witness of holiness of Black Catholic laity informs and inspires the homilies that they preach. Not all witnesses to lives of holiness will be as forthright as Mother Julia Jones; perhaps most will be subtle or inconspicuous. As a young man, I was fortunate to be aware of the "saints" among my faith community. Their examples of holiness and love for Jesus and the Church inspired my religious priesthood and spirituality. In *Be Glad and Rejoice*, Pope Francis highlights that "[w]e are all called to be holy by living our lives with love and by bearing witness in everything we do, and wherever we find ourselves."[21]

Pope Francis's words describe the lives of two "saints" who touched my life as a young man. They remind me of the elderly biblical figures of Simeon and Anna found in Luke 2:21–38. Although they did not literally live in the church, they did not rush in and out of our parish church but lingered there long after others had left the building. Their names were Adrian Johnson and Gladys Foster. They were holy Black Catholic lay persons. Adrian was a devout Catholic who had been a seminarian with the Divine Word Missionaries who operated the first seminary for Black men who aspired to the priesthood in Bay St. Louis, Mississippi. He felt called to married life and was drawn to be an organist and did not persevere in the seminary. Adrian Johnson was a classmate of the first four Black Society of Divine Word priests ordained at Bay St. Louis, Mississippi, in 1934.[22] Adrian had a strong baritone voice, and his singing bellowed throughout the church. During the time of racial segregation, he secured a job as the organist at a predominantly white parish, but he had to play the organ and sing the responses of the Latin High Masses from behind a

---

[20]Ibid., no. 132.

[21]Ibid., no. 14.

[22]First Black priests of the Society of the Divine Word. https://www.ncronline.org/news/people/first-Black-priests-us-opened-door-rest-us-pastor-says.

screen so that parishioners could not see that the melodious singing was coming from a Black man. Eventually, Adrian became the organist at St. Alphonsus Liguori "Rock" parish in St. Louis, Missouri, where I came to meet him. Now at a Black Catholic parish, he felt at home as he sang and directed a choir from the balcony of the beautiful Gothic church. For over thirty years he faithfully ministered in song at the St. Louis parish. Besides his music ministry, he had the habit of coming to church early dressed in suit and tie and kneeling on the high altar steps making a visit to the Blessed Sacrament, and when Mass ended and most of the parishioners had gone, he would kneel before the Blessed Sacrament again in prayer. This pious gesture inspired all who witnessed it. Adrian Johnson epitomized Black Catholic sanctity.

Adrian Johnson was not the last to leave the church building because lingering as she made her visits to the various side altars, prayed her rosary, and walked the stations of the cross was Gladys Foster. She was a very pious and quiet lady. When she spoke, her voice was soft and barely audible. Her very countenance exuded holiness. She always covered her head with a veil while in church. She also had a modest, pious habit. Gladys Foster would kiss the feet of Jesus on the large crucifix in back of the church. In fact, she would never pass any crucifix without kissing the feet of Jesus. This Black Catholic lady's holiness made me want to strive to live a holy life. Both Gladys's and Adrian's lives are prime examples of Pope Francis's words regarding holiness, "Let the grace of your baptism bear fruit in a path of holiness. Let everything be open to God; turn to him in every situation. Do not be dismayed, for you can do this in the power of the Holy Spirit, and holiness, in the end, is the fruit of the Holy Spirit in your life (cf. Galatians 5:22–23)."[23] The witness of their holy lives was a proclamation of good news to all who observed them. No words were ever spoken, but their witnesses were "sermons" that inspired, provided hope, offered the grace of steadfast perseverance, and will never be forgotten.

### Let the Church Roll On: The Enduring Faith of Catholic Hill

Historically, in more than one instance, Black Catholics maintained the fervor of their Catholic faith without a priest or preaching or the regular administration of the sacraments. There is an amazing story of a Black Catholic faith community in South Carolina at the outbreak of the Civil War that was essentially abandoned and forgotten. Benedictine historian

---

[23]*Gaudete et Exsultate*, no. 15.

Father Cyprian Davis best tells this inspiring, yet amazing, tale about a settlement at what is now known as Catholic Hill in Colleton County in the Diocese of Charleston, South Carolina:

> A church dedicated to St. James the Greater was established in 1833 in this area by Bishop John England for the several Catholic families who had plantations and slaves. In 1856 the church of St. James burned to the ground. Within the decade the Civil War broke out, the church was not rebuilt, and the slaveholding families moved away, leaving a small nucleus of Catholics among the Blacks in the area that had come to be known as Catholic Crossroads and is known today as Catholic Hill in Ritter, South Carolina. Without priest, church, or sacraments the Catholic faith was kept alive over a period of forty years through the efforts of a certain Vincent de Paul Davis, former slave and storeowner, who instructed the children.
>
> In 1897 a priest attached to the cathedral in Charleston, Father Daniel Berberich, discovered this community of "lost" Catholics. Eventually the church of St. James the Greater was rebuilt, and Father Berberich became a regular pastoral visitor until 1909. Following him, other priests came from other towns to serve the community. But always there was a core of laymen and laywomen who taught and led the community in worship during the periods when a priest was absent. In 1935 a new church was built and the school remodeled. . . . [The] church, the school, the cemetery, and the present congregation remain a visible monument to the tenacious faith of a community of Black Catholics. It is also another reminder of the fact that the preservation and the spread of Catholicism among the African American population has very often been the work of Black laymen and laywomen.[24]

What a remarkable story about a Black Catholic community's enduring faith. Abandoned and forgotten primarily because the white Catholic community had left, these Black Catholic laymen and laywomen could have easily abandoned Catholicism altogether, and yet they persevered. Vincent de Paul, a trained lay catechist, kept the Catholic faith flourishing on Catholic Hill by ringing a bell and calling the community together at the site of the burned-down church building every Sunday morning and leading prayer services that included songs, prayers, and preaching. He

---

[24]Cyprian Davis, *The History of Black Catholics in the United States* (New York: Crossroad, 1990), 209–210.

also continued to instruct the children in the catechism of the Church as well as trained other catechists in the community. St. James the Greater Church community remains today, although now it is a mission church of St. Anthony Church in Walterboro, South Carolina. They have about one hundred members now, but, more important, they remain a dedicated faith community born from Black Catholic laity's determination to keep the faith tradition alive through teaching, preaching, and praying.[25] Out of necessity, Vincent de Paul Davis adopted the role of a modern-day permanent deacon who provides spiritual care for his community. I have visited the descendants of Vincent de Paul Davis and the others of Catholic Hill, and they are proud of their ancestors' tenacity and perseverance.[26] Their mission church remains a vibrant community mostly due to committed laywomen. Given their incredible past, it is quite evident that giving up is not an option.

## Black Catholic Women Preach: Valuable Contributions to Catholic Preaching

Something must be said about the significant contributions that women make in the life of the African American Catholic community. As in many other ethnic groups, African American Catholic women are the majority of those who are active in the life of the parish. They bring a myriad of talents to the church, ranging from their intellectual capabilities, creativity, and diligence to their organizational skills, feminine spirituality, sensibilities, and perceptions. I believe that without the gifts and giftedness of women, the church would not achieve its full potential. Quite frankly, the absence of women's presence, knowledge, experiences, and voice is detrimental to "Mother Church" being truly complete. Although women are the majority of any parish's weekly attendance and serve in many liturgical roles from greeters, ushers, lectors, and altar servers to eucharistic ministers, cantors, and choir members, it is only on rare occasions that priests and parishioners hear their voices, their reflections, and interpretations of God's word. And we are the lesser for it. However, not deterred, women because of their genius and creativity, have historically opened themselves to more expansive ways of sharing their theologies, spiritualities, and biblical interpretations beyond the pulpit through testimonials, teaching, writing

---

[25] "Documentary of Catholic Hill Reveals a Journey of Faith," *Catholic Miscellany Newspaper,* Diocese of Charleston, August 19, 2020.

[26] During the Black Catholic Theological Symposium's annual meeting in Charleston, SC, October 2019, current members of St. James the Greater Church in Ritter, SC, came to share the parish history with our membership.

letters, prose, poems, and songs, the arts, and public actions on behalf of justice. Through their brilliance women have remained undeterred and unsilenced by patriarchal norms.

One only has to study the sacred scriptures to acknowledge and appreciate the place of women as missionaries—those who witnessed and told of God's revelation. It was our Blessed Mother, Mary, who gave her resounding, "Amen," her yes, her "so shall it be" when she was overshadowed by the Holy Spirit and became the mother of the Savior of the world, Jesus, the "Word made flesh and dwelt among us." Mary cried out, "My soul proclaims the greatness of the Lord, my spirit rejoices in God my savior" (Luke 1:46). Mary literally carried the Word in her womb during her pregnancy. It was Mary who encouraged the first miracle of Jesus at Cana in Galilee, with the words to the servers, "Do whatever he tells you" (John 2:5). It was Mary who lingered, lovingly, at the cross (John 19:26). Mary was present when they were gathered in one place on the day of Pentecost and was filled with the Holy Spirit and witnessed to its power along with Jesus's apostles and disciples (Acts 2:1).

It was another Mary, Mary of Magdala, who not only was compelled by the persuasion of Jesus's compassion and preaching, but who also first witnessed the resurrection and did not hesitate to announce, "He lives," making her an apostle of the resurrection. Eunjoo Mary Kim, in her book *Women Preaching: Theology and Practice through the Ages*, affirms Mary Magdalene as a missionary: "She shared what she had learned from Jesus from the time of Galilee, including the love of God manifested in the life, death, and resurrection of Christ Jesus, with those who had never met or heard him. In many paintings and artifacts of Mary Magdalene created during the early and medieval periods, she is depicted as a preacher holding the traditional preaching gesture of pointing her right index finger upward."[27]

Without entering into an exhaustive investigation of women preaching in the early centuries of the Church, we can state that apparently some women were preaching because in 1234, Pope Gregory IX legally forbade women to preach by inserting an article of prohibition into the Book of *Decretals*.[28] *Decretals* are papal letters, strictly those in response to a question. They have the force of law within the pope's jurisdiction. Evidently, the question of women preaching was posed to the pontiff, and

---

[27]Eunjoo Mary Kim, *Women Preaching: Theology and Practice through the Ages* (Eugene, OR: Wipf and Stock, 2004), 37.

[28]Nicole Bériou, "The Right of Women to Give Religious Instruction in the Thirteenth Century," in *Women Preachers and Prophets through Two Millennia of Christianity*, ed. Beverly Mayne Kienzle and Pamela J. Walker (Berkeley: University of California Press, 1998), 137.

he emphatically answered "no." However, Eunjoo Mary Kim notes that abbesses and nuns were officially allowed to

> teach and preach within their convents because this did not violate the seeming biblical injunctions against women teaching men[;] women preachers such as St. Hildegard of Bingen, St. Rose of Viterbo (1233–1252), St. Catherine of Siena (1347–1380) preached with full authority and sanctity both inside and outside monasteries. They preached not only to women but also to men without rousing opposition or censorship from the clergy, for their preaching had the authority of their mystical experiences of the divine.[29]

Suffice it to say that historically and officially some women have preached in the Catholic Church until its pontifical and canonical prohibitions. I turn now to African American Catholic women and their call to proclaim good news. From a woman's theological perspective on preaching, Kim asserts that a

> consensus among listeners can happen during the moment of preaching if the listeners grant sufficient respect to the different experiences of women and other oppressed people and are challenged by these experiences, recognizing that the lives of the various people are so intertwined that each is accountable to the other. Consensus among listeners is the result of both the preacher's honest speaking and the listeners' attentive, humble listening. If the listeners open themselves to differences and allow themselves the possibility of change, authentic solidarity grows within the congregation.[30]

I concur with Eunjoo Mary Kim's assertion also from a ministerial perspective. On those rare occasions when women have preached during Mass, I have witnessed the congregation come to a new or different understanding of a biblical text because of the message preached by a woman. Similarly, I have heard men outwardly attest to a new insight that they never recognized until it was preached by a woman. As a case in point, I recall both myself and an African American religious sister preaching on the Samaritan woman at the well narrative (John 4:1–42) using cycle A during the Lenten scrutinies of the catechumens a year apart and how the congregation reacted to our different insights on the text. We were both African Americans, but we had different perspectives because of

---

[29]Kim, *Women Preaching*, 56–57.
[30]Ibid., 14.

our genders. I must say that sister's feminine perspective of the Samaritan woman as an outcast woman because of her gender, ethnicity, and religion was far more influential than my limited insights. Many men commented how they appreciated the nuances that sister's reflection gave to the text, thus bringing about an authentic solidarity among the entire congregation.

To further illustrate the unique insights that come from Black Catholic women preaching, I turn to an excerpt from Thea Bowman's *Songs of My People*, a reflection on the woman at the well:

One day Jesus was going from Galilee to Jerusalem. Many Jews used to avoid Samaria like many Blacks used to avoid Mississippi, go miles around just to keep from passing through.

It was not by chance that Jesus stopped at a town in Samaria named Sychar and paused by the cooling, cleansing, refreshing water. He was tired. He was thirsty. He was hungry. He was human. His body needed rest. But he had work to do.

It was not by chance that a teacher, a Jewish rabbi without reproach, requested and accepted the ministry of a Samaritan, a stranger, a sinner, a woman. The well was deep, and he had no bucket. Jews did not ordinarily talk with Samaritans. Rabbis did not ordinarily speak with women in public. Holy people did not ordinarily consort with public sinners. But Jesus said to her, "Give me to drink." He asked her for a favor. He engaged her in conversation. He helped her to identify her own weakness and her strength. She gave him water from the well that was her Samaria. He, in return, gave her water that became in her a spring of living water giving eternal life.

She gave him herself as she was, without subterfuge or guile. He healed her guilt and restored her vitality. He transformed her and used her to bring all of Samaria to his feet.

When I acknowledge myself—my true self—weak, failing, incomplete, inconsequential, yet gifted and capable of transcendence, when I accept my neediness and come just as I am, I too can recognize the Messiah, and with joy I shall go running into *my* city crying, "Come! Come! Come see a Man who told me everything I have done!"[31]

These are the words of a Black Catholic religious sister who accentuated what it meant to be a woman who was transformed from a sinner, an outcast, a woman who once avoided crowds to a changed woman who

---

[31]Maurice J. Nutt, ed., *Thea Bowman: In My Own Words* (Liguori, MO: Liguori, 2009), 65.

became a missionary of good news to her village. Thea then moves from the text to her own testimony that she could go running to her own city crying, "Come see a Man who told me everything I have done."

Thea Bowman distinguished herself as both a teacher and preacher. In many ways she was exceptional, and her gift and persona provided opportunities for her to witness and evangelize as a woman, a Black Catholic woman, a Black Catholic religious sister. Yet there are others, namely, Black Catholic lay women who feel called to preach and face oppressive obstacles with little to no recourse. Much like Thea Bowman, Black Catholic lay womanist and liberation theologian Diana L. Hayes has distinguished herself within the Catholic Church as a theologian who also preaches. Hayes acknowledges:

> I have been challenged, in many ways, to prove not only the legitimacy of my existence but also the validity of my existence to face so many others who are not like me at all. As a Black, Catholic theologian who is very much a woman, I am, in many ways, doubly if not triply oppressed. It has been a constant struggle, therefore, for me to define not only who but whose I am. That struggle has included finding, acknowledging, and eventually rejoicing in my own voice, a voice unlike anyone else's because it arises out of the very depths of my being—who I am as Black, as Catholic, and as a woman and vowed celibate.[32]

Similar to Hayes's sentiments are the sentiments of Black feminist author, professor, and social activist bell hooks:

> For women within oppressed groups who have contained so many feelings—despair, rage, anguish—who do not speak, as poet Audre Lorde writes, "for fear our words will not be heard or welcomed," coming to voice is an act of resistance. Speaking becomes both a way to engage in active self-transformation and a rite of passage where one moves from being object to being subject. Only as subjects can we speak. As objects, we remain voiceless—our beings defined and interpreted by others.[33]

---

[32]Diana L. Hayes, *No Crystal Stair: Womanist Spirituality* (Maryknoll, NY: Orbis Books, 2016), 4–5.

[33]bell hooks, *Talking Back: Thinking Feminist, Thinking Black* (Boston: South End Press, 1989), 12.

An increasingly large number of African American Catholic religious sisters and lay women are seeking ways to share, reflect, and preach the good news of Jesus Christ. Many have academically prepared by earning degrees such as master of divinity, master of theology, and master of arts in pastoral or biblical studies. Included in their formation programs have been courses in lay presiding and leadership of worship classes. For these Black Catholic women their calling to preach is sincere and rooted in much prayer and discernment. They have a gift to share with the church grounded in their rich African American Catholic culture and spirituality, but it is continually rejected and unwanted. However, they are undaunted and have sought other opportunities to share their preaching gifts, even creating avenues for themselves. Within African American Catholic parishes across the country Black Catholic lay women preachers are starting ministries for women, offering retreats, sponsoring youth and young adult rallies, prayer services, and conferences, as well as preaching at parish missions and revivals. The resilience displayed by these faithful and spirit-filled Black Catholic women has sparked a needed renewal in many parishes that quite frankly were dying.

There are other creative initiatives that serve as platforms for lay women and religious women preaching. One in particular is the website preaching resource, Catholic Women Preach (www.catholicwomenpreach. org). According to their mission statement, they seek to raise voices and renew the church:

> Catholic Women Preach is an innovative project to address some of the most pressing challenges facing the Church today by responding to Pope Francis' call for broader and more active engagement of the baptized in the preaching mission of the Church. This project is a deeply faithful, hopeful, and joyful initiative intended to build up the church. Catholic Women Preach offers the theologically informed perspectives of Catholic women:
>
> - to serve as an inspirational, theologically based resource for ordained priests, deacons, catechists, and all involved in the ministry of the word in the Catholic Church.
> - to encourage Catholics, especially younger adult Catholics, with messages of hope to renew their faith, strengthen us and encourage active engagement in the life of the Church for our work in the world.
> - To provide a global platform for women's voices and faith re-

flections so that the fullness of our Catholic giftedness can be accessed by all Catholics.[34]

These Catholic lay and religious women from around the world offer a special gift to the universal Church. The contributors are genuinely a global association of Catholic women from various countries and nationalities serving the Church not only as preachers but also as theologians, scripture scholars, catechists, high school teachers, campus ministers, retreat leaders, pastoral program directors, pastoral ministers, parish administration, ministers in the Latinx community, the African community, the African American community, youth and young adult ministers, university and theology school administrators, writers and authors, journalists, spiritual directors, women development ministers, those ministering to those with intellectual disabilities, migrants and refugees, those serving on the leadership teams of their religious communities, those lobbying for Catholic social justice, community organizers working for affordable housing, social activists and human rights advocates, LBGTQ ministries, those working for Catholic nonviolence initiatives, those advocating for the environment and awareness of climate change, those seeking to eradicate poverty. This is merely a survey of the many ministries that these Catholic preaching women engage in. Imagine how informed, engaging, relevant, and compelling that their weekly scriptural reflections following the lectionary are! The wealth of their knowledge and lived experiences are amazing, and they offer it freely to the Church for its renewal and revitalization.

I am grateful for Catholic Women Preach because many of these religious and lay women have been my professors and are my colleagues, friends, and cherished confidants. I also rejoice in this preaching project because there are so many Black Catholic women religious and lay women sharing their cultural and spiritual gifts.[35] And finally, I must confess that I am an advocate for Catholic women preaching because I am a Catholic priest who preaches today because of the gracious Catholic

---

[34]Catholic Women Preach (https://www.catholicwomenpreach.org/about). A three-year series of homilies from this program is planned for publication by Orbis Books, beginning with *Catholic Women Preach: Raising Voices, Renewing the Church—Cycle A,* ed. Elizabeth Donnelly and Russ Petrus (Maryknoll, NY: Orbis Books, 2022).

[35]The Black Catholic women who are contributors to Catholic Women Preach are Dr. M. Shawn Copeland, Sr. Dr. Jamie T. Phelps, OP, Dr. timone davis, Dr. Marcia Chatelain, Dr. Shawnee M. Daniels-Sykes, Elyse Galloway, Sr. Dr. Anne Arabome, SSS, Kayla August, Sr. Anita P. Baird, DHM, Dr. Kim Harris, Dr. Diana L. Hayes, Dr. Valerie D. Lewis-Mosley, Dr. Kimberly Lymore, Vickey McBride, Joan F. Neal, Dr. Noelle Pratt, Olga Marina Segura, Sr. Nicole Trahan, FMI, Dr. C. Vanessa White, Dr. Julie Welborn, and Boreta A. Singleton.

religious women who taught me how to preach. Throughout my seminary formation and advanced academic studies, I never had a priest teach my preaching practicums, but rather I had three Catholic preaching women: Sister Kathleen Cannon, OP (Catholic Theological Union); Servant of God Sister Thea Bowman, FSPA (Institute for Black Catholic Studies—Xavier University of Louisiana); and Sister Joan Delaplane (Aquinas Institute of Theology). Sister Joan also served as president of the Academy of Homiletics. These are all remarkable women who challenged my preaching to be biblically based, theologically sound, and culturally and globally aware, while also being stimulating, motivating, and relevant.

It is somewhat baffling to me to imagine that these three "women of the word" would dedicate much of their lives and ministries to the formation of men to preach the Gospel—a ministry that officially at Mass they are not allowed to perform. What would make them do for others what they could not do themselves? The answer lies in their nurturing gifts as blessed women who deeply love their Church. I am forever grateful to "those preaching women!"

6

# Rhetorical Agency
# and the Black Prophetic Tradition

## Radical Rhetoric

Words have power. Words are transformative. Words have the agency
to both imagine and realize significant change in the lives and situations
of individuals and communities. The Black prophetic tradition is best promulgated by but is not necessarily exclusive to the Black church. From the
sacred sanctuaries and puissant pulpits of Black churches comes riveting
rhetoric that empowers and equips parishioners to work for and many
times realize needed change. Within the walls of most Black churches
are courageous and creative Black people who have navigated their way
through the treacherous terrains and wicked waters of economic exploitation, political gerrymandering, and racial disenfranchisement. Black
churches have long since been the locus of political meetings, organized
rallies, protests, and boycotts, voter registration and census participation
drives. These efforts are known as Black prophetic practices. The passionate prophetic sermons urged congregations to fearlessly march forward
toward moral victories. Cornel West observes that African American
"prophetic practices have been and, for the most part, remain ensconced
in a moralistic mood: that is, they are grounded in a moralistic conception
of the world in which the rightness or wrongness of human actions—be
they individually or collectively understood—are measured by ethical
ideas or moral standards."[1] After intense scrutiny, the Black prophetic
tradition essentially seeks a morally grounded sense of justice in both
personal and societal affairs.

The agency of the Black prophetic tradition is commonly embodied

---

[1]Cornel West and Eddie S. Glaude, Jr., eds., *African American Religious Thought: An Anthology* (Louisville: Westminster John Knox Press, 2003), 1040.

in preached sermons, pronouncements, declarations, and resolutions; the prophetic practices and actions of Black people seeking justice derive from the Black prophetic tradition. Myriad incidents can be told of Black oppression and the Black prophetic tradition employed, but I share one instance because of its monumental impact on past and future Black lives.

Over a century ago, East St. Louis, Illinois, was the scene of one of the bloodiest race riots of the twentieth century. Racial tensions began to increase when 470 African American workers were hired to replace white workers on strike against the Aluminum Ore Company. On July 2, 1917, Black men, women, and children were beaten and shot to death. That evening, white mobs began to set fire to the homes of Black residents. The residents had to choose between burning alive in their homes or running out of the burning houses only to be met by gunfire. In other parts of the city, white mobs began to lynch African Americans against the backdrop of burning buildings. Upwards of a hundred Black people were killed and thousands were driven from their homes; and more than sixty homes in Black Valley, the Negro district, were burned and nearly a half million dollars-worth of property was destroyed by fire.[2]

This heinous, chaotic event remains not only in the annals of our egregious American history of oppressing Black people, but this event for me is personal. My maternal grandparents, a Black Catholic family, parishioners of St. Augustine Catholic Church in East St. Louis, Illinois, barely escaped death with their young children as they crossed the Mississippi River into safety in St. Louis, Missouri.[3] For generations in my family, my grandparents' account of terror and surviving the 1917 East St. Louis massacre has been told and will continue to be told in the spirit of the Black prophetic tradition.

The 1917 East St. Louis massacre received swift national responses with the deployment of the National Guard, an investigation launched by the National Association for the Advancement of Colored People (NAACP), and written condemnation of the atrocities by W. E. B. Du Bois, Martha Gruening, and Ida B. Wells. In addition 8,000 African Americans silently marched from Harlem down New York City's famed Fifth Avenue with signs that read, "Mother, do lynchers go to heaven?" "Thou shall not kill," and "Give us a chance to live." The St. Louis Metropolitan branch

---

[2]Ida B. Wells, *The East St. Louis Massacre: The Greatest Outrage of the Century* (Amazon Kindle Edition, 2020), 3. This book was originally written by Wells in 1917.

[3]Maurice J. Nutt, CSsR, "A Sankofa Moment: Exploring a Genealogy of Justice," in *Ain't Gonna Let Nobody Turn Me Around: Stories of Contemplation and Justice*, ed. Therese Taylor-Stinson (New York: Church Publishing, 2017), 147.

of the National Urban League was created in the wake of the massacre. It is apparent that many of the African Americans who marched in New York City that day were members of churches where preachers preached against the racist killings and lynchings that happened in East St. Louis. Although they marched in silence, fierce resolve and steadfast determination were in their stride.

On July 3, the day after the East St. Louis race riot, the Negro Fellowship League of Chicago met and passed the following resolution:

> RESOLVED, That we, the colored citizens of Chicago, in the shadow of the awful calamity at East St. Louis, hereby express our solemn conviction that the wholesale slaughter of colored men, women, and children was the result of the reckless indifference of public officials, who, with the power of the police, sheriff and governor, could have prevented this massacre if they had discharged the duty which the law imposed upon them, and we call upon press, pulpit and moral forces to demand the punishment of the officials who failed to their duty.[4]

This scathing indictment of the reprehensible crimes committed illustrates how Black people used their agency to name the havoc wreaked upon an innocent Black community. Although their rhetoric was non-threatening, it nevertheless morally castigated the purveyors of violence and oppression and demanded punishment for those who failed to uphold the law. Thus, the Negro Fellowship League of Chicago's rhetorical agency substantiates Cornel West's claim that "moral integrity, political consistency, and systemic analysis sit at the center of the Black prophetic tradition."[5] To be clear in this case and others, the prophetic rhetorical agency is employed for the sake of the greater community—it is other-centered—and not for individualistic ambition or gain.

## Prophetic Imagination

Prophetic imagination offers an alternative to the way things simply "are" and the belief in the way in which God "intends" that they should be. Prophetic imagination is not wishful thinking or a fanciful hope, but

---

[4]Wells, *The East St. Louis Massacre*, 3.
[5]Cornel West, *Black Prophetic Fire: A Dialogue with and Edited by Christa Buschendorf* (Amazon Kindle Edition, 2015), 160.

rather it is rooted in biblical assurances and biblical prophetic promises. Within the Black prophetic tradition and Black preaching, the preacher can make prophetic claims not as conjecture but with absolute assurance that the same God that performed miracles, fought battles, and brought liberation in biblical times is the same God who is on the side of the oppressed today. In other words, within the Black prophetic tradition problematic realities are subdued and certitude assured by prophetic promises. To elaborate, I offer the following illustrations: A person is berated with derision and constant setbacks; that's the problematic reality, and yet the prophetic promise is found in Isaiah 54:17: "Every weapon fashioned against you shall fail; every tongue that brings you to trial you shall prove false." To those facing and fighting against racism and inequality, that's the problematic reality, but the prophetic promise provides solace in Psalm 34:18–19: "The righteous cry out, the Lord hears, and he rescues them from all their afflictions. The Lord is close to the brokenhearted, saves those whose spirit is crushed." For those who are despondent, listless, and in despair who cannot find relief, that is their unequivocal situation, their problematic reality, but there is a word from the Lord found in John 10:10 giving them unspeakable joy when Jesus says, "I came so that they might have life and have it more abundantly." The problematic reality is in the uncontrollable circumstances that people face, and the prophetic imagination enables the hearers of the preaching or declaration to hear and experience an alternative way—the reality that God intends. When one encounters the transforming power of the gospel, his or her entire world has changed because Jesus represents newness and change; he represents transformation and liberation.[6]

## The Prophetic Rhetorical Agency of Baldwin, King, Bowman, and Massingale

Throughout the history of America, there are numerous instances in which Black people have employed their rhetorical agency to speak unbridled truth to power. Within the Black prophetic tradition, rhetorical agency is not solely relegated to preachers and not exclusively to the Protestant Black church. In the following I provide a cursory survey of the vigorous rhetorical agency of four twentieth- and twenty-first-century African Americans: three men and one woman, two from the Protestant tradition and two from the Roman Catholic tradition; one geographically

---

[6]James H. Harris, *Preaching Liberation* (Minneapolis: Fortress Press, 1995), 21.

from the East, one from the North, and two from the South; three reared among the economically middle class and one reared among the urban poor. All four have preached the gospel, and yet one later professed to be non-religious. Three earned terminal degrees and one is without any academic degree, yet all four are considered highly intelligent and cogently prophetic. Three are deceased, and one is alive. All possess(ed) an abiding love and commitment to the African American community and the quest for justice and equality. Their names are James Baldwin (1924–1987), Martin Luther King Jr. (1929–1968), Thea Bowman (1937–1990), and Bryan Massingale (1957–).

## James Baldwin

Reared in the impoverished tenements of Harlem, New York, James Arthur Baldwin was an African American novelist, playwright, essayist, poet, and activist. Baldwin's writings critically examined the complex intricacies of race, religion and religious hypocrisy, sexuality, masculinity, Black oppression, white supremacy and white privilege, and class distinctions. His stepfather was a preacher, and to appease him he became a "junior minister" as a teenager. Speaking of his truncated tenure as a preacher, Baldwin notes, "I was fourteen when I entered [the ministry] and seventeen when I left."[7] Baldwin was repelled by Christianity because of how white people justified the exclusivity of their religion by purporting the whiteness of Jesus and the kingdom of heaven as no place for Black people. Baldwin confessed that the irreverent and appalling behavior of white Christians caused him to "regard white Christians and, especially, white ministers with a profound and troubled contempt. And indeed, the terror that I could not suppress upon finally leaving the pulpit was mitigated by the revelation that now, at least, I would not be compelled—allowed—to spend eternity in their presence."[8]

Baldwin exerted his rhetorical agency through his writings and speeches. The genius of his craft is best encapsulated by a reviewer in the *New York Times Book Review*, who stated: "The best essayist in this country—a man whose power has always been in his reasoned, biting sarcasm; his insistence on removing layer by layer the hardened skin with which Americans shield themselves from their country."[9]

---

[7]James Baldwin, "To Crush a Serpent," in *The Cross of Redemption: Uncollected Writings*, ed. Randall Kenan (New York: Pantheon Books, 2010), 195.

[8]Ibid., 159.

[9]This review is on the back-jacket cover of James Baldwin's *The Cross of Redemption: Uncollected Writings*.

In the following excerpt from his 1963 essay *The Fire Next Time*, his rhetorical agency is reflected in the terror that every Negro child has in preparing for the unknown, the day that they will encounter the debilitating force of racial hatred and violence. The child has no idea when it will arrive, but the child is assured by his or her parents that it will come. The child is simply left to await it. James Baldwin's prophetic rhetoric gives testimony that this is the lot of every Black child in America: racism will come, prepare to meet it.

> Long before the Negro child perceives this difference, and even longer before he understands it, he has begun to react to it, he has begun to be controlled by it. Every effort made by the child's elders to prepare him for a fate from which they cannot protect him causes him secretly, in terror, to begin to await, without knowing that he is doing so, his mysterious and inexorable punishment. He must be "good" not only in order to please his parents and not only to avoid being punished by them; behind their authority stands another, nameless and impersonal, indefinitely harder to please, and bottomlessly cruel. And this filters into the child's consciousness through his parents' tone of voice as he is being exhorted, punished, or loved; in the sudden, uncontrollable note of fear heard in his mother's or father's voice when he has strayed beyond some particular boundary. He does not know what the boundary is, and he can get no explanation of it, which is frightening enough, but the fear he hears in the voices of his elders is more frightening still.[10]

In the following excerpt from his 1964 essay "What Price Freedom?" Baldwin sends a stern warning, an impassioned word of caution to white America that the racial oppression, unrelenting segregation, horrific violence, and incessant subjugation of Black people will lead to their demise. Unequivocally, James Baldwin was a prophetic voice in the Black literary tradition; his rhetoric spoke fiercely to the structural power imbalances and injustices of the social order. He readily denounced the terror the white dominant culture evoked in the dominated Black culture. Baldwin leaves open the possibility of a recourse from self-sabotage under certain conditions. He vehemently urges America to make a collective and comprehensive examination of conscience of its sins against Black humanity. He implicitly implores the nation to confess its sins, repent and

---

[10]James Baldwin, "Down at the Cross," in *The Fire Next Time* (New York: Vintage, 1992), 26.

do penance for its evil ways, and pledge to amend its hard-heartedness; then and only then would America save itself from perishing. However, because of centuries of Black suffering, be it physical, psychological, or symbolic, Baldwin thinks that it might be too late for the United States to make this necessary metamorphosis.

> In order for us to survive and transcend the terrible days ahead of us, the country will have to turn and take me in its arms. Now, this may sound mystical, but at the bottom that is what has got to happen, because it is not a matter of *giving me* this or that; it is not yours to give. Let us be clear about that. It is not a question of whether they are going to give me any freedom. I am going to take my freedom. That problem is resolved. The real problem is the price. Not the price I will pay, but the price the country will pay. The price a white woman, man, boy, and girl will have to pay in themselves before they look on me as another human being. This metamorphosis is what we are driving toward, because without that we will perish—indeed, we are almost perishing now.[11]

## Martin Luther King Jr.

This son and grandson of Baptist preachers was reared in the Sweet Auburn neighborhood of Atlanta, Georgia. Martin Luther King Jr. was destined to one day be a preacher himself. He balanced well his inherent curiosity for study and knowledge and his empathy for people, most especially for those less fortunate than himself. At a young age Martin was mesmerized by the profound words preachers used to make biblical characters and situations come to life, how a preacher's sonorous voice and commanding stance in the pulpit were able to engage and persuade a congregation to both accept the truth of the gospel and to put that truth into practice. As an erudite preacher himself, Martin understood the power of the preached word. He used his rhetorical agency to move his listeners beyond complacency to places of empowerment. King's sermons often concluded with memorable prophetic images of a renewed universe and a lovelier dwelling with God's providential care ushering in a realm of peace.[12]

---

[11]James Baldwin, "What Price Freedom?" in *The Cross of Redemption: Uncollected Writings*, ed. Randall Kenan (New York: Pantheon Books, 2010), 70.

[12]Valentino Lassiter, *Martin Luther King in the African American Preaching Tradition* (Cleveland: Pilgrim Press, 2001), 63.

Unquestionably, it was King's innate intelligence, ability to resonate with all classes of people, intense prayer life, and capacity to invigorate congregations with his riveting preaching that encouraged the citizens of Montgomery, Alabama, to select the young pastor of Dexter Avenue Baptist Church to lead the 1955 Montgomery bus boycott and ignite the Civil Rights Movement. As leader of the Civil Rights Movement, confronted with menacing violence fraught with terror and degradation, King adopted nonviolent resistance as his approach to achieving racial justice. King insisted that violent retaliation and the use of weaponry would make matters worse for Black people. Throughout his iterations of marches, protests, boycotts, physical attacks, and incarcerations, Martin Luther King's writings, speeches, sermons, and actions reinforced his nonviolent position. In accepting the Nobel Prize for Peace in 1964, King asserted, "I refuse to accept the view that mankind is so tragically bound to the starless midnight of racism and war that the bright daybreak of peace can never become a reality. . . . I believe that unarmed truth and unconditional love will have the last word."[13]

King was clear how he used his rhetorical agency. Although he was praised for his prophetic and persuasive rhetoric, he did not bow to the adulation because he knew that his cause was not about self-aggrandizement but about banishing racial segregation and racial injustice and bringing peace to an out-of-control violent nation. King embodied the proposition that rhetorical agency was other-centered, and he preached prophetic imagination until the very end, when less than twenty-four hours before an assassin's bullet claimed his life, he uttered these words:

> But I'm not concerned about that now. I just want to do God's will. And he's allowed me to go the mountain and I've looked over. And I've seen the promised land. I may not get there with you. But I want you to know tonight, that we as a people, will get to the promised land. I'm happy tonight. I'm not worried about anything. I'm not fearing any man. Mine eyes have seen the glory of the coming of the Lord.[14]

Martin Luther King Jr.'s concern for "the other," meaning the poor, the marginalized, and the disenfranchised, reverberates throughout his

---

[13]Martin Luther King Jr., Nobel Peace Prize Acceptance Speech, Oslo, Norway, December 10, 1964.

[14]Martin Luther King Jr., "The Mountaintop," sermon at Mason Temple Church of God in Christ, Memphis, TN, April 3, 1968.

sermons and speeches. In the following sermon excerpt, King makes a preferential option for and an irrefutable identification with the poor.

> I choose to identify with the underprivileged, I choose to identify with the poor, I choose to give my life for the hungry, I choose to give my life for those who have been left out of the sunlight of opportunity. . . . This is the way I'm going. If it means suffering a little bit, I'm going that way. If it means sacrificing, I'm going that way, because I heard a voice saying, "Do something for others."[15]

In the quote below, King argues that during "this period of social transition," meaning the ongoing violence, terror, and racism, he is not so concerned with those who malign him and the movement by spewing aspersions of racial hatred; he expects that. But rather, King employs his rhetorical agency to rail against those "so-called" good people who remain silent amid the insidious racism that Black people are forced to endure. King reminds America that its inactions will be not be forgotten; in fact, they will be recorded in history.

> History will have to record that the greatest tragedy of this period of social transition was not the strident clamor of the bad people, but the appalling silence of the good people.[16]

## Thea Bowman, FSPA

A self-described "old folks" child, Thea (her birth name was Bertha) Bowman was the only daughter born of the union of middle-aged parents: a physician father and an educator mother. Thea was a proud native of Canton, Mississippi. She attributes the Canton community, most especially the elders, for influencing and rearing her. In later life, the influence of the elders was evident in Thea's own rhetoric, as she frequently referred to the wisdom of the old folks. She would say, "Mrs. Ward said . . . or Mother Ricker taught me. . . ." At a very early age Thea was learning what would eventually become her hallmark—bringing faith alive through preaching, teaching, singing, and praising. Thea's father was a member of the United Methodist denomination, and her mother was an Episcopalian,

---

[15]Martin Luther King Jr., "The Good Samaritan," sermon at Ebenezer Baptist Church, Atlanta, August 28, 1966, quoted in David J. Garrow, *Bearing the Cross: Martin Luther King, Jr., and the Southern Christian Leadership Conference* (New York: Vintage, 1988), 524.

[16]Martin Luther King Jr., *Stride toward Freedom: The Montgomery Story* (New York: Harper and Row, 1958), 202.

and although Thea was christened in the Episcopal church, she attended churches of various denominations in her formative years. When she was nine years old, Thea through her own volition converted to Catholicism. She attended Holy Child Jesus Catholic school in Canton, and the sisters who taught her left an indelible mark on her. Thea would later reflect that it was not necessarily the teachings of the church or the liturgy that drew her to Catholicism; rather it was the personal witness of the priests, sisters, and laity at her parish that greatly influenced her conversion.[17] She saw their commitment to the poor and marginalized, their sense of community and earnest care for the greater community; these things made a deep impression on her. Thea witnessed "faith in action" on behalf of the oppressed poor by these devoted Catholic Christians. Her desire to be a witness for Jesus and to help those most in need were paramount in her decision at fifteen years old to enter the convent and begin her trajectory of becoming a Franciscan Sister of Perpetual Adoration.

It was apparent that Sister Thea would use her rhetorical agency in preaching, teaching, and singing to bring healing, intercultural awareness, and racial reconciliation to a troubled nation. From among the US Black Catholic priests and religious, Thea would emerge as an immanent prophetic voice for Black people, especially Black Catholics. Although her rhetorical gifts were certainly innate, Thea was educated in linguistics, literature, storytelling, and Black orality, drama, musicality, and vocal training. She wanted to be used by God, and that God did. God used Thea to go to places to bring healing, resolve conflicts, urge the apathetic, humble the arrogant, challenge the ignorant and intolerant, castigate the wicked, console the sorrowful, and encourage the downtrodden. Thea's words and songs brought life and joy to the multitudes.

Thea Bowman's rhetoric enthralled, but she also used her pronouncements to teach. Her most notable teaching oration was to the United States Conference of Catholic Bishops at their biannual meeting in June 1989 at Seton Hall University. She was invited to address the bishops on what it means to be Black and Catholic. Thea's mantra was "each one, teach one." She would often say, "If you know something, teach someone else." Thea used this address to the bishops as an opportunity to teach them something that perhaps they didn't know or at least needed to be reminded of: that Black Catholic lives matter. Essentially, she instructed and enlightened the bishops on African American history and spirituality. She challenged the bishops to continue to evangelize the African American community,

---

[17]Maurice J. Nutt, *Thea Bowman: Faithful and Free* (Collegeville: Liturgical Press, 2019), 19.

to promote inclusivity and full participation of Blacks within Church leadership, and to understand the necessity and value of Catholic schools in the African American community.[18] She asked the rhetorical question, "What does it mean to be Black and Catholic? It means that I come to my church fully functioning. That doesn't frighten you, does it?"[19] In the richness of the Black prophetic tradition, Thea, with self-determination, not asking permission to be acknowledged, fearlessly defined herself and her intentions before the bishops. If not frightening for a group of mostly white men, it surely must have made some feel uncomfortable. However, Thea's disarming candor and persuasive speech moved the bishops emotionally and spirituality. On November 14, 2018, at another meeting of the Catholic bishops of the United States, twenty-nine years after Thea's consequential address, the bishops celebrated the phenomenal prophetess and holy Black religious woman who stirred their hearts, unanimously approving the opening of her cause for canonization.

In the two following quotes from Thea Bowman, she unapologetically with bold rhetoric self-defines as well as offers a stirring indictment against the racism, sexism, paternalism, and hypocrisy that Black people experience from the Church they profess and love.

> I like being Black. I have friends who are white and brown and yellow and red—all the colors in between. I love being with my friends, and I love sharing with them, but I love being myself. And I thank God for making me my Black self.[20]
>
> Black people who are still victims within the church of paternalism, of a patronizing attitude, Black people who within the church have developed a mission mentality—they don't feel called, they don't feel responsible, they don't do anything. Let Father do it, let the sisters do it, let the friends and benefactors from outside do it. That's the mission mentality. And it kills us, and it kills our churches. And so, within the Church, how can we work together so that all of us have equal access to input, equal access to opportunity, equal access to participation? Go into a room and look around and see who's missing, and send some of your folks out to call them in so that the Church can be what she claims to be, truly Catholic.[21]

---

[18]Ibid., 111.

[19]Thea Bowman, "To Be Black and Catholic: Address to the US Catholic Bishops," *Origins* 19, no. 8 (July 6, 1989), 114–118.

[20]Thea Bowman, *Sr. Thea: Her Own Story* (DVD) (Florissant, MO: Oblate Media and Communication, 1990).

[21]Bowman, "To Be Black and Catholic," 114–118.

## Bryan N. Massingale

This Milwaukee-born Black Catholic moral theologian is unique in that there are very few Black Catholic moralists in the nation. Bryan Massingale is a "cradle Catholic." His father converted to Catholicism in the late 1940s, and his mother converted when they married. His home life was structured and faith-filled as his parents sought to provide him and his four siblings the best opportunities within their means. Besides his parents, Massingale's grandmother was very influential in his life and on his life decisions. A strong sense of morality pervaded the Massingale household; Bryan understood the consequences of not assuming personal responsibility and always sought to act justly. Bryan Massingale was thoroughly Catholic educated, attending Catholic grade school, high school, and university. Bryan was an extremely intelligent young man and excelled in all his academic endeavors. Early in his life he had aspirations to the Catholic priesthood and eventually entered the diocesan seminary.

Throughout his life Massingale has been completely aware of the pervasive sin of racism that festers in the church and society. His vocation as a priest of the Archdiocese of Milwaukee afforded him the opportunity to pursue graduate studies in moral theology. Bryan ultimately earned his sacred theology doctorate in moral theology from the Redemptorists' pontifical school of moral theology, the Academia Alphonsianum in Rome. He has taught with distinction at St. Francis Seminary and Marquette University in Milwaukee, the Institute for Black Catholic Studies at Xavier University of Louisiana in New Orleans, and he is currently the James and Nancy Buckman Professor of Theological and Social Ethics as well as the Senior Fellow in the Center for Ethics Education at Fordham University in New York. He is a past convener of the Black Catholic Theological Symposium, a former president of the Catholic Theological Society of America, and president-elect of the Society of Christian Ethics.

Massingale is uniquely tri-vocational: he is a priest (preacher), scholar (theologian), and activist. In the immortal words of the late Civil Rights icon and US Congressman, John Lewis, Massingale doesn't mind getting involved in some "good trouble." Although a majority of his time is spent lecturing in a classroom, he travels extensively giving lectures, offering consultations, doing research and writing, and providing pastoral ministry by presiding and preaching at churches locally and throughout the country. Commenting on his identity as a Catholic priest, Massingale notes, "There was just this deep-down sense that being a priest would enable me to help people but also be a force for justice, too."[22] This scholar-preacher-activist has quickly emerged as the preeminent voice advocating for racial justice in the Catholic Church. His seminal book, *Racial Justice and the Catholic Church* (Orbis Books, 2010), explores how Catholic social teaching has been used—and not used—to combat racism and promote reconciliation and justice. Be clear that Massingale's research on racial justice is not relegated to books and documents; no, he is an activist very much connected to current news reports and is in constant conversation with people who are devalued and marginalized by racism and homophobia. His writings and rhetorical agency reflect his immersion in the fray of the struggle for racial justice as well as the subjugation of the LGBTQ community. His current research projects explore the contribution of Black religious radicalism to Catholic theology; the notion of "cultural sin" and its challenge to Catholic theological ethics; and the intersections of race and sexuality in both social life and Catholicism.[23] Bryan Massingale's courageous voice is long overdue within Catholicism. His critique and challenge of some Church positions and teachings come from places of both love and pain: a genuine love for the Church of his baptism and priesthood and pain from the Church's racism long inflicted on Black and brown Catholics and the Church's perceived lack of understanding and full acceptance of LGBTQ Catholics.

The advent of the Black Lives Matter movement amid the inhumane, senseless, and unwarranted killings of Black bodies by some police officers has ignited global protests and demonstrations seeking the firing and arrest of those police officers for the crime of murder. While the ordinaries of a majority of US (arch)dioceses remained eerily silent about the matter, Massingale could not be silent. He was infuriated and used his rhetorical agency and prophetic witness to condemn the increasing murders of Black people as racist and immoral. The priest-scholar-activist denounced the unwarranted killings from the pulpit, by writing articles, giving interviews to television, radio, magazine, and newspaper outlets, offering lectures, and speaking at anti-racism webinars. Father Bryan Massingale, like the prophets of old, spoke fierce words that excoriated the evils of racism and flagrantly disparaged those who continue to perpetuate racism.

---

[22] Olga Segura, "Meet Father Bryan Massingale: A Black, Gay, Catholic Priest Fighting for an Inclusive Church: A Profile of a Progressive Leader in the Catholic Church Working for Racial and LGBTQ Justice," *The Revealer*, a review of religion and media, published by the Center for Religion and Media at New York University, June 3, 2020.

[23] Bryan N. Massingale, biographical profile on the Fordham University website (www.fordham.edu).

In this excerpt from *Racial Justice and the Catholic Church* Massingale discusses how white dominance is viewed as normative and that "others," meaning those who are non-white, must simply conform to that which is considered the standard. He emphatically submits that the catholicity of the Church is in question if only Western European cultural expressions are the standard and anything outside of that norm is tacitly deemed inferior or unacceptable—thus the Church isn't truly universal.

> Recall that I argued that the key component of Black culture is "the expectation of struggle," and that a core element of white culture is the presumption of dominance, that is, the presumption of being the norm or standard to which all "others" should conform. Now we can better understand the phrase "white church culture" and what Black Catholics mean when we say that the Catholic Church is a "white institution." It entails more than the obvious fact that a Western European culture has shaped the culture of the Catholic Church in the United States. What makes this a "white" church culture is deeper than the cultural roots of its liturgical music or rubrics. It is the presumption that these—and *only* these—particular cultural expressions are standard, normative, universal, and thus really "Catholic."[24]

As a critical African American Catholic thought-leader, in the following article published by the *National Catholic Reporter*, Massingale argues for an expanded understanding of the conditions of being considered "pro-life." He submits in the following excerpt that being authentically "pro-life" explicitly means holding sacred *all* human life even beyond the womb. Massingale reproves those who are advocates of racial intolerance and who claim to be unwaveringly pro-life.

> Be "unconditionally pro-life." These are the words of St. Pope John Paul II from his final pastoral visit to the United States. He summoned Catholics to "eradicate every form of racism" as part of their wholehearted and essential commitment to life.
>
> This has a very serious consequence: You cannot vote for or support a president who is blatantly racist, mocks people of color, separates Latino families and consigns brown children into concentration

---

[24]Bryan N. Massingale, *Racial Justice and the Catholic Church* (Maryknoll, NY: Orbis Books, 2010), 79.

camps, and still call yourself "pro-life." We need to face, finally and at long last, the uncomfortable yet real overlap between the so-called "pro-life" movement and the advocates of racial intolerance.

In the name of our commitment to life, we must challenge not only these social policies, but also the attitude that cloaks support for racism under the guise of being "pro-life." John Paul II declared that racism is a life issue. Ahmaud Arbery, Breonna Taylor, George Floyd and the many Black and brown victims of COVID 19 prove it. It is way past time for Catholics to become "unconditionally pro-life."[25]

Walter Brueggemann suggests that the task of rhetorical agency and prophetic ministry is not found solely in the process of nurturing and nourishing but in evoking a "consciousness and perception alternative" to the existing dominant culture that surrounds us.[26] I concur with Brueggemann's assessment of the function of rhetorical agency in light of the Black prophetic tradition. How could the African American community for centuries endure the physical and psychological abuse of white supremacy and remain "in their right mind" (sane)? For that matter, how do African Americans survive the resurgent, horrific, and overt racism today? I submit that the answers to these questions are one and the same. Certainly, African American ancestors had the assurance that God was with them through dangers seen and unseen, and yet I believe that the soothing prophetic alternative reality provided by African American preachers confirmed for them that they were much more than what white people thought about them or said about them. The preachers' words gave them an inner spiritual strength to overcome any obstacle that came their way. Their ability to resist and remain resilient was derived from the preacher's prophetic promise that "trouble don't last always."

---

[25]Bryan N. Massingale, "The Assumption of White Privilege and What We Can Do about It," *National Catholic Reporter* (Kansas City, MO), June 1, 2020.

[26]Walter Brueggemann, *The Prophetic Imagination* (Philadelphia: Fortress Press, 1978), 13.

# 7

# Toward An African American
# Catholic Theology of Preaching

What does it mean to preach specifically to the African American Catholic community? This is not a rhetorical question but one that deserves an answer. A community fraught with seemingly insurmountable challenges, suffering, and pain. And yet bolstered with fortitude, an uncommon faithfulness, and an unyielding sense of self-determination, Black Catholics have persevered and in most cases thrived. Like a pot of New Orleans gumbo, Catholicism in the United States has been well seasoned by the presence of Black Catholics: adding the richness of our culture in song and music, intellect and insights, devotion and dance, art and aesthetics, piety, prayer, and praise. The Black Catholic community has also enriched the church with the uniqueness of its preaching—a preaching that has evolved as an idiosyncratic African American Catholic theology of preaching. Thus, this chapter delineates the common ground between Black preaching and the directives promoted in the United States Catholic Bishops' document on preaching, *Fulfilled in Your Hearing*. The topics presented in pursuit of an African American Catholic theology of preaching include The Holy Spirit and Preaching, Preaching and Ecumenism, Preaching as Celebration, and Preaching for Liberation, which includes prophetic preaching, preaching on social issues, and anti-racism preaching.

Before exploring an *African American Catholic* theology or understanding of preaching, one must first ask if there is an "official" *Catholic* theology of preaching. Dominican theologian Mary Catherine Hilkert maintains that with the liturgical renewal of the 1950s and 1960s and the Second Vatican Council, the Catholic Church officially reclaimed a theology of revelation centered on the word of God. Hilkert asserts, "The Dogmatic Constitution on Revelation, *Dei Verbum*, urged a return to the word of God as the source of renewal for the entire church. While the Catholic Church has consistently moved toward a stronger emphasis on preaching and its importance, we still have no fully developed theology of preaching."[1]

Therefore, Catholics look to their theology of revelation prescribed by *Dei Verbum* to glean insights into a possible Catholic theology of proclamation. *Dei Verbum* describes an understanding of grace and a sacramental theology of revelation as "the mystery of God's self-communication in love which occurs in and through creation and human history—a mystery recognized and named in salvation history and culminating in Jesus Christ."[2]

Any Christian theology of preaching centers on Jesus Christ as Word of God. According to Hilkert, an appropriate starting point of any Catholic theology of preaching is the incarnation—the mystery of God's fullest word has been spoken in history, in a human being, in human experience. Rather than beginning with the power of God's word as something totally other and beyond our experience, Hilkert proposes we begin with the revelation of God which is to be discovered in the midst of—and depths of—what is human. She asks the question: "Can we reflect on the mystery of preaching as the naming of grace in human experience?"[3] Implicit in this quotation is the additional question as to whether we can announce God's path of liberation from the midst of the disgrace of our experience. As we move toward articulating characteristics of an African American Catholic theology of preaching, African Americans answer these questions with a resounding, "Yes, we must!"

## The Holy Spirit and Preaching

Holy Spirit–filled preaching is a requisite for many African American Catholics. In fact, the person who preaches the gospel makes a statement about the Holy Spirit just by standing at the ambo. Even before the first word is uttered, presuppositions and definitions from across the centuries speak volumes about the Spirit-led event to be experienced by the preacher and the congregation. According to Rev. Dr. James Forbes, "The preaching event itself—without reference to specific texts and themes—is a living, breathing, flesh-and-blood expression of the theology of the Holy Spirit."[4] In formulating an operative theology of proclamation, Forbes maintains:

---

[1]Mary Catherine Hilkert, OP, "Naming Grace: A Theology of Proclamation," *Worship* 60 (1986): 440.

[2]Pope Paul VI, *The Dogmatic Constitution on Divine Revelation [Dei Verbum]* (November 18, 1965), no. 6.

[3]Hillkert, 49.

[4]James Forbes, *The Holy Spirit and Preaching* (Nashville: Abingdon Press, 1989), 19.

The preaching event is an aspect of the broader work of the Spirit to nurture, empower, and guide the church in order that it may serve the kingdom of God in the power of the Spirit. It is a process in which the divine-human communication is activated and focused on the word of God and is led by a member of the community of faith [the preacher] who has been called, anointed, and appointed by the Holy Spirit to be an agent of divine communication. That person's authority is grounded in the self-revealing will of God as articulated and elaborated in the biblical witness. In addition, the preacher's authority is confirmed or ordained by the community of faith in response to the continuing counsel of the Holy Spirit.[5]

If preachers intend to preach the Gospel of Jesus Christ, who calls them to serve the kingdom in our time, they need all the power available to them. We live in a culture that has lost contact with the living spirit of Jesus. We need preaching that is more than delightful rhetoric. At the other end of the spectrum, mere ranting, raving, and excitement from some spirited preacher will also not suffice. The people of God need and want some sense of the Spirit accompanied by power sufficient to comfort and sustain them in the struggle of their Christian journeys.

Pope Paul VI, in his exhortation *On Evangelization in the Modern World*, emphasizes the important role of the Holy Spirit in Catholic preaching by maintaining that the Holy Spirit impels each individual, as evangelizer, to fervently proclaim the gospel. The Pontiff in his teaching was thoroughly convinced that without the Holy Spirit powerfully present in our preaching and Christian witness, Catholic evangelization would be ineffective. "Without the Holy Spirit the most convincing dialectic has no power over the heart of [human beings]."[6]

Additionally, *Fulfilled in Your Hearing* encourages Catholic preachers under the inspiration of the Holy Spirit to preach so as to lead the faithful to praise God. This document contends that preachers must first recognize the active presence of God in their own lives, as broken and shattered as they may be, and out of that brokenness affirm and witness to the congregation that it is still good to praise him and even give him thanks. There is a clear mandate from the Roman Catholic Church that urges Catholic preachers to be Spirit-filled preachers. Unfortunately, in many cases, the urgency of this message has not been received by Catholic preachers. Therefore, it is a fallacy that the Catholic Church does not promote Holy Spirit–filled preaching. It suffices to say that many preachers

---

[5]Ibid., 20.
[6]Pope Paul VI, *Evangelii Nuntiandi,* apostolic exhortation (December 8, 1975), no. 75.

refuse to receive the Church's message and thus the anointing.

Within the context of Black preaching the preacher is expected to be anointed by the power of the Holy Spirit before there is any attempt to preach the word. The preacher cannot preach without the Holy Spirit. Regardless of one's ability, strength, or study habits, the sermon or homily is ultimately a product of the power of the Holy Spirit, which enables the preacher to utter "what thus says the Lord." James Cone indicates that there can be no preaching unless the preacher is called by the Holy Spirit.

> In order to separate the preached Word from ordinary human discourse and thereby connect it with prophecy, the Black church emphasizes the role of the Spirit in preaching. No one is an authentic preacher in the Black church tradition until he or she is called by the Spirit.[7]

Cone is on target. Preaching in the Black preaching tradition is indeed dependent on the Holy Spirit. The challenge for preachers in the African American Catholic community is to free themselves to be used by the Holy Spirit and to cease trying to quench the Spirit. An African American Catholic theology of preaching requires Spirit-filled proclamation—a requirement that is certainly non-negotiable.

### Preaching and Ecumenism (Pastoral Considerations)

Ecumenism—promoting unity among the world's Christian denominations and religions—is a vital aspect in the formulation of an African American Catholic theology of preaching. Effective pastoral ministry is never done in a vacuum or in isolation. Many Black Catholics have relatives who are members of various Christian denominations as well as from the Muslim faith. Recall that Catholicism was late in its evangelization efforts among the Black community. Therefore, it is commonplace for African American Catholics to have relatives, both immediate and distant from various faith traditions. In my own family religious lineage, my mother was a devout Catholic and my father was a dutiful Baptist. In fact, my father's uncle was pastor of the "family church," New Star Missionary Baptist Church in St. Louis. Due to their firm religious differences, they were not married initially by a priest or minister but rather by a justice of the peace. My father agreed to have their four sons baptized into and practice the Catholic faith, and even to have their marriage convalidated,

---

[7]James H. Cone, *Speaking the Truth* (Grand Rapids, MI: William B. Eerdmans, 1986), 23.

but he himself remained a steadfast member of the Baptist faith.

In many instances, Black Catholics have to defend and justify their being Catholic. There remain many misconceptions about the Catholic faith among Protestants and other religions. Among the many misconceptions is the enduring notion that the Catholic Church is a "white religion" and that Black people have no place there. Fortunately, most Black Catholics have persevered while being assailed by those lacking knowledge of the polity and teachings of the Roman Catholic Church. Although ecumenism is about unity and cooperation with other Christians, in some cases, Black Catholics fervent in their faith have used these moments of opposition as teachable moments of opportunity to evangelize Protestants to join the Catholic Church. In many Black Catholic parishes those invited to enter the Rite of Christian Initiation of Adults (RCIA) are typically relatives and coworkers of Catholics faithfully attending a particular parish.

The Second Vatican Council sought to promote Christian unity and understanding among other Christian traditions and non-Christian religions through the promulgation of its decree on ecumenism. The framers of the ecumenism decree adduce the importance of finding common ground for the sake of unity by being open to the movement of the Holy Spirit in the process; they state:

> Today, in many parts of the world, under the influence of the grace of the Holy Spirit, many efforts are being made in prayer, word and action to attain that fullness of unity which Jesus Christ desires. The Sacred Council exhorts, therefore, all Catholic faithful to recognize the signs of the times and to take an active and intelligent part in the work of ecumenism.[8]

It is to this end that Pope Paul VI called the Church when he stated:

> As Catholics our best ecumenical efforts are directed both to removing the causes of separation that still remain, as well as to giving adequate expression to the communion which already exists among all Christians. We are sustained and encouraged in this task because so many of the most significant elements and endowments "that are Christ's gift to his Church are the common source of our strength.[9]

---

[8]Second Vatican Council, Decree on Ecumenism (*Unitatis Redintegratio*), November 21, 1964, no. 4.

[9]Pope Paul VI, Message to the World Council of Churches General Assembly at Nairobi, *Doing the Truth in Charity: Statements of Pope Paul VI, John Paul I, John Paul II, and the Secretariat for Promoting Christian Unity, 1964–1980* (New York: Paulist Press, 1982), 291.

Pope John Paul II echoed these same sentiments during a papal visit to the Black community in Harlem, New York: "I wish to greet in you the rich variety of your nation, where people of different ethnic origins and creeds can live, work, and prosper together in mutual respect."[10]

It is important to note that the work of ecumenism is not a "one-sided endeavor" but rather one inextricably linked by mutuality and respect. The Black church, aside from theological, doctrinal, and cultural differences, has Christ as the center of its mission, ministry, and message. In the 1960s the Black church sought ecumenical outreach among other Christian churches. However, their purposes, unlike those of Roman Catholicism, were not aimed at a reunion with the Catholic Church but rather simply dialogue and cooperation to achieve respectful equity with the Catholic Church and so together to banish injustices from society and the church. Mary R. Sawyer asserts in her book *Black Ecumenism: Implementing the Demands of Justice*:

> Contemporary Black ecumenical movements are in large part a product of the Black consciousness movement of the 1960s. Their agenda is empowerment and liberation. Their goal is participation as equals among equals in an ethnically pluralistic American society *and* a universal Christian Church comprised of culturally defined particularities. Their strategy is cooperative, interdenominational action involving the historic Black denominations, both Protestant and Catholic.[11]

Perhaps as a belated response to the Black ecumenical movement, the Black Catholic bishops in their 1984 pastoral letter said, "We wish to encourage our Black Catholics to deepen their awareness and understanding of the whole Black church, inasmuch as the majority of Black Christians in this country are separated from Catholic unity."[12] Although the Black Catholic bishops' statement is a noble gesture, I find that it falls short of authentic ecumenism. To a large extent Black Catholics are keenly aware of other Black Christians because of family relationships and attending their church services and events. Some of our Black Catholic gospel choirs participate in Black church gospel concerts; some Black Catholics attend Black Protestant prayer services; and still others attend social gatherings

---

[10]Pope John Paul II, "The Ideal of Liberty, a Moving Force," U.S.A.: *The Message of Justice, Peace, and Love* (Boston: Daughters of St. Paul, 1979), 96.

[11]Mary R. Sawyer, *Black Ecumenism: Implementing the Demands of Justice* (Valley Forge, PA: Trinity Press International, 1994), 63.

[12]*What We Have Seen and Heard: A Pastoral Letter on Evangelization From the Black Bishops of the United States* (Cincinnati: St. Anthony Messenger Press, 1984), 15–16.

at Black churches. Black Catholics should be encouraged to find ways to interact and engage with not only Black churches, but white Protestants and Jewish and Muslim communities. As a pastor, I actively sought ways to make these vital connections: be it working on neighborhood beautification projects, addressing and finding solutions to neighborhood gang violence, or opening a computer center to bridge the digital divide with Black Christian churches, working with a Jewish synagogue to provide academic tutoring for urban youth, or participating in anti-racism marches and peaceful protests with the Muslim community. Differences begin to dissipate, and commonalities are created with human interaction, discussion, and cooperation. However, ecumenical contact will never occur if it is not valued and deeply intentional.

Those called to preach and minister within the Black Catholic community must not simply tolerate those from other Christian faith traditions or non-Christian religions; rather, they must attain a respectful appreciation for who they are and their beliefs. Inevitably, at some point Black Catholic parishioners will expect their Catholic priest, religious sister, brother, or permanent deacon to visit a sick non-Catholic relative in the hospital, attend and perhaps preach and preside at a non-Catholic relative's wake or funeral. These are moments not only to be pastoral and compassionate but important times, spaces, and "openings" for evangelization within the Black community. I believe that Catholic preachers should always preach their very best, but most especially at funerals and weddings. That's when you have a captive audience within the African American community. Typically, there are unchurched people sitting in the pews for these occasions, and an inspiring homily might encourage them to inquire more about the Catholic Church. Furthermore, excellent preaching would quell their assumption that Catholic preaching is notoriously uninspiring.

Not long after I became a pastor of a parish in a predominantly African American neighborhood, an opportunity occurred that enabled me to be a witness of Jesus Christ and to demonstrate what it means to be actively ecumenical. One Sunday while celebrating Mass with the parishioners, just before distributing communion, our church lights began to flash off and on and we heard the sirens of fire trucks coming down the street. The president of the parish council approached me at the altar and whispered in my ear that the Baptist church across the street was on fire and was burning to the ground. I calmly announced the news to the parishioners, asked the deacon to distribute communion and lead the congregation in prayer for our Baptist neighbors while the parish council president and I would go and stand in support of the Baptist pastor with his distraught congregation facing this tragedy. I had a good relationship with the pastor, since I had worked with him on various community projects and had even preached at his church revival. While we stood there watching the church burn due to faulty electric wiring, I offered our parish gymnasium as a place for his congregation to worship as long as they wished to be there. The first Sunday that they worshipped at our gymnasium, our Catholic parishioners were there to welcome them and to serve them breakfast after their service and to fellowship with them. This is what ecumenism in action looks like—being one in the name of the One whom we all profess!

## Preaching as Celebration

In African American preaching, the preacher always presents a revelation. This revelation is always communicated with inspiration and celebration. It is a matter of glorifying God and involving the hearers.

The preacher is not just an impartial reporter of what happens between God and God's people in human history as recorded in scripture. The preacher is one who has also experienced what those in the stories experienced, and therefore the preacher is both recorder and witness of the story being related. The biblical story is the preacher's story, and it becomes the congregation's story as well. When deliverance, healing, hope, or miracles come to the biblical story, the same goodness is experienced by the preacher and the congregation alike. The chorus of the old hymn, "Blessed Assurance," serves as a good example of this: "This is *my* story. This is *my* song. Praising *my* Savior all the day long."

In gratefulness for these manifold blessings, African Americans tend to shout; they celebrate with the abiding conviction, "If I don't praise him, the rock's gonna cry out."[13] Celebration is an integral, authentic, and wholesome aspect of worship in African American preaching and worship. The point of celebration comes when the biblical story becomes the preacher's and the people's story. The preacher and the people are in a celebrative mode because the testimonies of the participants in the story also become their testimonies. In other words, there is a "blessed assurance" that what God did for the biblical characters of old, God is doing for them right now.

*Celebration* is a word commonly used by Roman Catholics in reference to the celebration of the Eucharist. Roman Catholics refer to the priest presiding at the eucharistic celebration as the celebrant. In many

---

[13]This is one line from the song, "Don't Want No Rocks," by Rev. Paul Jones (San Francisco, CA: PPMG-SoSouth Recording, 1993).

instances, however, the experience of Mass in many Catholic parishes has been anything but a celebration. Lifeless preaching has contributed to this valid criticism. Yet the aim of celebrating Eucharist is to remember and celebrate the salvation that Jesus offers through his paschal mystery. *Fulfilled in Your Hearing* contends that the "challenge to preachers is to reflect on human life with the aid of the Word of God and to show by their preaching, as by their lives, that in every place and at every time it is indeed right to praise and thank the Lord."[14]

African American sermons or homilies do not only end in celebration, but the whole preaching event itself is a celebration. So the meaning of celebration as climax must be reexamined. This meaning is often too limited. According to Henry Mitchell, "We in the African American tradition have cultural roots which demand that the sermon end in celebration."[15] It is true that climax might be that concluding portion of the sermon in which phrases and sentences are presented in ascending order of rhetorical forcefulness. However, this might or might not be the point of highest celebration of the preacher and audience.

I argue that the conclusion is not the only point of celebration in "good" traditional Black preaching. If celebration means ecstatic talking and hearing and involvement in the story, then in most Black sermons the celebration is interspersed throughout, with greater intensity toward the end. Olin P. Moyd states, "When the preacher engages in narration and storytelling with imagination and with celebration at several places throughout the proclamation, the preacher and the audience are drawn into an identification with the biblical characters in the story, and the historical event becomes an existential event. Thus, celebration is the natural response."[16]

If the sermon or homily is celebration, there is a substance in the proclamation that elicits celebration, and that substance is the kerygma, the Good News. An African American Catholic theology of preaching affirms celebration within the preaching event. African American sermons reflect Black people's lived experience of the Word. Through both Black sermons and Black preaching, the faithful are theologically informed; they are inspired; and they are empowered to "run on just a little while

---

[14]Bishops' Committee on Priestly Life and Ministry, National Conference of Catholic Bishops. *Fulfilled in Your Hearing: The Homily in the Sunday Assembly* (Washington, DC: United States Catholic Conference, 1982), 28.

[15]Henry H. Mitchell, *Celebration and Experience in Preaching* (Nashville: Abingdon Press, 1991), 12.

[16]Olin P. Moyd, *The Sacred Art: Preaching and Theology in the African American Tradition* (Valley Forge, PA: Judson Press, 1995), 109.

longer," knowing that by God's grace everything will be all right: this is something to celebrate.

## Preaching for Liberation

For liberation theologians, God intends to liberate the world from oppression. African American homiletics professor Carolyn Ann Knight defines oppression as "a form of sin in which a person or community exploits other persons or communities. Oppression is frequently systemic, that it results from patterns of thought, feeling, and behavior that are transpersonal."[17] The oppressive tendency is so deeply embedded in some social structures that oppressors do not even know that they are oppressors! Among the most common and deeply entrenched systems of oppression are racism, sexism, poverty, classism, homophobia, xenophobia, ageism, oppression of those living with physical or mental disabilities, and ecological abuse. More specific examples include the national health care debate, reform of welfare and other governmental services, the national debt and economy, the drug culture, abortion, the death penalty, human trafficking, mass incarceration and prison reform, police reform, climate change, attitudes and laws regarding sexuality and same-sex marriage. Religion, too, can be used to oppress. African Americans are victims not only of racism; they are victims of *all* of the aforementioned oppressions.

Liberation preachers, including those who preach in African American Catholic parishes, believe that God operates through the processes of history to free humankind and nature from oppression. Knight posits that "God aims for all people and all elements of the natural world to have their own integrity, secure living conditions, freedom, opportunities to relate with all created entities in love and justice. The best liberation preachers are aware that oppressors are oppressed by their oppressive ideas, feelings and actions."[18] Those preaching for liberation alert both oppressed and oppressor to God's present activity in using individuals and groups to move toward a world in which all live together in love, justice, dignity, and shared material resources.

Pope Paul VI expressed similar sentiments in regard to preaching and living the truth that truly liberates. He states, "The Gospel entrusted to us is also the word of truth. A truth that liberates and which alone gives

---

[17]Carolyn Ann Knight, "Preaching from the Perspective of Liberation Theology," in *Patterns of Preaching*, ed. Ronald J. Allen (St. Louis: Chalice Press, 1998), 223.

[18]Ibid.

peace of heart is what people are looking for when we proclaim the Good News to them."[19] In the same vein as Pope Paul VI, Pope John Paul II urged us to "defend with force the dignity and the rights of every [person] against the oppressions and vexations of the powerful. Set oneself to true reconciliation among [humanity] and Christians."[20]

The US bishops assert in *Fulfilled in Your Hearing* that faith leads to an active response and a transformation of one's life.

> A response can take on many forms. Sometimes it will be appropriate to call people to repentance for the way they have helped to spread the destructive powers of sin in the world. At other times the preacher will invite the congregation to devote themselves to some specific action as a way of sharing in the redemptive and creative word of God.[21]

## Preaching on Social Issues

Unfortunately, in most American Catholic parishes, preaching on social issues, especially racism, is either weak or nonexistent. A social issue is public. The issue affects communities and has social and communal consequences. Some preachers mention social issues, but few preachers give detailed attention to them. When a social issue is mentioned in a typical homily or sermon, it appears only as an illustration or a fleeting example. Even the statement in *Fulfilled in Your Hearing* concerning the need for Catholic preachers to address societal ills seems patronizing at best. In the context of liberation preaching as it is best promoted by our Protestant brothers and sisters, there is never a directive such as, "*Sometimes* it will be appropriate to call people to repentance for the way they helped to spread the destructive powers of sin in the world." Injustice in the world must *always and at all times* be condemned by the Christian preacher, Catholic or Protestant. Ronald Allen offers this insight of preaching on a social issue: "The preacher is called to help the congregation interpret social issues and a Christian response from the perspective of the gospel. The church seeks for every social world to conform to the gospel, that is, to manifest relationships that are loving and just."[22]

In addition to the emotion so important to the African American

---

[19]*Evangelii Nuntiandi*, no. 78.

[20]John Paul II, *Fear Not: Thoughts on Living in Today's World*, ed. Alexandria Hatcher (Kansas City, MO: Andrews McMeel, 1999), 73.

[21]*Fulfilled in Your Hearing*, 19.

[22]Ronald Allen, *Patterns for Preaching* (St. Louis: Chalice Press, 1998), 199.

preaching style, preachers in African American settings have a moral and theological responsibility to develop a sound hermeneutical approach to the gospel. This demand, while not exclusive to the African American community, is an expectation of the people because of their constant struggle with racial, economic, and political oppression. The preacher is compelled to say something that addresses the needs of the people—directing the message to their heads and hearts. This holistic message will teach Blacks how to live as Christians and how to relate their religion to freedom practices.

An argument for caring for the poor and the oppressed and bringing those social concerns to the attention of the greater community is firmly rooted in sacred scripture. From a biblical perspective, the Jewish people's religious consciousness grew out of the memory of the exodus from slavery in Egypt, when they believed that God intervened directly and overwhelmingly to liberate them as a chosen people. The Israelites did not liberate themselves from their bondage. They did not fight in a revolution to win their freedom. In the biblical account, God intervened in extraordinarily dramatic fashion to force Pharaoh to release them. Justice in the Bible is thus fundamentally a matter of preserving this relationship with God, manifested especially in how the poor are treated.[23]

Because humanity was made in the image and likeness of God, human beings are the only image of God that God allows and recognizes. Australian Redemptorist theologian and social justice advocate Bruce Duncan asserts, "But God expects us to recognize and reverence this image in each other, and so to treat each other with respect and concern. This message powerfully reinforces the central message about what living justly in society entails, especially care for those in distress or affliction."[24]

Likewise, Jesus was profoundly imbued with the sentiments of justice, righteousness, and liberation for the poor and oppressed in the Hebrew scriptures that he read and studied. Jesus saw himself as the embodiment of the hopes of the Jewish people and the promises of the One he called Father. The evangelist Luke in his gospel saw the social implications of Jesus's message as a vital component to the ministry of Jesus. In Jesus's "inaugural sermon," conveying his mission and ministry, he emphasized that because the Spirit of the Lord was upon him, he was anointed to bring good news to the poor, release to captives, sight to the blind, freedom to those in the bondage of oppression, proclaim a year of favor, of jubilee from the Lord (cf. Luke 4:18–19). William J. Barber II asserts, "But eventually they [killed] Jesus because he preached the Kingdom of

---

[23]Bruce Duncan, *Social Justice: Fuller Life in a Fairer World* (Mulgrave, Victoria, Australia: Garratt, 2012), 7.
[24]Ibid., 10.

love, care for the sick, the stranger, and the imprisoned over against the world's principles of greed, hate, division, and injustice. Jesus was killed because his preaching set him against the empire of his day."[25]

Preaching the tenets of social concerns and social justice is not foreign to Catholic preaching. A precedent has been set because of Catholic social teaching. Duncan explains:

> Social justice as a term began to be used in the late 19th century and was adopted by Pope Pius XI in the 1920s as a more accurate way to speak of what St. Thomas Aquinas in the 13th century had termed "general" or "legal" justice. Social justice is the virtue that directs all our actions to the common good, and covers the whole economy, including production and distribution, as well as the public institutions of society.[26]

Indubitably, the nucleus of Catholic social teaching is a preferential option for the poor, meaning that those who are least advantaged, oppressed, and suffering the most have an important and rightful claim on the church. Catholic preachers thus have an inherent obligation to preach against powers, policies, and practices that harm the Body of Christ. Pope Francis has warned church members from becoming "single-issue Catholics" at the expense of negating other major social concerns. Although opposition to abortion is an irrefutably distinctive aspect of the Catholic faith, it should not be used to supersede the plethora of other social justice issues. Critiquing those for whom "the only thing that counts is one particular ethical issue or cause that they themselves defend,"[27] Pope Francis wrote:

> Our [defense] of the innocent unborn, for example, needs to be clear, firm and passionate, for at stake is the dignity of a human life, which is always sacred and demands love for each person, regardless of his or her stage of development. Equally sacred, however, are the lives of the poor, those already born, the destitute, the abandoned and the underprivileged, the vulnerable infirm and elderly exposed to covert euthanasia, the victims of human trafficking, new forms of slavery, and every form of rejection.[28]

---

[25]William J. Barber II, "Foreword: The Terrible Joy of Dangerous Preaching," in *How to Preach a Dangerous Sermon*, by Frank A. Thomas (Nashville: Abingdon Press, 2018), foreword, xiii.

[26]Duncan, *Social Justice*, 51.

[27]Pope Francis, *Gaudete et Exsultate (Be Glad and Rejoice), On the Call to Holiness in Today's World,* apostolic exhortation (March 19, 2018), no. 101.

[28]Ibid.

To preach on a social issue is assuredly risky, even dangerous, but preaching the truth of the gospel is a dangerous proposition. If one accepts the call to the preaching ministry in order to be liked, that person has chosen the wrong profession. One preaches not for adulation but out of an unwavering conviction that the truth will set both the preacher and the congregation free. Frank Thomas argues:

> Preach the moral base of issues, though you will be accused of preaching politics, you will in fact be preaching dangerous sermons. Preaching healthcare for all, at least in some communities, is a dangerous sermon. Preaching about the care and concern of God's green earth is a dangerous sermon. Preaching about white supremacy and white privilege is a dangerous sermon. This is not to suggest that every sermon that is preached is to be a dangerous sermon, but at least some of the sermons one preaches should be dangerous.[29]

## Practice What You Preach:
## Preaching and Living Racial Justice in the Catholic Church

Those who sit in the pews need to hear a word of power and spirit— a word of liberation. With the help of the preacher, Blacks are able to celebrate despite the reality of oppression and injustice because they believe that God is faithful and just. Preaching without celebration is de facto a denial of the good news in any culture. The preacher celebrates and encourages others to celebrate; however, the preaching ministry must also include liberation. Without liberation, there can be no authentic celebration. And authentic celebration has been far from the minds and hearts of church-going African Americans amid the increasingly overt and pervasive anti-Black racial animus in the United States. Admittedly, racism was mentioned among the many societal ills of the nation, yet it remains conspicuous as a multiheaded hydra—a persistent problem that must be continually addressed.

There is a legitimate perception by some, and an irrefragable reality for most Black people, that there is an all-out racial assault on African American communities and other communities of color. Seemingly permission has been granted for vitriolic insults, racist rancor, and malicious killings of Black and brown bodies. As the world contended with a global COVID-19 pandemic, there was also an uptick in Asian hate crimes and

---

[29]Thomas, *How to Preach a Dangerous Sermon*, 90.

killings. Asians were scapegoated as the cause of the coronavirus. People of color, most especially in the United States, have been made to feel as "other"—meaning non-white, non-American, and perceived as inferior. Bryan Massingale submits, "We know how our culture frames whiteness and folks of color. We know how race works in America. The fundamental assumption behind all the others is that white people matter, or should matter, more than people of color. Certainly, more than Black people. That Black lives don't matter, or at least not as much as white lives."[30] He further posits, "A key component of Black culture is 'the expectation to struggle,' and that a core element of white culture is the presumption of dominance, that is, the presumption of being the norm or standard to which all 'others' should conform."[31] While racism and racist behavior is ever-existent, it is evermore blatantly insidious. In his book *Black Suffering: Silent Pain, Hidden Hope*, James Henry Harris confronts the pervasiveness of anti-Blackness and "otherness" in America and beyond; he argues:

> The structural inequalities in society due to injustices and racial discrimination toward Blacks and minorities are seen in the disproportionate numbers of Black folk dying from chronic diseases, including coronavirus, in cities like New York, Chicago, Detroit, and New Orleans. The problem is that the fact of this reality doesn't seem to ever change regardless of who is in the White House, Congress, or the Governors' mansion. It appears that governments and businesses tend to be unconcerned about the blatant presence of racism in every corner of the world. Black suffering is seen every day and in every place where the sun seems to shine, where the rain falls, and wherever the wind blows. And, yet we act as if it does not exist.[32]

Although the dominant white culture may want to "act as if racism doesn't exist" in America, people of color do not have the luxury or privilege to live in such a "dream world" because they suffer the pain of hatred and modern-day lynching—lynching not always by hanging from a tree but when driving, walking, jogging, selling single cigarettes, coming out of a convenience store, attending Bible study, on a playground playing with a toy gun, sitting in the back seat of a car listening to music, standing

---

[30]Bryan N. Massingale, "The Assumptions of White Privilege and What We Can Do about It," *National Catholic Reporter* (Kansas City, MO), June 1, 2020.

[31]Bryan N. Massingale, *Racial Justice and the Catholic Church* (Maryknoll, NY: Orbis Books, 2010), 79.

[32]James Henry Harris, *Black Suffering: Silent Pain, Hidden Hope* (Minneapolis: Fortress Press, 2020), 5.

in a garage, standing in a backyard, at home playing video games with a nephew, at home eating a bowl of ice cream, or at home in bed asleep. Beautiful Black people—all senselessly killed.

If we have ears to hear and hearts to hold, there are desperate cries reverberating from the streets of cities large and small throughout the world. These global cries of anguish, anger, and agony are from the oppressed and those who stand in solidarity with those who suffer injustice and inequality. In 2020, literally the world watched the excruciating smartphone video of a forty-six-year-old African American man apprehended by four Minneapolis police officers, handcuffed face down on the ground as one of the police officers, Derek Chauvin, relentlessly pressed his knee into his neck for nine minutes and twenty-nine seconds. The man, George Floyd, in anguish cried out "Please, I can't breathe" twenty-seven times to no avail and became unconscious and died of asphyxiation. Moments after George Floyd's murder protests erupted globally. The protesters were multiracial and intergenerational, indicating that they were united in their quest for justice and racial harmony. An incalculable number of unwarranted killings of Black people have occurred at the hands of those sworn to protect and serve our communities. Pope Francis expressed concern for this murder, saying: "I have witnessed with great concern the disturbing social unrest in your nation in these past days, following the tragic death of Mr. George Floyd," he said. "We cannot tolerate or turn a blind eye to racism and exclusion in any form and yet claim to defend the sacredness of every human life."[33] Pope Francis added that he joins the Church in Saint Paul and Minneapolis, and throughout the entire United States, "in praying for the repose of the soul of George Floyd and of all those others who have lost their lives as a result of the sin of racism."[34] Perhaps Pope Francis from afar understands better than some in this country, the anger and frustration of sacred human *Black lives* being so violently lost. Black families having to express public grief to have their Black humanity acknowledged—and yet racial injustice has a way of stealing Black folks' right to eulogy and to respectfully mourn. Justice like breath ought always be recognized as a human right. It should be understood why seemingly voiceless and unheard people protest in the streets crying out and saying the names of Trayvon Martin, Rekia Boyd, Tamir Rice, Atatiana Jefferson, Michael Brown, Eric Garner, Tyisha Miller, Rayshard Brooks, Sandra Bland, Alton Sterling, Ahmaud Arbery, Breonna Taylor,

---

[33]Pope Francis, "Pope Francis: No Tolerance for Racism, But without Violence," https://www.vaticannews.va/en/pope/news/2020-06/pope-francis-usa-george-floyd-protests-no-racism-violence.html.

[34]Ibid.

Philando Castile, George Floyd, Deborah Danner, Daunte Wright, and . . . the next name . . . when will it end?

When the grief and pain of Black suffering becomes so entrenched and there are no words left to utter, thankfully Dr. Ernest L. Gibson, III, associate professor of English and co-director of Africana studies at Auburn University, provides the words that must be spoken:

> America's greatest reckoning has always been, and will continue to be, its relationship to Blackness. This country's struggle, or, more precisely, its unwillingness to resolve, make amends, or atone for its history of and contemporary commitment to antiBlack violence is rooted in the very core of its national identity. The great American irony lies in recognizing how every morsel of its beauty is born out of the residue of its ugliness, every freedom stolen by means of oppressing others. When we understand that America's sense of self is tethered to a perpetual violence towards Black folks, we will learn that the type of justice and change and transformation we seek requires for America to let go of herself. While such "a-letting-go-of" is an act of vulnerability, it is also an act of surrender and sacrifice. I am not convinced that America has learned to be that unselfish; I am not convinced America thinks such a reckoning worthwhile.[35]

Besides contending with the debilitating 2020–2021 coronavirus pandemic, the world was also faced with the enduring and debilitating plight of racism. Beyond the courageous statements condemning racism and the promise of corrective actions, people are yearning for a moral compass, a way forward by which their lives and actions are informed by their faith. For African Americans, faith and racial justice have long intersected—the church has been a place to pray, find comfort, receive a message of hope, to discuss and strategize about political and civic actions. This is not the case for predominantly white congregations. The litany of excuses for avoiding sermons about the sin of racism includes not wanting people to feel uncomfortable, racism is a politically charged topic, and people will leave the church or worse yet withhold their money from the collection baskets. Yet there is a word from God.

God's word is replete with scriptural texts that castigate oppression, hatred, and malfeasance. Otis Moss III, pastor of Chicago's Trinity United

---

[35]Ernest L. Gibson, III, Associate Professor and Co-Director of Africana Studies at Auburn University. This quote was posted on Dr. Gibson's personal Facebook page in November 2020. Quote used with permission.

Church of Christ, in his book *Blue Note Preaching in a Post-Soul World: Finding Hope in an Age of Despair*, brilliantly equates in sermonic form Black suffering with the suffering of Christ. He preaches,

> Why does he understand my predicament? Jesus lived a life as a colonized person and as a minority in a community that was under siege by an occupying army. Jesus understands poverty created by an empire, Jesus knows about racial profiling, Jesus understands mass incarceration, Jesus is frustrated with the traditional church, Jesus experiences state-sponsored torture, knows what it's like to have a public defender who lacks competency, was executed for a crime that he did not commit and understands character assassination in the media before and after his death. Jesus even knows what it is like to be stopped and frisked. Jesus is acquainted with patriarchy, since not a single brother would listen to any of the sisters when they announced, "Guess what ya'll, the tomb is empty!" Jesus knows all about our troubles. . . . Jesus wrestles with tragedy but does not fall into despair.[36]

Note the modern-day parallels that Moss makes with contemporary Black suffering and the brutal treatment of the biblical and historical Christ. Yes, indeed, Jesus knows all about Black folks' troubles.

When preaching against racism or any other oppression that hinders the Body of Christ, the Christian preacher is called to shepherd the congregation to a place of contrition, conversion, and reconciliation. White preachers and white congregations must repent of *their* sin. Do not have a Black priest or minister come to a white congregation and preach on the sin of racism. What sense does it make to have the victim of racism come to provide solutions to racism in America? I believe it is the white preacher's responsibility to muster the temerity to convey a message that not only refutes racist behavior and structures but moves the congregation to sincere contrition. People are not born racists; it is a learned behavior. One sermon indicting racism is inadequate; perhaps a preaching series is more beneficial. Once racist behavior is acknowledged and remorse expressed, preachers must invite their congregations to personal conversion, to change and make amends for their attitudes and actions. It is advantageous for preachers to admit in their sermons their own complicity in racism and their need for ongoing recovery; then congregations can come

---

[36]Otis Moss III, *Blue Note Preaching in a Post-Soul World: Finding Hope in an Age of Despair* (Louisville: Westminster John Knox, 2015), 19.

to a point of authentic reconciliation—healing with and commitment to oppressed people.[37]

Kenyatta Gilbert understands that which constitutes Black prophetic preaching as being a biblically informed, contextually shaped mode of discourse that offers clear and crucial indicators. In essence Black preaching:

(1) unmasks systemic evils and deceptive human practices by means of moral suasion and subversive rhetoric; (2) remains interminably hopeful when confronted with human tragedy and communal despair; (3) connects the speech-act with just actions as concrete praxis to help people freely participate in naming their reality; and (4) carries an impulse for beauty in its use of language and culture.[38]

This schema that Gilbert develops provides the criteria that enable the preacher to name the injustice that is present locally, nationally, and globally as well as to name what justice should be. It is vitally important that the preacher who wishes to preach prophetically not only consider but intentionally unpack and incorporate these salient directives into his or her preaching.

As the senseless killings of Black and brown bodies by law enforcement officers continue to happen, there is something else that occurs, like it or not. Once again is heard that incessant and clarion declaration: Black Lives Matter. Why does this mantra infuriate some in the dominant culture? Is it not a prerogative of any ethnic group to affirm its right to exist and not be killed? When people rebuff the purpose of the Black Lives Matter movement by insisting, "all lives matters," they not only miss the point that all lives are not at risk but also further diminish the realities of racism and oppression in our country. The Black Lives Matter Movement challenges traditional norms of social movements. It is decentralized and creative: it has no one single leader; it is innovative with new media; it has modernized civil disobedience; and it maintains political and social pressure in the streets and at the policy table simultaneously. The Black Lives Matter Movement is a movement that shows no signs of fading.

The United States Catholic bishops have directly addressed the sin of racism in varying degrees by publishing four pastoral letters within the past sixty years from 1958 to 2018. In the document "Discrimination and

---

[37]Maurice J. Nutt, "Preaching in a Time of Crisis," *Preacher Magazine* (College of Preachers of the United Kingdom, London, England), August 2020.

[38]Kenyatta R. Gilbert, *A Pursued Justice: Black Preaching from the Great Migration to Civil Rights* (Waco, TX: Baylor University Press, 2016), 6.

the Christian Conscience" (1958), the bishops expressed their concern that the "transcendent moral issues" involved in seeking racial justice and equality had been obscured. They noted this was a multifaceted problem that had been analyzed from the disciplines of law, history, economics, and sociology. The bishops declared the time has come to cut through the maze of less essential issues and to come to the heart of the problem— meaning that the race question is both a moral and religious question.[39] Notably the bishops issued this statement years after Brown v. Board of Education (1954), the brutal killing of Emmett Till in Money, Mississippi (1955), and the Montgomery Bus Boycott (1955); their tardiness speaks of their reluctance to address racism in America during the Civil Rights era. A decade later the bishops issued another statement on race titled "The National Race Crisis" (1968). Massingale observes that there were three contributing factors to the promulgation of this pastoral letter: the racially motivated rioting and civil disobedience in major urban cities across the nation, the release of the Kerner report outlining the devastating and volatile nature of the country's racial problem, and perhaps the most obvious, the assassination of Martin Luther King Jr. in Memphis on April 4, 1968. His death opened the possibility that more militant "Black Power" advocates would seize the leadership of the Civil Rights Movement.[40] "Racism is an evil which endures in our society and in our church. Despite apparent advances and even significant changes in the last two decades, the reality of racism remains."[41] These sobering, yet realistic, opening words of the US Catholic bishops' pastoral letter *Brothers and Sisters to Us* (1979) asserts that not enough has been done by society and the church to quell racism. In my estimation, *Brothers and Sisters to Us* is the strongest condemnation of racism by the bishops. Although the mandates within this document are both veracious and courageous, the title given to this pastoral letter is problematic. The title holds the understanding of people of color by many in the Catholic Church in the United States, especially by its largely white leadership (presumably the "us" of the title). Such language implies that people of color are the "other," effectively outside the community, which is understood to be, as a rule, white. Perhaps a more suitable title would have "Brothers and Sisters to One Another." However, of the many significant attributes of the

---

[39]Massingale, *Racial Justice and the Catholic Church*, 52.

[40]Ibid., 56–57.

[41]United States Conference of Catholic Bishops (USCCB), *Brothers and Sisters to Us: US Bishops' Pastoral Letter on Racism in Our Day* (Washington, DC: National Conference of Catholic Bishops, 1979), 1.

document, I like that it forthrightly names racism as a sin that destroys the Body of Christ; it names the church as complicit in the sin of racism; and it provides salient recommendations for action on all ecclesial levels from the parish to the pastoral center.[42]

However, this poignant pastoral letter was never fully publicized, preached, or put into practice. In the wake of the unrelenting murders of Black and brown people by police, recurrent instances of police brutality, the advent of the Black Lives Matter movement, the sustained protests of Americans of all ethnicities, the chaotic and irresponsible rhetoric of the US president, after individual prelates had made stirring statements condemning racism and some even attending protests, and after Pope Francis weighed in on the social unrest and racism in America, in November 2018 the US Catholic bishops issued the document *Open Wide Our Hearts: The Enduring Call to Love—A Pastoral Letter against Racism*. To be fair on the timing of this pastoral letter, it went through several drafts and iterations by the committee. As a whole *Open Wide Our Hearts* is comprehensive in condemning racism and naming it as sin, but there are more than a few deficiencies that must be acknowledged. Systematic theologian Father Daniel P. Horan, OFM, in his column for the *National Catholic Reporter* thoroughly analyzed the pastoral letter and in part made the following observations:

> It is striking that the word "sin" appears at least 14 times in the document and "racism" more than 50, but the terms "privilege" or "supremacy" are never mentioned. When "white" appears in the body of the text, it is only in reference to historical eras long gone—those "white European immigrants" who arrived to find Native Americans, a white priest who disparaged Fr. Augustus Tolton in the 19th century, white parishioners who once upon a time received communion ahead of Black Catholics in segregated parishes of yesteryear. While the document states "some have called" racism in the United States "our country's original sin," it nevertheless fails to name the sinner. Whether intended or not, this document does not challenge white Catholics to consider their role in a systemically racist society and church, it lets whites too easily off the hook by failing to name the other side of the coin of racist oppression: white privilege.
>
> The specter that haunts the new document is the unacknowledged reality that racism is a white problem and that while systemic racism does affect everybody, it benefits white folk to the disadvantage of

---

[42]Ibid., 66.

people of color. Most people know that overt racial oppression and discrete racist acts are wrong. Another pastoral document to reiterate this point is not needed. Instead, what is needed—but wasn't delivered—is a strong statement with a clear message exhorting those in the position of social and cultural dominance that they must change if there is any hope of a different future.[43]

I concur with Horan's assessment, but I would add that while the pastoral letter issued mandates and firm recommendations, and even established an ad hoc committee against racism that promoted listening sessions, study guides, encounters, interactions, and dialogues among various ethnic groups in the hope of individual, societal, and ecclesial conversion and transformation regarding racist actions and racism as a whole, yet there was no accountability, evaluation, or monitoring provided in the document. If people and structures are not held accountable for their racist malfeasance, attitudes, behaviors, practices, and people, and there are no consequences for this amoral behavior, institutions and structures are not likely to change, and *Open Wide Our Hearts* will be the racism pastoral letter *de jour* until the US bishops issue the next one. If the Catholic Church put forth vigor toward mandatory and rigorous ongoing training, accountability, monitoring, and evaluation of racism and racist practices by its clergy, religious, personnel, and parishioners, perhaps we would witness real transformation. I commend bishops that in some instances suspended priests from the ministry who were guilty of malicious racist comments or actions.

The US Catholic bishops in *Open Wide Our Hearts* committed themselves and priests and deacons to preach against racism. The bishops state, "We commit to preach with regularity homilies directed to the issue of racism and its impact on our homes, families, and neighborhoods, particularly on certain feast days and national holidays. We direct our priests and deacons to do the same."[44] Prior to the publication of the 2018 pastoral letter on racism, Archbishop Robert Carlson directed all priests and deacons of the St. Louis Archdiocese to preach an unprecedented message condemning the sin of racism on the first Sunday of Lent in 2018 when 500,000 Catholics would hear this message as they began their Lenten

---

[43]Daniel P. Horan, OFM, "The Bishops' Letter Fails to Recognize That Racism Is a White Problem," *National Catholic Reporter* (Kansas City, MO), February 20, 2019, https://www.ncronline.org/news/opinion/faith-seeking-understanding/bishops-letter-fails-recognize-racism-white-problem.

[44]United States Conference of Catholic Bishops, *Open Wide Our Hearts: The Enduring Call to Love—A Pastoral Letter against Racism*, November 2018, https://www.usccb.org/issues-and-action/human-life-and-dignity/racism/upload/open-wide-our-hearts.pdf.

observances. As a follow-up to the archbishop's requests, some priests of the archdiocese shared their anti-racism message with the archdiocesan newspaper. Here is a sampling of the messages of three white priests:

> Racism is contrary to our faith. We all know that God created each and every human being with an inviolable dignity, and that racism is a sin because it attacks that dignity.
>
> Most people who hear the word "racism," think of extreme examples such as the Ku Klux Klan or Neo-Nazis. But there are subtler forms of racism.
>
> Confronting racism starts within. Racism comes out in many different ways, some more explicit, some more covert. It shows itself in comments made about people of different races or about other countries and nationalities. It shows itself in the many ways that we treat people differently because of their race. While it is uncomfortable to admit having subconscious racist thoughts, when we are uncomfortable, we can grow. When we allow the Holy Spirit to make us uncomfortable, He can do amazing things in our lives.[45]
>
> —Father William Dotson

> Fear lives among us for many reasons, including changing demographics and shifting populations, racial profiling, overt xenophobia and injustices, including in our laws and in the workplace, for example.
>
> "We must repent, by naming our fears and renouncing them in Jesus' name." He also called on others "to renounce the obstacles presented within ourselves and the Church that keep us from proclaiming a kingdom of justice and brotherhood.[46]
>
> —Father John O'Brien

> Being pastor of a mostly African American community in north St. Louis broadened my vision and opened my heart more, helping me understand the community more and some of their pains and sorrows as well as their gifts.
>
> Black Catholics at one time had to sit in the back of church and receive Communion last. He cited a priest in the Diocese of Wichita, Kan., who wasn't allowed to become a priest in the St. Louis Arch-

---

[45] Joseph Kenny, "Priests, Deacons Share Varied Perspectives about the Sin of Racism at Masses across the Archdiocese," *St. Louis Review* (St. Louis, MO), March 5–11, 2018, https://www.archstl.org/priests-deacons-share-varied-perspectives-about-the-sin-of-racism-at-masses-across-the-archdiocese-2268.

[46] Ibid.

diocese because at the time Cardinal Joseph Glennon didn't allow African Americans to be ordained here. 'He had to shop around for another diocese.'

Instead of debating whether or not someone is racist, Father Scheble prefers to ask people to just open their hearts more to others.[47]

—Father Carl Scheble

Coincidentally and perhaps providentially, the St. Louis Archdiocese was also the locus of a historical, prophetic, and bold summons by Pope John Paul II during his January 1999 pastoral visit to the United States. In his homily[48] challenging Catholics to be "unconditionally pro-life," the pontiff also declared:

> As the new millennium approaches, there remains another great challenge facing this community . . . [and] the whole country: *to put an end to every form of racism, a plague which . . . [is] one of the most persistent and destructive evils of the nation.*[49]

This historic event where a pope came to the United States and publicly denounced the sin of racism is marked in *Racial Justice and the Catholic Church*, in which author Bryan Massingale notes the adverse and dismissive comments by the Catholic faithful and news pundits regarding the pope's unsettling mention of racism in his homily. Massingale observes:

> However, the pontiff's prophetic call was not universally embraced by the Catholic faithful. Indeed, a major Catholic commentator speaking on EWTN, the Catholic cable network program, immediately after the pope's [homily], lauded John Paul's uncompromising stances concerning the death penalty and euthanasia but noted that the pope's "curious remarks about racism" demonstrated "how ill-

---

[47]Ibid.

[48]Prior to the papal visit to St. Louis, I served as pastor of St. Alphonsus Liguori "Rock" Catholic Church, a predominantly African American Redemptorist parish. I also served as the priest adviser to the St. Charles Lwanga Center, a center for African American Catholic evangelization. I was asked by the staff and board of directors, including Jane Brown, Gloria Green, Norman Williams, Corliss Cox, Barbara Hancock, and Leon Henderson, to attend a meeting in the fall of 1998 where I was asked to go speak with Archbishop Justin Regali and to implore him to have Pope John Paul II address the sin of racism that was a festering cancer within St. Louis and its region during his papal visit. Although the archbishop made no guarantee to have the Holy Father mention the racism that plagued St. Louis, I was very pleased when he did so in his homily.

[49]Pope John Paull II, "Homily in the Trans World Dome," *Origins* 28 (February 11, 1999), 601; emphasis added.

served the Holy Father is by his advisors, since racism is no longer a pressing social issue in the United States."

This moment is important for two reasons. First, this particular cable network (EWTN) is the self-styled "media presence" of the U.S. Catholic Church. That such statements could be aired on a network renowned for its orthodoxy, and that they were not officially repudiated or challenged, suggests that standing against racism is not a major mark of Catholic identity or orthodoxy. Second, this event illustrates a recurring dynamic in the U.S. Catholic engagement with racism, namely, that the church of Rome has been more vigilant, solicitous, concerned, and forthright regarding racial injustice and the plight of racial minorities in the United States than have U.S. Catholics and their leaders. Rome has shown a willingness to confront racial inequality in a way that the U.S. church has yet to muster.[50]

Acknowledging that many members of the Catholic hierarchy have made profound statements rebuking racism, racist comments and actions, providing illustrations of how white priests have homiletically decried racism during the Sunday liturgy, and even describing how a pope stunned a local city by exposing its and the country's sin of racism, I now turn to how African American preachers revile racism in their preaching. I chose to survey three African American men and one African American woman from the predominantly white Catholic and Episcopalian denominations because their homilies and addresses are contextualized from both a Black and religious perspective from their respective faith traditions. These excerpts are coming from preachers who experience racism and other forms of discrimination firsthand from "society and sanctuary." Pay close attention to how the excerpts from their sacred rhetoric come from places that are direct, honest, uncompromising, and unapologetic—places of suffering and pain, and yet places of hope and promise. These plain truth-telling homilies call their listeners to a metanoia, a real conversion of lives and to solidarity:

The gospel is good news because it radically calls into question a world built without the recognition of the God whose inherent nature is justice and whose intrinsic nature does not value things that are contrary to God's will as revealed in the life and ministry of Jesus, who said that love of God and love of neighbor were the

---

[50]Massingale, *Racial Justice and the Catholic Church* (Maryknoll, NY: Orbis Books, 2010), 46–47.

two commandments on which hung the Law and the Prophets. When one believes in and proclaims this message, confrontation with principalities and powers of this world is unavoidable. A gospel that bothers no one and questions nothing is no longer the gospel.[51]

—Homily "Following Jesus while Black,"
Rev. Vincent Powell Harris

The warring soul of this nation is most recently manifested by the fact that though we have boldly declared that all are created equal and endowed with the inalienable rights of "life, liberty and the pursuit of happiness," we elected a "Make America Great Again" vision defined by a racially chauvinistic agenda and inhumane xenophobic policies, and one that also traffics in toxic misogynistic and LGBTQ-phobic realities. There is no getting around it: we are a nation with a warring soul.

Such a soul is intrinsic to our country's very identity. Thus, throughout our nation's history, we have been challenged by the reality of two unreconciled strivings, two warring ideas. Are we going to be a slave nation or a free nation? Are we going to be a Jim and Jane Crow nation or a just and equal nation? Are we going to be a xenophobic and intolerant nation or a multiracial, multiethnic, welcoming nation? Until we as a nation—as a people—make a decision, we will continually find ourselves in warring soul times of chaos and crisis.[52]

—Homily "The Work Our Soul Must Do,"
Rev. Dr. Kelly Brown Douglas

We have a responsibility as faith communities to lead the way to God. Therefore, we must TELL THE TRUTH—REPENTANT TRUTH. Not just *mea culpa, mea culpa, mea maxima culpa,* but the truth that then compels us to action, to do something different. Truth that leads to metanoia, truth that protects human dignity from the human condition. Truth that reveals where we stand with God who appears when humanity is being denied. We need to tell the truth of the past and our complicity with what undergirds white supremacy, so we can understand all its complexities that strike out against Black/Brown bodies that don't conform to Anglo-Saxon exceptionalism.

---

[51] "Following Jesus While Black," homily by Vincent Powell Harris, in *Preaching Black Lives Matter,* ed. Gayle Fisher-Stewart (New York: Church Publishing, 2020), 42.
[52] "The Work Our Souls Must Do," homily by Kelly Brown Douglas, in *Preaching Black Lives Matter,* ed. Fisher-Stewart, 234–235.

This notion of what it means to be a faithful citizen fits the mold of what has been described as the default setting for the American white male heterosexual—and this feeds white supremacy. Systemic racism is an immoral monster. The root problem is our incapacity to confront this brutal immoral monster who violates Black people and people of color.[53]

—Address, "Let the Church Roll On,"
Bishop Fernand J. Cheri III, OFM

At no point in the history of the Catholic community in this country is it more imperative that those charged with teaching the faith and shepherding the faithful to listen intently to the Spirit of God, the basic gospel message—the kerygma—and the voices and experiences of the women and men whose perspectives and wisdom they too often ignore or resist. I believe the Catholic Church has a critical role to play in making this nation more just and humane. Hard truths and discussions must be had. Animosity to President-elect Biden and Vice President-elect Harris over the one issue of choice as an abdication of their solemn duty to protect all life is rooted in the intransigence and arrogance that oft times accompanies whiteness, maleness, money, and power to the detriment of their teaching authority. We need to hear the sound voices of the successors of the Apostles. Father Augustus Tolton, Pierre Toussaint, Mother Mary Lange, OSP, Mother Henriette DeLille, SSF, Julia Greeley, and Sister Thea Bowman, FSPA, pray for us![54]

—Homily "The Call to Prophecy,"
Father Manuel B. Williams, CR

Any attempt to formulate an African American Catholic theology of preaching must take into consideration at least four salient directives. First, an African American Catholic theology of preaching is null and void without the anointing of the Holy Spirit. Only under the influence of the Holy Spirit can a preacher boldly speak a prophetic message of consolation and challenge to God's people. Second, African American Catholics are rarely monolithic as a singular faith tradition—many have relatives from various Christian denominations. Thus, preaching to African American

[53]Fernand J. Cheri, III, OFM, Auxiliary Bishop of New Orleans, address to the Conference of Major Superiors of Men, "Let the Church Roll On," August 4, 2020. Used with permission.
[54]Manuel B. Williams, CR, Pastor and Director of Resurrection Catholic Parish and Mission, Montgomery, AL, homily, "A Call to Prophecy," December 13, 2020. Used with permission.

Catholics requires a sensitivity to and a familiarity with Protestant faith traditions. Being ecumenical is a desired prerequisite to preaching within the Black Catholic community. Third, an African American Catholic theology of preaching is one of celebration. The preacher in African American Catholic settings must identify—become one with God's Word and God's people—and announce and experience the good news of God's ongoing deliverance. Finally, an African American Catholic theology of preaching is de facto liberation preaching. Preachers in African American Catholic settings are charged with helping the community envision the practical implications of liberation and encourage the people to join God's liberating initiatives. Black preaching is a quest for securing justice and peace for God's oppressed people. To be clear, there are those who seek premature paths to promoting peace among the races before committing themselves to the painful acknowledgment of systemic racism and white supremacy in our nation and their unwillingness to take the sometimes long journey toward making the necessary social, economic, and political systematic and institutional changes to true and lasting peace. But peace is not a polite conversation between the oppressor and the oppressed. Peace is dismantling the hierarchies of oppression. Peace is the redistribution of economic and social power. Peace does not come from seeking the lowest common denominator but in seeking radical and universal principles that will be fair to all.[55] Homilies must encourage oppressors to repent, to turn away from complicity in oppression and to turn toward God's liberating work in history. Preachers must uplift the oppressed with God's message of hope and with the assurance that "trouble don't last always."[56]

---

[55]Maurice J. Nutt, "When Will It End? Why the 'Black Lives Matter' Movement Matters," opinion editorial, WWL News, New Orleans, July 7, 2016.
[56]This is one line of a verse from the African American Spiritual, "Hush, Somebody's Calling My Name."

# Conclusion

## *Go Forth and Announce the Good News*

Black Catholics have a distinct and storied history in the United States. Much like life in general, African American Catholics have endured more than their share of trials and tribulations along with some moments of productivity and progress. My own genealogy attests to seven contiguous generations of African American Catholics. The dream of my maternal grandfather, Edward Louis Duvall, born ten years after slavery, was to become a Catholic priest. It was to be a dream deferred simply because of the color of his skin, or more precisely, the melanin in his skin. And yet fifty-three years after his death divine providence would see his dream fulfilled as his grandson received the sacrament of Holy Orders. In my thirty-plus years as a religious missionary priest, I have had the unique vantage point of viewing Black Catholic life in America from the perspectives of pastor, mission, revival, and retreat preacher, academic and pastoral program administrator, and serving on several national Black Catholic organization boards. I have witnessed firsthand both the growth and waning of Black Catholics in the church. During the 1970s and '80s there was much hope and excitement as Black Catholic parishes were growing and Black Catholic school enrollment was increasing; more young Black people were entering seminaries and convents; the Black Catholic Theological Symposium and the Institute for Black Catholic Studies began; National Black Catholic History Month was created to be celebrated each November; programs and conferences emerged for youth and young adults; liturgical and music conferences were launched; parish and diocesan-wide revivals were preached; active lay participation was promoted; *What We Have Seen and Heard*, a pastoral letter on evangelization by the then ten Black Catholic bishops, was promulgated; *Lead Me, Guide Me*, a Black Catholic hymnal, was inaugurated; the National Black Catholic Congress was reestablished; a Black Catholic pastoral plan commenced; catechetical and lay formation programs were initiated; *The*

*History of Black Catholics in the United States* was published; charismatic clergy, religious, and lay leadership abounded; and more Black bishops were consecrated than ever before. During that time, it seemed as if every aspect of Black Catholic life was esteemed, honored, and held as sacred.

What happened? In my estimation Black Catholic self-determination happened. When Sister Thea Bowman, while addressing the United States Catholic bishops, posed the question, "What does it mean to be Black and Catholic? It means that I come to my church fully functioning. That doesn't frighten you, does it? I come to *my church* fully functioning. I bring myself, *my Black self*, all that I am. . . ." While her Black Catholic self-determined sacred rhetoric was applauded and celebrated in that moment, Thea died. Courageous and visionary Black bishops, religious women and men, clergy, and laity also died, and with them much of their wisdom, fortitude, and vision has gradually yet steadily dissipated. Perhaps Thea's beautiful, bold Blackness did frighten the hierarchy. We see that much of what she asked of the bishops in their pastoral care of Black Catholics has shifted or ended—there are fewer Black Catholic parishes, schools, bishops, offices for Black Catholic ministry, significant Black chancery personnel, and above all, limited evangelization efforts.

And yet through it all, as an African American Catholic who loves his church and comes fully functioning to my church, I remain hopeful. The good Lord knows that Black Catholics have endured and survived far worse than our current circumstances. This book is aptly titled *Down Deep in My Soul*. It is a book about race, religion, ritual, and rhetoric—but it is also a resource. It is a resource about the resiliency of Black Catholics who have in ages past and in times to come stand on the promises of Holy Scripture, lean into our faith and the teachings of our Catholic faith, and who reach way down deep into the reservoir of our sanctified souls for blessed assurance. Black Catholics are grateful too for those *Sankofa moments*, those times, as our Ghanaian ancestors taught us, when we must reach back and fetch what was lost or forgotten. I am grateful, too, that Benedictine Father Cyprian Davis, our Black Catholic griot, historian, storyteller, repository of our traditions, and now ancestor, told us about a Catholic, Spanish-speaking slave, an Arabian Black native of Azamor in Morocco, who came to what would become the United States in the year 1536 along with three other men, Catholic explorers from Spain. His name was Esteban or Stephen.[1] Esteban was here as a Black Catholic man long before the *Mayflower* landed, or any other European immigrants arrived.

---

[1] Cyprian Davis, OSB, *The History of Black Catholics in the United States* (New York: Crossroad, 1990), 28.

Knowing about my spiritual ancestor Esteban is good news for me because it affirms the place and presence of Black Catholics in the United States.

In recent years, Black Catholics have also experienced affirmation and a "kindred spirit" in the person of Pope Francis, who is culturally and socially aware of the experiences of Black people in America, both Catholics and Protestants alike. The Black Catholic community was overjoyed when Pope Francis in 2020 elevated Washington, DC's Archbishop Wilton Daniel Gregory to the College of Cardinals—making him the first African American cardinal. Commenting on this historic event, Black Catholic historian Shannen Dee Williams states:

> To be sure, Pope Francis' appointment of Cardinal Gregory is first and foremost a recognition and celebration of the pioneering Black prelate's long and distinguished record of moral and servant leadership in the white-dominated and former slaveholding U.S. Church. An unyielding champion of racial equality and advocate for the church's marginalized, neglected and abused, he has consistently demonstrated a commitment to the common good and all humanity without distinction. This is why news of his elevation heartened a large cross section across the U.S. Catholic community.[2]

The number of African Americans who make up the Roman Catholic population in the United States is relatively small, and an alarming number of these feel isolated and unwanted. African American Catholics seek recognition, not for recognition's sake, but because we are here, and we have been here; we are Esteban's spiritual progeny; and we have gifts to present to a church that is our home. We are elated for providing the American Catholic Church with gifts of Black sanctity and Black sacred witness in the persons of Pierre Toussaint, Mother Mary Lange, Mother Henriette DeLille, Father Augustus Tolton, Julia Greeley, and Sister Thea Bowman—all on the path to sainthood. With the gifts we bring to the Church, we seek an even exchange of spiritual and pastoral services. Nearly four decades ago the Black bishops of the United States issued an affirmation that as Black Catholics "we have come of age." Part of the process of maturing or "coming of age" is the ability to speak for ourselves and firmly articulate our needs.

As African American Catholics of the twenty-first century, we are

---

[2]Shannen Dee Williams, "Why the Nation's First Black Cardinal Matters," *Central Minnesota Catholic Magazine* (St. Cloud, MN), November 29, 2020, https://thecentralminnesotacatholic. org/shannen-dee-williams-why-the-nations-first-Black-cardinal-matters/.

responding to the call to come and share the richness of our culture and spirituality. We come to the Church with our unity and our diversity, with our strengths and weaknesses. By no means are we monolithic in our worship, preaching, or service. Sister Eva Marie Lumas, SSS, contends that for too long our presence in the Church has been taken for granted or ignored:

> But we are here because we have chosen to synthesize our Catholicism with our Blackness in ways that are life-giving and authentic, and we trust the Holy Spirit to teach us new ways of being Black while teaching the whole Church new ways of being Catholic! Isn't this the whole point of Roman Catholic evangelization with the Black community? Shouldn't it enable us to grow into a fuller understanding of ourselves as an image and likeness of the Blackness of God? And shouldn't it engage our help so that the whole Church can better understand how to renounce the cultural idolatries that obscure its mission and obstruct its ministry?[3]

Olga M. Segura, in her book *Birth of a Movement: Black Lives Matter and the Catholic Church*, offers a pragmatic, albeit some might think utopian, suggestion, when she states:

> The Catholic Church has a crucial role to play in the struggle for liberation. . . . [The] United States bishops must appoint a Black liberation consultant who can liaise between the church and various organizers involved in the fight for Black liberation. This will help American bishops to understand the issues communities of color are most concerned with outside of just the issues they believe matter to us.[4]

Although I agree with Segura's suggestion, it would mean the bishops opening themselves to listening and heeding the advice of those from whom they do not typically seek consultation. I believe that it requires this kind of initiative on the part of the church for constructive change and healing to occur between the church and communities of color.

Those who wish to preach within the African American Catholic com-

---

[3]Eva Marie Lumas, SSS, "Choosing the Better Part: Liturgy, Black and Catholic," *Liturgy* 90 (July 1999): 6.

[4]Olga M. Segura, *Birth of a Movement: Black Lives Matter and the Catholic Church* (Maryknoll, NY: Orbis Books, 2021), 130.

munity will be prepared to preach only when they are able to confront their personal prejudice and racist attitudes, are *willing* and want to minister in our community, are truly open to our culture in its various expressions, are willing to study formally the history, theology, and preaching style and culture of our people, and enter as listeners and learners into our lives in order to be good pastors and teachers in the faith. Agreeing with my analysis, Massingale opines, "The Catholic Church cannot be a proactive force for racial justice unless its teaching, catechesis, [preaching] and practices forthrightly address the reality of white privilege and embrace an understanding of racism beyond its personal and intentional manifestations."[5] And he further elaborates, "Catholic reflection, witness, and action for racial justice will be neither credible nor effective unless this faith community and its leadership cultivate intentional racial solidarity with, and 'transformative love' for, Black Catholics and other Catholics of color."[6]

Finally, it must be said that African American cultural preaching preparation is not only for white priests and deacons ministering in our community but also for the growing influx of Asian and African priests and sisters sent to our community. Although we have an honored and respected African bond, we have many distinctive cultures and differing lived experiences both secular and ecclesial. Without knowledge or conversation with the community, our beloved African brothers and sisters are sent to our community and are expected to thrive simply because they share our same hue. They too must learn our culture and prepare to preach to us. Likewise, we must strive to understand their cultural reality.

What is the future for African American Catholics? Without an in-depth analysis, we will still be present but in a different way—and perhaps have an even stronger presence in the church. I believe the future of Black Catholicism in America will be stronger only if the church will embrace and enrich its preaching ministry within the Black community. That means embracing the powerful art and effectiveness of Black preaching in Catholic worship through Black cultural, theological, and liturgical education. With the declining number of Black Catholic priests, and religious women and men, the future will be the ministry of Black permanent deacons and their wives and lay ecclesial ministers. But they must be sufficiently prepared to lead Black Catholics in a manner that is culturally, spiritually, and theologically appropriate to who we are.

---

[5] Bryan N. Massingale, *Racial Justice and the Catholic Church* (Maryknoll, NY: Orbis Books, 2010), 179.

[6] Ibid.

Preaching is holy work with holy expectations. Only those who dare to preach radically and prophetically can truly usher people into God's sanctuary and once they have received the living and liberating word of God, send them forth to announce the good news.

# Bibliography

Allen, Ronald J., ed. *Patterns of Preaching*. St. Louis: Chalice Press, 1998.

Arbuckle, Gerald A., SM. "Inculturation and Evangelization: Realism or Romanticism?" in *Anthropologists, Missionaries and Cultural* Change. Williamsburg, VA: Studies in Third World Societies, 1985.

Asante, Molefi Kete. *The Afrocentric Idea*. Philadelphia: Temple University Press, 1987.

Baldwin, James. "Down at the Cross." In *The Fire Next Time*. New York: Vintage, 1992,

———. "To Crush a Serpent." In *The Cross of Redemption: Uncollected Writings*, edited by Randall Kenan. New York: Pantheon Books, 2010.

———. "What Price Freedom?" In *The Cross of Redemption: Uncollected Writings*, edited by Randall Kenan. New York: Pantheon Books, 2010.

Baldwin, Lewis V. "Black Christianity in the South in the Nineteenth Century: Its Development and Character." In *Religion in the South Conference Papers*. Mobile: Alabama Humanities Foundation, 1986.

Bartlett, Gene B. *The Audacity of Preaching*. New York: Harper and Row, 1961.

Blasingame, John W. *The Slave Community*. New York: Oxford University Press, 1972.

Bishops' Committee on Priestly Life and Ministry, National Conference of Catholic Bishops. *Fulfilled in Your Hearing: The Homily in the Sunday Assembly*. Washington, DC: United States Catholic Conference, 1982.

Boyack, Kenneth, CSP, ed. *Catholic Evangelization Today: A New Pentecost for the United States*. New York: Paulist Press, 1987.

———, ed. *The New Catholic Evangelization*. New York: Paulist Press, 1992.

Bowman, Thea, FSPA, ed. *Families: Black and Catholic—Catholic and Black*. Washington, DC: United States Catholic Conference, 1985.

———. *Sr. Thea: Her Own Story*. DVD. Florissant, MO: Oblate Media and Communication, 1990.

———. "To Be Black and Catholic: Address to the U.S. Catholic Bishops." *Origins* 19, no. 8 (July 6, 1989).

Braxton, Edward K. "The View from the Barbershop: The Church and African American Culture." *America* 178, no. 4 (1998).

Brown, Joseph A., SJ. *A Retreat with Thea Bowman and Bede Abram: Leaning on the Lord.* Cincinnati: St. Anthony Messenger Press, 1997.

———. *To Stand on the Rock: Meditations on Black Catholic Identity.* Maryknoll, NY: Orbis Books, 1998.

Brueggemann, Walter. *The Prophetic Imagination.* Philadelphia: Fortress Press, 1978.

Buttrick, David. *Homiletic: Moves and Structures.* Minneapolis: Fortress Press, 1987.

Cade, John B. "Out of the Mouths of Ex-Slaves." *Journal of Negro History* 20 (July 1935).

Cepress, Celestine, FSPA, ed. *Sister Thea Bowman, Shooting Star: Selected Writings and Speeches.* Winona, MN: St. Mary's Press, 1993.

Chernoff, John Miller. *African Rhythm and African Sensibility.* Chicago: University of Chicago Press, 1979.

*Code of Canon Law: Latin-English Edition.* Washington, DC: Canon Law Society of America, 1983.

Cone, James H. *For My People.* Maryknoll, NY: Orbis Books, 1984.

———. *God of the Oppressed.* New York: Seabury Press, 1975.

———. *Speaking the Truth.* Grand Rapids, MI: William B. Eerdmans, 1986.

Conwill, Giles A. "The Word Becomes Black Flesh: A Program for Reaching the American Black." In *Evangelizing Blacks*, ed. Glenn C. Smith. Wheaton, IL: Tyndale House, 1988.

Copeland, M. Shawn, ed., with LaReine-Marie Mosley, SND, and Albert J. Raboteau. *Uncommon Faithfulness: The Black Catholic Experience.* Maryknoll, NY: Orbis Books, 2009.

Costen, Melva Wilson. *African American Christian Worship.* Nashville: Abingdon, 1991.

Crawford, Evans E. *The Hum: Call and Response in African American Preaching.* Nashville: Abingdon, 1995.

Davis, Cyprian, OSB. "The Black Contributions to a North American Spirituality." *New Catholic World* 225 (July–August 1982).

———. *The History of Black Catholics in the United States.* New York: Crossroad, 1990.

Duncan, Bruce, CSsR. *Social Justice: Fuller Life in a Fairer World.* Mulgrave, Victoria, Australia: Garratt, 2012.

Eslinger, Richard L. *The Web of Preaching: New Options in Homiletic Method.* Nashville: Abingdon, 2002.

Fishel, Leslie H., Jr., and Benjamin Quarles. *The Negro American: A Documentary History*. Glenview, IL: Scott, Foresman, 1967.

Fisher-Stewart, Gayle, ed. *Preaching Black Lives Matter*. New York: Church Publishing, 2020.

Flannery, Austin, OP, ed. *Vatican Council II: The Conciliar and Post Conciliar Documents*. Northpoint, NY: Costello, 1975.

Forbes, James. *The Holy Spirit and Preaching*. Nashville: Abingdon, 1989.

Francis, Mark R., CSV. *Liturgy in a Multicultural Community*. Collegeville, MN: Liturgical Press, 1991.

Frazier, E. Franklin. *The Negro Church in America*. New York: Schocken Books, 1974.

Fry Brown, Teresa L. *Delivering the Sermon: Voice, Body, and Animation in Proclamation*. Minneapolis: Fortress Press, 2008.

Gilbert, Kenyatta R. *The Journey and Promise of African American Preaching*. Minneapolis: Fortress Press, 2011.

———. *A Pursued Justice—Black Preaching from the Great Migration to the Civil Rights Movement*. Waco, TX: Baylor University Press, 2016.

Glaude, Eddie S., Jr. *Begin Again: James Baldwin's America and Its Urgent Lessons for Our Own*. New York: Crown, 2020.

Gregory, Wilton D., ed. *In Spirit and Truth: Black Catholic Reflections on the Order of Mass*. Washington, DC: United States Catholic Conference, 1988.

Griffin, James. "Racism: A Tarnished Reflection of Ourselves." *Origins* 27, no. 2 (May 29, 1997).

Hanis, W. T., and Henry Sawyer. *The Springs of the Mende Belief and Conduct*. Freetown: Sierra Leone University Press, 1968.

Harris, James Henry. *Black Suffering: Silent Pain, Hidden Hope*. Minneapolis: Fortress Press, 2020.

———. *Pastoral Theology: A Black Church Perspective*. Minneapolis Fortress Press, 1991.

———. *Preaching Liberation*. Minneapolis: Fortress Press, 1995.

———. "Preaching Liberation: The Afro-American Sermon and the Quest for Social Change." *Journal of Religious Thought* 46 (Winter–Spring 1995).

———. *The Word Made Plain: The Power and Promise of Preaching*. Minneapolis: Fortress Press, 1995.

Hayes, Diana L. *Forged in the Fiery Furnace: African American Spirituality*. Maryknoll, NY: Orbis Books, 2012.

———. *No Crystal Stair: Womanist Spirituality*. Maryknoll, NY: Orbis Books, 2016.

———. *Standing in the Shoes My Mother Made: A Womanist Theology*. Minneapolis: Fortress Press, 2011.

Hayes, Diana L., and Cyprian Davis, eds. *Taking Down Our Harps: Black Catholics in the United States*. Maryknoll, NY: Orbis Books, 1998.

Hecht, Michael L., Mary Jane Collier, and Sidney A. Ribeau. *African American Communication: Ethnic Identity and Cultural Interpretation*. Newbury Park, CA: Sage, 1993.

Heille, Gregory, OP. *The Preaching of Pope Francis: Missionary Discipleship and the Ministry of the Word*. Collegeville, MN: Liturgical Press, 2015.

Hilkert, Mary Catherine, OP. "Naming Grace: A Theology of Proclamation." *Worship* 60 (1986): 434–48.

———. *Naming Grace: Preaching and the Sacramental Imagination*. New York: Continuum, 1997.

hooks, bell. *Talking Back: Thinking Feminist, Thinking Black*. Boston: South End Press, 1989.

———. *Teaching to Transgress: Education as the Practice of Freedom*. London: Routledge, 1994.

Horan, Daniel P., OFM. "The Bishop's Letter Fails to Recognize That Racism Is a White Problem." *National Catholic Reporter*, February 20, 2019.

Huels, John M. *The Pastoral Companion: A Canon Law Handbook for Catholic Ministry*. Chicago: Franciscan Herald Press, 1986.

Kenny, Joseph. "Priests, Deacons Share Varied Perspectives about the Sin of Racism at Masses across the Archdiocese." *St. Louis Review*, March 5–11, 2018.

Kienzle, Beverly Mayne, and Pamela J. Walker, eds. *Women Preachers and Prophets through Two Millennia of Christianity*. Berkeley: University of California Press, 1998.

Kim, Eunjoo Mary. *Women Preaching: Theology and Practice Through the Ages*. Eugene, OR: Wipf and Stock, 2004.

King, Martin Luther, Jr. "The Good Samaritan." Sermon at Ebenezer Baptist Church, Atlanta, August 28, 1966. Quoted in David J. Garrow, *Bearing the Cross: Martin Luther King, Jr., and the Southern Christian Leadership Conference*. New York: Vintage, 1988.

———. "The Mountaintop." Sermon at Mason Temple Church of God in Christ, Memphis, TN, April 3, 1968.

———. Nobel Peace Prize Acceptance Speech, Oslo, Norway, December 10, 1964.

———. *Stride toward Freedom: The Montgomery Story*. New York: Harper and Row, 1958.

LaRue, Cleophus J. *The Heart of Black Preaching*. Louisville, KY: Westminster John Knox, 2000.

Lassiter, Valentino. *Martin Luther King in the African American Preaching Tradition*. Cleveland, OH: Pilgrim Press, 2001.

Lincoln, C. Eric, and Lawrence H. Mamiya. *The Black Church in the African American Experience*. Durham, NC: Duke University Press, 1990.

Lowry, Eugene L. *The Homiletical Plot: The Sermon as Narrative Art Form*. Exp. ed. Louisville, KY: Westminster John Knox Press, 2001.

Lumas, Eva Marie, SSS. "Choosing the Better Part: Liturgy, Black and Catholic." *Liturgy* 90 (July 1999).

MacGregor, Morris J. *The Emergence of a Black Catholic Community: St. Augustine's in Washington*. Washington, DC: Catholic University of America Press, 1999.

Massey, James Earl. *Designing the Sermon: Order and Movement in Preaching*. Abingdon Preacher's Library. Nashville: Abingdon, 1980.

Massingale, Bryan N. "The Assumption of White Privilege and What We Can Do about It." *National Catholic Reporter*. June 1, 2020.

———. *Racial Justice and the Catholic Church*. Maryknoll, NY: Orbis Books, 2010.

May, William E., ed. *The Church's Mission of Evangelization*. Steubenville, OH: Franciscan University Press, 1996.

Mays, Benjamin E. *The Negro's God*. New York: Russell & Russell, 1968.

McClory, Robert. "Black and Catholic Are Joint Ventures at Chicago Parish." *National Catholic Reporter*, March 13, 1998.

McMickle, Marvin A. *Shaping the Claim: Moving from Texts to Sermon*. Elements of Preaching. Minneapolis: Fortress Press, 2008.

Mintz, Sidney, and Richard Price. *The Birth of African American Culture: An Anthropological Perspective*. Boston: Beacon Press, 1976.

Mitchell, Henry H. *Black Preaching*. San Francisco: Harper and Row, 1979.

———. *Black Preaching: The Recovery of a Powerful Art*. Nashville: Abingdon, 1990.

———. *Celebration and Experience in Preaching*. Nashville: Abingdon, 1990.

Moss, Otis, III. *Blue Note Preaching in a Post Soul World: Finding Hope in an Age of Despair*. Louisville, KY: Westminster John Knox, 2015.

Moyd, Olin P. *Redemption in Black Theology*. Valley Forge, PA: Judson Press, 1979.

———. *The Sacred Art: Preaching and Theology in the African American Tradition*. Valley Forge, PA: Judson Press, 1995.

Mueller, J. J., SJ. *Practical Discipleship: A United States Christology.* Collegeville, MN: Liturgical Press; 1992.

Nutt, Maurice J., CSsR, "Preaching in a Time of Crisis." *Preacher Magazine* (London: College of Preachers of the United Kingdom), August 2020.

———. "A Sankofa Moment: Exploring a Genealogy of Justice." In *Ain't Gonna Let Nobody Turn Me Around: Stories of Contemplation and Justice,* edited by Therese Taylor-Stinson. New York: Church Publishing, 2017.

———. *Thea Bowman: Faithful and Free.* People of God Series. Collegeville, MN: Liturgical Press, 2019.

———, ed. *Thea Bowman: In My Own Words.* Liguori, MO: Liguori Publications, 2009.

———. "When Will It End? Why the 'Black Lives Matter' Movement Matters." Opinion editorial, WWL News, New Orleans, July 7, 2016.

O'Connell, Gerard. *The Election of Pope Francis: An Inside Account of the Conclave That Changed History.* Maryknoll, NY: Orbis Books, 2019.

Orobator, Agbonkhianmeghe E. *Theology Brewed in an African Pot.* Maryknoll, NY: Orbis Books, 2008.

Parachini, Patricia A. *Lay Preaching: State of the Question.* American Essays in Liturgy Collegeville, MN: Liturgical Press, 1999.

Parrinder, Geoffrey. *West African Psychology.* London: Lutterworth Press, 1951.

Pascoe, C. F. *Two Hundred Years of the Society for the Propagation of the Gospel: An Historical Account of the Society for the Propagation of the Gospel in Foreign Parts.,* vol. 1. Oxford: Oxford University Press, 1901.

Phelps, Jamie T., OP, ed. *Black and Catholic: The Challenge and Gift of Black Folk.* Milwaukee: Marquette University Press, 1997.

———. "Black Spirituality." In *Taking Down Our Harps,* ed. Diana L. Hayes and Cyprian Davis, OSB. Maryknoll, NY: Orbis Books, 1998.

———. "Caught between Thunder and Lightning: A Historical and Theological Critique of the Episcopal Response to Slavery." In *Many Rains Ago: A Historical and Theological Reflection on the Role of the Episcopate in the Evangelization of African American Catholics.* Washington, DC: United States Catholic Conference, 1990.

———. *Spiritual Traditions for the Contemporary Church.* Nashville: Abingdon, 1989.

———. "The Theology and Process of Inculturation: A Theology of Hope for African American Catholics in the United States." *New Theology Review* 7, no.1 (1994).

Pope Francis. Chrism Mass Homily, St. Peter's Basilica, Vatican City, Holy Thursday, March 28, 2013.

———. *Evangelii Gaudium (The Joy of the Gospel)*. Washington, DC: USCCB Communications, 2013.

———. *Gaudete et Exsultate (Rejoice and Be Glad)*. Washington, DC: USCCB Communications, 2018.

———. Homily for the Solemnity of Pentecost, St. Peter's Basilica, Vatican City, Sunday, May 19, 2013.

———. Homily on the Sunday of the Word of God, St. Peter's Basilica, Vatican City, January 24, 2021.

———. "Meeting with the Poor Assisted by Caritas." Assisi, Italy, October 4, 2013.

Pope John Paul II. *The Ad Limina Addresses of His Holiness Pope John Paul II to the Bishops of the United States* (February 1998–October 1998). Washington DC: United States Catholic Conference, 1998.

———. *The Church Is a Creator of Culture*. Melbourne: Australian Catholic Theological Society, 1983.

———. *Fear Not: Thoughts on Living in Today's World*. Edited by Alexandria Hatcher. Kansas City, MO: Andrews McMeel, 1999.

———. "Goree Island—Twin Symbol: Excerpts from Pope John Paul II's Address on Goree Island." *Catholic International*, February 1992.

———. "Homily in the Trans World Dome." *Origins* 28 (February 11, 1999).

———. "The Ideal of Liberty, a Moving Force." In *U.S.A.: The Message of Justice, Peace, and Love*. Boston: Daughters of St. Paul, 1979.

Pope Paul VI. Message to the World Council of Churches General Assembly at Nairobi. *Doing the Truth in Charity: Statements of Pope Paul VI, John Paul I, John Paul II, and the Secretariat for Promoting Christian Unity, 1964–1980*. Mahwah, NJ: Paulist Press, 1982.

———. *On Evangelization in the Modern World*. Washington, DC: United States Catholic Conference, 1975.

Posey, Thaddeus J., OFM Cap., ed. *Portrait in Black: Black Catholic Theological Symposium*. Washington, DC: National Black Catholic Clergy Caucus, 1978.

Proctor, Samuel D. *How Shall They Hear?* Valley Forge, PA: Judson Press, 1992.

Raboteau, Albert S. *A Fire in the Bones: Reflections on African American Religious History*. Boston: Beacon Press, 1995.

———. *Slave Religion*. Oxford: Oxford University Press, 1978.

Randolph, Peter. *Sketches of Slave Life or, Illustrations of the Peculiar Institution*. Boston, 1855.

Rawick, George P. *God Struck Me Dead*. Philadelphia: Pilgrim Press, 1969.

Ray, Benjamin. *African Religions*. Englewood Cliffs, NJ: Prentice-Hall, 1976.

Reumann, John. "A History of Lectionaries: From the Synagogue at Nazareth to Post–Vatican II." *Interpretation*, April 1977.

Riccardi, Andrea. *To the Margins: Pope Francis and the Mission of the Church*. Maryknoll, NY: Orbis Books, 2018.

Sawyer, Mary R. *Black Ecumenism: Implementing the Demands of Justice*. Valley Forge, PA: Trinity Press International, 1994.

Scarborough, Dorothy. *On the Trail of Negro Folk-Songs*. Cambridge, MA: Harvard University Press, 1925.

Schineller, Peter. *A Handbook on Inculturation*. New York: Paulist Press, 1990.

Secretariat for the Liturgy and Secretariat for Black Catholics, National Conference of Catholic Bishops. *Plenty Good Room: The Spirit and Truth of African American Catholic Worship*. Washington, DC: United States Catholic Conference, 1990.

Segura, Olga M. *Birth of a Movement: Black Lives Matter and the Catholic Church*. Maryknoll, NY: Orbis Books, 2021.

———. "Meet Father Bryan Massingale: A Black, Gay, Catholic Priest Fighting for an Inclusive Church: A Profile of a Progressive Leader in the Catholic Church Working for Racial and LGBTQ Justice." *The Revealer*. New York: New York University, June 3, 2020.

Sernett, Milton C. *Black Religion and American Evangelism*. Metuchen, NJ: Scarecrow Press, 1975.

Shorter, Aylward. *Toward a Theology of Inculturation*. Maryknoll, NY: Orbis Books, 1988.

Smith, Glenn C., ed. *Evangelizing Blacks*. Wheaton, IL: Tyndale House, 1988.

Smith, J. Alfred. *Preach On: A Concise Handbook of the Elements of Style in Preaching*. Nashville: Broadman Press, 1984.

Smith, J. Alfred, Walter B. Hoard, and Milton E. Owens, eds. *Outstanding Black Sermons*, vol. 1. Valley Forge, PA: Judson Press, 1978.

Spadaro, Antonio. "Wake Up the World: Conversations with Pope Francis about Religious Life." In *La Civiltà Cattolica* 165, no. 1, trans. Donald Maldari, SJ (2014).

Taylor-Stinson, Therese, ed. *Ain't Gonna Let Nobody Turn Me Around: Stories of Contemplation and Justice*. New York: Church Publishing, 2017.

*Tell It Like Is!* Oakland: National Black Sisters' Conference, 1983.

Thomas, Frank A. *How to Preach a Dangerous Sermon*. Nashville: Abingdon, 2018.

———. *Introduction to the Practice of African American Preaching*. Nashville: Abingdon, 2016.

———. *They Like to Never Quit Praisin' God: The Role of Celebration in Preaching*. Cleveland: United Church Press, 1997.

United States Conference of Catholic Bishops (USCCB). *Brothers and Sisters to Us: US Bishops' Pastoral Letter on Racism in Our Day*. Washington, DC: National Conference of Catholic Bishops, 1979.

———. *Here I Am, Send Me. A Conference Response to the Evangelization of African Americans and The National Black Catholic Pastoral Plan*. Washington, DC: United States Catholic Conference, 1990.

———. *Open Wide Our Hearts: The Enduring Call to Love—A Pastoral Letter against Racism*. Washington, DC: USCCB Communications, 2018.

Untener, Ken. *Preaching Better: Practical Suggestions for Homilists*. Mahwah, NJ: Paulist Press, 1999.

Warren, Mervyn. *Black Preaching: Truth and Soul*. Washington, DC: University Press of America, 1977.

Waznak, Robert P. *An Introduction to the Homily*. Collegeville, MN: Liturgical Press, 1998.

West, Cornel. *Black Prophetic Fire: A Dialogue with and Edited by Christa Buschendorf*. Amazon Kindle Edition, 2015.

West, Cornel, and Eddie S. Glaude, Jr., eds. *African American Religious Thought: An Anthology*. Louisville, KY: Westminster John Knox Press, 2003.

*What We Have Seen and Heard: A Pastoral Letter on Evangelization From the Black Bishops of the United States*. Cincinnati: St. Anthony Messenger Press, 1984.

Williams, Clarence, CPPS. *The Black Man and the Catholic Church*. Detroit: Academy of the Afro-World Community, 1981.

———. "Pastoral Strategy for Evangelization from a Global Pan-African Perspective." *New Theology Review* 7, no. 1 (1994): 14–27.

Williams, Shannen Dee. "Why the Nation's First Black Cardinal Matters." *Central Minnesota Catholic Magazine*, November 29, 2020.

Wilmore, Gayraud S., ed. *African American Religious Studies: An Interdisciplinary Anthology*. Durham, NC: Duke University Press, 1989.

———, ed. *Black Theology: A Documentary History, 1966–1979*. Maryknoll, NY: Orbis Books, 1979.

# Selected Bibliography
# of African American Preaching

Alcantara, Jared E. *Crossover Preaching: Inter-Cultural-Improvisational Homiletics in Conversation with Gardner C. Taylor*. Downers Grove, IL: InterVarsity Press, 2015.

Allen, Donna E. *Toward a Womanist Homiletic: Katie Cannon, Alice Walker, and Emancipatory Proclamation*. New York: Peter Lang, 2014.

Andrews, Dale P. *Practical Theology for Black Churches: Bridging Black Theology and African American Folk Religion*. Louisville, KY: Westminster John Knox, 2002.

Bailey, E. K., and Warren W. Wiersbe. *Preaching in Black & White: What We Can Learn from Each Other*. Grand Rapids, MI: Zondervan, 2003.

Bond, Adam L. *The Imposing Preacher: Samuel DeWitt Proctor and Black Public Faith*. Minneapolis: Fortress Press, 2013.

Bond, L. Susan. *Contemporary African American Preaching: Diversity in Theory and Style*. St. Louis: Chalice Press, 2003.

Brogdon, Lewis. *The Spirituality of Black Preaching: Advice to Young Preachers on the Heart of Black Preaching*. Lanham, MD: Seymour Press, 2016.

Cannon, Katie Geneva. *Teaching Preaching: Isaac Rufus Clark and Black Sacred Rhetoric*. New York: Continuum International Publishing Group, 2002.

Collier-Thomas, Bettye. *Daughters of Thunder: Black Women Preachers and Their Sermons, 1850–1979*. San Francisco: Jossey-Bass, 1997.

Crawford, Evans E., and Thomas H. Troeger. *The Hum: Call and Response in African American Preaching*. Nashville: Abingdon, 1995.

Davis, Gerald L. *I Got the Word in Me and I Can Sing It, You Know: A Study of the Performed African-American Sermon*. Philadelphia: University of Pennsylvania Press, 1985.

Fisher-Stewart, Gayle, ed. *Preaching Black Lives Matter*. New York: Church Publishing, 2020.

Forbes James A. *The Holy Spirit and Preaching*. Nashville: Abingdon, 1989.

Fry Brown, Teresa L. *Delivering the Sermon: Voice, Body, and Animation in Proclamation*. Minneapolis: Fortress Press, 2008.

———. *Weary Throats and New Song: Black Women Proclaiming God's Word*. Nashville: Abingdon, 2003.

Gilbert, Kenyatta R. *Exodus Preaching: Crafting Sermons about Justice and Hope*. Nashville: Abingdon, 2018.

———. *The Journey and Promise of African American Preaching*. Minneapolis: Fortress Press, 2011.

———. *A Pursued Justice—Black Preaching from the Great Migration to the Civil Rights Movement*. Waco, TX: Baylor University Press, 2016.

Harris, James Henry. *Beyond the Tyranny of the Test: Preaching in Front of the Bible to Create a New World*. Nashville: Abingdon, 2019.

———. *Black Suffering: Silent Pain, Hidden Hope*. Minneapolis: Fortress Press, 2020.

———. *Preaching Liberation*. Minneapolis: Fortress Press, 1995.

———. *The Word Made Plain: The Power and Promise of Preaching*. Minneapolis, 1995.

Haywood, Chanta M. *Prophesying Daughters: Black Women Preachers and the Word, 1823–1913*. Columbia: University of Missouri Press, 2003.

Howard, Gregory. *Black Sacred Rhetoric*. Dallas: Borderstone Press, 2010.

Jackson, Cari. *For the Souls of Black Folks: Reimagining Black Preaching for Twenty-First Century Liberation*. Eugene, OR: Wipf and Stock, 2013.

Johnson, James Weldon, Aaron Douglas, and C. B. Falls. *God's Trombones: Seven Negro Sermons in Verse*. Chapel Hill: University of North Carolina at Chapel Hill Libraries, 2004.

Johnson, Kimberly P. *The Womanist Preacher: Proclaiming Womanist Rhetoric from the Pulpit*. Burlington, MA: Lexington Books, 2019.

Jones, Kirk Byron. *The Jazz of Preaching: How to Preach with Freedom and Joy*. Nashville: Abingdon, 2004.

LaRue, Cleophus J. *The Heart of Black Preaching*. Louisville, KY: Westminster John Knox, 2000.

———. *I Believe I'll Testify: The Art of African American Preaching*. Louisville, KY: Westminster John Knox, 2011.

———, ed. *More Power in the Pulpit: How America's Most Effective Black Preachers Prepare Their Sermons*. Louisville, KY: Westminster John Knox, 2009.

———. *Rethinking Celebration: From Rhetoric to Praise in African American Preaching*. Louisville, KY: Westminster John Knox, 2016.

————, ed. *This Is My Story: Testimonies and Sermons of Black Women in Ministry*. Louisville, KY: Westminster John Knox, 2005.

Lassiter, Valentino. *Martin Luther King in the African American Preaching Tradition*. Cleveland, OH: Pilgrim Press, 2001.

Lischer, Richard. *The Preacher King: Martin Luther King, Jr. and the Word That Moved America*. New York: Oxford University Press, 1995.

Martin, Lerone A. *Preaching on Wax: The Phonography and the Shaping of Modern African American Religion*. New York: New York University Press, 2014.

Massey, James Earl. *Designing the Sermon: Order and Movement in Preaching*. Abingdon Preacher's Library. Nashville: Abingdon, 1980.

————. *The Responsible Pulpit*. Anderson, IN: Warren Press, 1974.

McClain, William B. *Come Sunday: The Liturgy of Zion*. Nashville: Abingdon, 1990.

McMickle, Marvin Andrew. *Preaching to the Black Middle Class: Words of Challenge, Words of Hope*. Valley Forge, PA: Judson Press, 2000.

————. *Shaping the Claim: Moving from Texts to Sermon*. Elements of Preaching. Minneapolis: Fortress Press, 2008.

————. *Where Have All the Prophets Gone: Reclaiming Prophetic Preaching in America*. Cleveland: Pilgrim Press, 2019.

Miller, Keith D. *Voice of Deliverance: The Language of Martin Luther King Jr. and Its Sources*. New York: Free Press, 1992.

Mitchell, Ella Pearson. *Those Preaching Women*. 3 vols. Valley Forge, PA: Judson Press, 1985.

Mitchell, Henry H. *Black Preaching: The Recovery of a Powerful Art*. Nashville: Abingdon, 1990.

————. *Celebration and Experience in Preaching*. Nashville: Abingdon, 1990, rev. 2008.

————. *The Recovery of Preaching*. San Francisco: Harper & Row Publishers, 1977.

Mitchell, Stephanie Y. *Name It and Claim It: Prosperity Preaching in the Black Church*. Cleveland, OH: Pilgrim Press, 2007.

Moss, Otis, III. *Blue Note Preaching in a Post Soul World: Finding Hope in an Age of Despair*. Louisville, KY: Westminster John Knox, 2015.

Moyd, Olin P. *The Sacred Art: Preaching and Theology in the African American Tradition*. Valley Forge, PA: Judson Press, 1995.

Pipes, William H. *Say Amen, Brother! Old-Time Negro Preaching: A Study in American Frustration*. Detroit: Wayne State University Press, 1992.

Powery, Luke. *Dem Dry Bones: Preaching, Death, and Hope*. Minneapolis: Fortress Press, 2012.

———. *Spirit Speech: Celebration and Lament in Preaching.* Nashville: Abingdon, 2009.

Proctor, Samuel D. *The Certain Sound of the Trumpet: Crafting a Sermon of Authority.* Valley Forge, PA: Judson Press, 1994.

———. *"How Shall They Hear?" Effective Preaching for Vital Faith.* Valley Forge, PA: Judson Press, 1992.

Redmond, Eric C. *Say It! Celebrating Expository Preaching in the African American Tradition.* Chicago: Moody, 2020.

Rieder, Jonathan. *The Word of the Lord Is Upon Me: The Righteous Performance of Martin Luther King Jr.* Cambridge, MA: Belknap Press of Harvard University, 2008.

Roberts, Samuel K., ed. *Born to Preach: Essays in Honor of the Ministry of Henry and Ella Mitchell.* Valley Forge, PA: Judson Press, 2000.

Rosenberg, Bruce A. *Can These Bones Live? The Art of the American Folk Preacher.* Rev. ed. Urbana, IL: University of Illinois Press, 1988.

Salvatore, Nick. *Singing in a Strange Land: C. L. Franklin, the Black Church, and the Transformation of America.* Urbana: University of Illinois Press, 2006.

Simmons, Martha, ed. *Preaching on the Brink: The Future of Homiletics.* Nashville: Abingdon, 1996.

Simmons, Martha, and Frank A. Thomas. *Preaching with Sacred Fire: An Anthology of African American Preaching, 1750 to the Present.* New York: W. W. Norton, 2010.

Smith, J. Alfred. *Preach On!* Nashville: Broadman Press, 1984.

Smith, Kelly Miller. *Social Crisis Preaching.* Macon, GA: Mercer University Press, 1984.

Spencer, Jon Michael. *Sacred Symphony: The Chanted Sermon of the Black Preacher.* New York: Greenwood Press, 1987.

Stephens, Alfred. *Homiletics from the Underside: The Art of Contextual Preaching.* Madurai, India: ECHO, 2014.

Stewart, Warren H. *Interpreting God's Word in Black Preaching.* Valley Forge, PA: Judson Press, 1984.

Taylor, Gardner C. *How Shall They Preach?* Elgin, IL: Progressive Baptist Publishing House, 1977.

Thomas, Frank A. *God of the Dangerous Sermon.* Nashville: Abingdon, 2021.

———. *How to Preach a Dangerous Sermon.* Nashville: Abingdon, 2018.

———. *Introduction to the Practice of African American Preaching.* Nashville: Abingdon, 2016.

———. *Preaching as Celebration Digital Lecture Series and Workbook.* Indianapolis: Hope for Life Press, 2015.

———. *Surviving a Dangerous Sermon.* Nashville: Abingdon, 2020.

———. *They Like to Never Quit Praisin' God: The Role of Celebration in Preaching.* Cleveland, OH: United Church Press, 1997.

Thomas, John L., Jr. *Voices in the Wilderness: Why Black Preaching Still Matters.* Eugene, OR: Cascade Books, 2018.

Titon, Jeff Todd. *Give Me This Mountain: Life, History, and Selected Sermons of C. L. Franklin.* Urbana: University of Illinois Press, 1989.

Travis, Sarah. *Decolonizing Preaching: The Pulpit as Postcolonial Space.* Eugene, OR: Cascade Books, 2014.

Turner, William Clair, Jr. *Preaching That Makes the Word Plain: Doing Theology in the Crucible of Life.* Eugene, OR: Cascade Books, 2008.

Warren, Mervyn A. *King Came Preaching: The Pulpit Power of Dr. Martin Luther King, Jr.* Downers Grove, IL: InterVarsity Press, 2001.

*What We Have Seen and Heard: A Pastoral Letter on Evangelization from the Black Bishops of the United States.* Cincinnati: St. Anthony Messenger Press, 1984.

Wherry, Peter M. *Preaching Funerals in the Black Church: Bringing Perspective to Pain.* Valley Forge, PA: Judson Press, 2014.

# Index